West of the Border

West of the Border

The Multicultural Literature
of the Western American Frontiers

 Noreen Groover Lape

Ohio University Press
ATHENS

Ohio University Press, Athens, Ohio 45701

© 2000 by Noreen Lape

Printed in the United States of America

All rights reserved

09 08 07 06 05 04 03 02 01 00   5 4 3 2 1

Library of Congress Cataloging-in-Publication Data

Lape , Noreen Groover, 1966–
   West of the border : the multicultural literature of the Western American frontiers /
Noreen Groover Lape.
      p. cm.
   Includes bibliographical references and index.
   ISBN 0-8214-1345-7 (alk. paper) — ISBN 0-8214-1346-5 (pbk. : alk. paper)
      1. American literature—West (U.S.)—History and criticism. 2. American
literature—Minority authors—History and criticism. 3. Women and literature—West
(U.S.)—History. 4. Multiculturalism in literature. 5. Ethnicity in literature. 6. Frontier
and pioneer life in literature. 7. West (U.S.)—In literature. I. Title.

PS271 .L37 2000
810.9'3278—dc21

                                                                00-028569

For Dale

Contents

Acknowledgments

Any serious act of writing, as I try to teach my freshman composition students, is truly a social and collaborative interaction. What I value most about having written this book is the satisfying intellectual and social connections I formed with people who so generously aided and guided me.

In 1993, I was having a conversation with my mentor Carolyn L. Karcher when the idea for this book was generated. I thank her for meticulously reading and commenting on the entire manuscript, teaching me how to shape a book, offering heartfelt encouragement, and always being extremely generous with her time. I also thank Lynda Hill, Susan Wells, and Jeannie Pfaelzer for reading the manuscript and offering countless helpful suggestions. As a result of this collaboration, I published a version of the fifth chapter in *Breaking Boundaries: New Perspectives on Women's Regional Writing*, edited by Sherrie A. Inness and Diana Royer (reprinted here by permission of the University of Iowa Press), and a version of the first chapter in the summer 1998 issue of *American Indian Quarterly* (published by the University of Nebraska Press).

I would also like to thank Gillian Berchowitz and David Sanders at Ohio University Press. They approached me about publishing my manuscript even before I had begun to contact publishers, gave me important editorial advice about crafting a book, and adroitly guided the project through to its completion.

Over the last few years, Dan Ross read the entire manuscript, listened to me rattle on endlessly about the changes I was making, helped me sort through and address various reader comments, and constantly assured me that I was on the right track. My gratitude extends not only to him but also to Cindy, Melanie, and Benjamin Ross, Cheryl Yatsko (true to her profession, she kept me sane), and Patrick McHenry for their friendship, enthusiasm, and support.

The crack secretarial staff in the Department of Language and Literature at Columbus State University deserves thanks. Tracy Autry and Deirdre Brown typed the notes section as well as other supporting documents for the book. Several librarians at Simon Schwob Memorial Library offered their co-operation and assistance at a grueling point in the process. Terry Townsend filled out scores of interlibrary loan cards and Cheryl Hewitt managed the influx of interlibrary loan books so I could check the quotes and facts quickly and efficiently.

Finally, I thank my family, James and Patricia Groover and Erin Groover, who always encouraged me in my goals. But I owe the biggest debt of gratitude to Dale Lape, who read much of my work, listened to me complain about my various writer's blocks, and always offered helpful suggestions (including well-planned diversions). Throughout the years, he made countless sacrifices that enabled me to complete this book. I am forever thankful for his emotional, intellectual, and financial support.

West of the Border

Introduction

*Rites of Passage, Contact Zones,
and the American Frontiers*

In an essay entitled "The Melting Pot," Robert Laxalt describes the borders and boundaries of a small "copper company town" that evolved into a "real international settlement" fraught with cultural divisions. Laxalt observes, "There were some other words, not so nice, for it then.... There was Greek Town, Hunky Town, Jap Town, Wop Town, and Mid Town. That meant the middle of town, and it was where all the 'white people' lived. The rest of us were cheap labor for the copper mines and the smelter. The 'foreigners' stuck together for the most part, but once in a while, you could get a scrap if you were a Hunky and you crossed the line into Greek Town. Our common enemy was Mid Town. Anytime you crossed that line, you were in for big trouble."[1] Laxalt's "Melting Pot" essay recalls a central myth of American cultural formation, a myth first applied to frontier life by Frederick Jackson Turner, the historian whose famous paper "The Significance of the Frontier in American History" (1893) sparked the systematic study of the frontier. In his "frontier melting pot thesis," Turner postulates that "the frontier promoted the formation of a composite nationality for the American people.... In the crucible of the frontier the immigrants were Americanized, liberated, and fused into a mixed race, English in neither nationality nor characteristics."[2] In the passage from Laxalt, however, the emphasis is on divided cultures, the crossing of lines, and the threat of "big trouble"—

highlighting the struggles for power among American cultural groups as they mediate their multiple ethnicities to construct a national identity that is neither inherently separatist nor homogeneously unified. In Laxalt's image of cultural "others" building lives for themselves on the periphery of Mid Town—the place where "'white people'" (really the Anglo community) reside—we find the idea of the frontier borderlands as social rite of passage.

For the fin-de-siècle historian, the social rite of passage occurs when sundry ethnicities conjoin, intermingle, lose their individual identities, and form a whole new nationality on the frontiers. Of course, Turner's immigrants are largely of Scotch and German descent. The peripheral communities Laxalt describes, too, with the exception of the Japanese, are all European. And Laxalt explains that eventually "all the barriers broke down. They [the 'whites'] finally accepted us as human." He ends his essay with the bittersweet observation that as the inevitable process of Americanization occurs, "the old-country people would be only a dimming memory ... and the melting would be done."[3] Laxalt evokes Turner's belief that the melting pot narrative ends when immigrants are "Americanized" and "liberated."

However, the fictional and nonfictional writings of some immigrant and nonimmigrant Americans on the frontiers call into question the myth of melting-pot liberation. In the literature of non-European frontier cultures—Asian, Mexican, and Native American—melting-pot "liberation" is not often the corollary of culture contact. The frontier dynamics of a burgeoning America were highly intricate and complicated during Turner's time. In the nineteenth century and at the turn into the twentieth, Anglo immigrants from the East Coast confronted aboriginal Native Americans, African captives, Asians immigrating from further west, and Mexicans who had become aliens in their own land after the Mexican-American War. As Gloria Anzaldúa states of the Chicano people: "They'd like to think I have melted in the pot. But I haven't, we haven't."[4] Instead, the mestiza (mixed) people "sustain contradictions" and tolerate ambiguity; they "juggle cultures" and "operat[e] in a pluralistic mode."[5] Yet in spite of the conflicts and contradictions that erupt, such mediation can be potentially dynamic, invoking creativity and social rejuvenation.

Fusion into a mixed race and inclusion in U.S. society was not possible for some groups, like Mexicans and Asians, who were deemed inherently unassimilable despite their attempts to become "Americanized." By the early twentieth century, many federal officials concluded that regardless of the U.S. government's efforts, Native Americans failed to assimilate. Further, melting-pot liberation presumes a mechanical, unidirectional movement of society toward integration. In some cases, cultures compromised assimilation by merging their traditions and Anglo cultural customs, a process anthropologists call syncretism. This intermingling of traditions from disparate cultures can denote either cultural tolerance or resistance.[6] For instance, whereas the Okanogan novelist and folklorist Mourning Dove considers the points of correspondence between Okanogan and Anglo traditions when she rewrites trickster tales for a white readership, conversely, Native American prophets put up resistance by appropriating Christianity only to reject it. At times, the appropriation and subversion of the dominant culture occur simultaneously in syncretic forms. Subversion may be an unintended consequence of adopting the dominant culture.[7] James Beckwourth, the half-black fur trapper and adopted Crow tribal member, sanctions Anglo rule when he passes as white in his autobiography. Narrating his experiences with the Crow tribe and with white fur traders, Beckwourth endorses frontier conquest even as he reveals the humanity of the Crows. Ultimately, the merging of cultural and literary traditions occurs within culturally fluid contexts.

Many nineteenth-century and turn-of-the-century U.S. authors—Native American, Asian American, African American, and Anglo American—lived in the culturally fluid contexts of the contact zones at the frontier. Residing "west of the border," the frontier cultural others encountered Anglo Manifest Destiny and wrote about their imagined fates. "West of the border" is then not so much a geographical place as zones of culture contact and conflict in which writers negotiated their positions between cultures. As the nation was being formed, there was not a single frontier event in which white frontiersmen undertook a continual, "heroic" push to the Pacific coast as they "civilized" society; instead, multiple frontiers were occupied by diverse cultural groups at disparate geographical points. Employing Victor Turner's theory of rites of passage in conjunction with borderland theory, *West of the Border* analyzes the works of writers who live between cultures and negotiate their new American identities through cross-cultural dialogues.

Following Frederick Jackson Turner's pronouncement of his frontier thesis, U.S. history departments engaged in a heated debate that resulted in a mound of substantial scholarship.[8] However, his thesis also influenced frontier studies in U.S. literature. In his "frontier thesis," Turner states: "The existence of an area of free land, its continuous recession, and the advance of American settlement westward, explain American development."[9] Turner's emphasis on the land and the westering frontiersman was mirrored in the literary scholarship on the U.S. frontier.

Scholars, at first, studied literature depicting "the advance of American settlement westward" by self-reliant, individualist frontiersmen who encountered the "wild, uninhabited" territories and transformed them into cultured "civilizations."[10] Their perspectives often coincided with the frontiersman's monolithic view of Native Americans as a mass of faceless savages who were merely obstacles to frontier settlement. More recently, the Turnerian position has been extended as interest has arisen in the fiction and journals of pioneer women: literary critics and historians alike consider whether the frontier experience empowered or alienated women in liberating them from restrictive gender conventions.[11] Other frontier literary studies emphasize "the existence of an area of free land" in analyzing the relationship between pioneers and the landscape: Henry Nash Smith's groundbreaking study *Virgin Land* traces the impact of "free land" on the American consciousness.[12] Combining gender and landscape studies, Annette Kolodny's *The Lay of the Land* and *The Land Before Her* examine the gendered metaphors employed by male and female explorers, fiction writers, travelers, and pioneers who first experienced and wrote about the U.S. frontier landscape.[13]

Currently, ethnohistorians are reconceiving the frontier as a human, intercultural zone, and their view is beginning to inform literary studies. According to James Axtell, ethnohistory is the study of "multiple and shifting frontiers between different cultures." Ethnohistorians view frontiers not as "geographical spaces accidentally occupied by people" but as "human spaces" where "diverse cultures came together."[14] Similarly, in introducing their collection *The Frontier in History: North America and South Africa Compared*, Leonard Thompson and Howard Lamar define the frontier as "a territory or zone of interpenetration between two previously distinct societies." They say that "usually, one of the societies is indigenous to the region, or at least has occupied it for many generations; the other is intrusive."[15] An implication of Thompson and Lamar's definition is that there is a potential threat of colonialism—the subjugation of native people by invaders.

In *Imperial Eyes: Travel Writing and Transculturation,* Mary Louise Pratt's discussion of the "contact zone" in colonial encounters resembles the ethnohistorians' "frontier." Borrowing the concept from linguistics, Pratt states that contact zones are "social spaces where disparate cultures meet, clash, and grapple with each other, often in highly asymmetrical relations of domination and subordination—like colonialism, slavery, or their aftermaths as they are lived out across the globe today."[16] Similarly, in her cultural autobiography *Borderlands/La Frontera: The New Mestiza,* Anzaldúa describes borderlands as "physically present wherever two or more cultures edge each other"; in their coming together, "*un choque,* a cultural collision" is formed.[17] Both historians and critics suggest that frontiers are characterized by the clash of cultures, sometimes in unequal power relations.

West of the Border, then, draws on this view of frontiers as places where cultures make contact rather than on the Turnerian notion of the frontier as an "area of free land" traversed by westering pioneers. Within the context of culture contact, the U.S. frontier experience is like a rite of passage for groups west of the border. Many literary scholars have viewed the frontier as a rite of passage for white frontiersmen. Richard Slotkin asserts that the frontier myth depicts the frontiersman's "initiation" into "a higher state of being or manhood."[18] Eric Heyne declares, "Crossing the frontier is a quintessentially American act, our national (male) rite of passage...."[19] Victor Turner, the anthropologist, theorized about rites of passage in several works throughout his life. His theories were inspired by Arnold van Gennep's *Rites de Passage* (1908). Van Gennep distinguishes three stages in these rites: the initiand's separation from his social group, his experience in the transitional or liminal state, and his reincorporation into the original culture.[20] According to Turner, the liminal realm is unlike the initiand's past or future state since he exists in no well-defined cultural space but is "necessarily ambiguous." Hence, in the liminal realm, individuals are "neither here nor there; they are betwixt and between the positions assigned and arrayed by law, custom, convention, and ceremonial."[21] For the multicultural writers discussed in *West of the Border,* the American frontiers are like the liminal or transitional phase in a rite of passage. Kolodny proposes a redefinition of the frontier "as a specifiable first moment on that liminal borderland between distinct cultures."[22] Ronald Takaki asserts that "America represented liminality" to immigrants in that it was a place for them "to become new people in a society still being defined and formed."[23]

The experience of liminality or transition, for the authors discussed in this book, characterizes the borderlands and shapes their writings.

Following Victor Turner's theories, how, we can ask, do initiands in the U.S. frontier rite of passage function in the borderlands? Existing in transitional or in-between states, initiands are mediators within their cultures; yet prior to adopting a new status, they also receive the prescriptions of their cultures.[24] Turner describes the transitional realm as lacking structure: the initiand is an outsider in society and he temporarily loses his social and cultural status. Because the initiand separates from his culture, the transitional state is "potentially a period of scrutinization of the central values and axioms of the culture in which it occurs";[25] hence, the initiand engages in "speculation and criticism" of society.[26] Ronald Grimes compares the traditional understanding of ritual with Turner's view of ritual: "Ritual had been portrayed as the most backward-looking, foot-dragging of cultural forms. It was hardly capable of acting on society; rather, it was a 'repository' or 'reflection' of it. Always it was passive, inert. Turner painted another picture, that of a cultural 'agent,' energetic, subversive, creative, socially critical."[27] Rites of passage are not only "subversive" and "socially critical," but "seedbeds of cultural creativity"; during the transitional phases of ritual, initiands experience "an instant of pure potentiality when everything, as it were, trembles in the balance."[28] In fact, Turner maintains, liminal conditions often generate "myths, symbols, rituals, philosophical systems, and works of art."[29]

West of the Border explores the literary works produced by writers who are themselves "betwixt and between" cultural identities. They write from the experience of culture contact in which the U.S. frontier is like the transitional phase in a social, cultural, and historical rite of passage. Van Gennep observes that rites of passage "'accompany every change of place, state, social position and age'" in an individual or cohort.[30] Turner views rites of passage as social and historical when he states that there are "phases of history that are in many respects 'homologous' to the liminal periods of important rituals in stable and repetitive societies, when major groups or social categories in those societies are passing from one cultural state to another."[31] Producing works that mediate between disparate cultures on the frontiers, the writers negotiate social, cultural, and identity frontiers through cross-cultural dialogues.

Further, the writers experience the frontiers and embody borders in their culturally ambiguous identities. Like the initiands in rites of passage, they are "threshold people" who are socially marginal because of their mixed identities. Both the Paiute translator Sarah Winnemucca Hopkins and Beckwourth are cross-cultural negotiators in their autobiographies. In her role as translator, Hopkins linguistically mediates between white and Paiute societies—her bilingualism results in her being between cultures; and Beckwourth incorporates frontiers into his identity—a biracial fur trapper of black and white parentage, he passes as both white and Crow. Also, Trickster, a character from Native American mythology, mediates between white, Native American, and Mexican groups in the postcontact milieu. Employing the Trickster character in his novel, the Cherokee author John Rollin Ridge encodes his experience of Cherokee Removal in the character of a Mexican trickster/bandit. Sui Sin Far and Onoto Watanna, Eurasian sisters of British and Chinese ancestry, arbitrate their mixed identities on the Asian frontier. Moreover, Onoto Watanna, Mary Austin, and James Beckwourth act as "transethnics": Onoto Watanna adopts Japanese clothing and persona; Austin and Beckwourth do likewise with Native American. Victor Turner finds that the "transvestism" of initiands in rites of passage is an emblem of their loss of status. For instance, "the passive attitude of the male initiands may be symbolized by the wearing of female apparel."[32] Onoto Watanna masks her Chinese cultural heritage by wearing Japanese garments. Beckwourth's transvestism, ironically, supports his status as a heroic "Indian chief." Similarly, Austin, the southwestern writer and ethnographer, purposely appropriates Native American cultural forms to foster her life's aesthetic project.

Like the authors' mixed "American" identities, their writings are formal hybrids, works composed from a variety of cultural sources. As the frontier is a zone of cultural conflict, so is hybrid frontier literature; two accents, voices, consciousnesses therein "come together and consciously fight it out on the territory of the utterance," according to Bakhtin.[33] For example, David Murray states that autobiography was not a traditional Native American form.[34] Hopkins appropriates the autobiography in order to reach an Anglo audience but uses that form to convey the collective life of the Paiutes. She also includes within her autobiography two traditional Native American genres: the tribal origin story and historical narrative. Beckwourth's as-told-to autobiography includes a Native American coup tale and war narrative as well as European essay and poetical verse. The postcontact trickster tale "White Men Are Snakes" evinces hybridity by incorporating biblical narrative into its structure. Also,

Mourning Dove revises Okanogan trickster tales for an audience of white children by excising scatological and "superstitious" details. Finally, Austin employs Native American myths, tropes, and translations in many of her novels and essays. Undoubtedly, that the authors inhabit the borderlands as "threshold people" effects their construction of hybrid works.

If the American borderlands are like thresholds to a new state of being, they differ from the transitional states described by Turner in his theories of ritual. As I stated above, Turner finds that in the transitional phase, initiands are subversive and socially critical; yet he is ambiguous about whether they can sustain cultural critique. For Turner, the liminal or transitional stage is resolved when the initiand returns to the structure of society.[35] Because the initiands return to the same tribal society from which they separate in a rite of passage, Turner claims the action in the transitional state is not much more than "a subversive flicker" instantly contained in the status quo.[36] At the same time, he postulates exceptions to this rule; for instance, he describes the Tallensi shaman who may experience "the transformation of what is essentially a liminal or extrastructural phase into a permanent condition of sacred 'outsiderhood'" from which he may "criticize" and "mediate" between members of society.[37] Turner's theories arise from his investigation of rites of passage in which initiands separate from and return to the same tribal status quo. The frontiers allow for social critique because many of the writers in this study do not rejoin the same cultural group from which they separate. Native Americans, for example, separate from tribal culture only to become reincorporated into an Anglo American–dominated social order. Turner states, "What the initiand seeks through rite and myth is not a moral *exemplum* so much as the power to transcend the limits of his previous status."[38] In the homogenous social structure that embraces ritual, the initiand can enjoy transcendence, knowing the return to social order is inevitable. Frontier writers west of the border seek out or even create moral exempla as they confront not a return to their own traditional social structure but further immersion in antistructure as they are defined by Anglo American culture. Of necessity, then, the borderlands become a place of social critique in which some writers, unlike Turner's initiands, shape and influence the dominant culture rather than succumb to its inscription (Beckwourth being a notable exception).

Given the creative and transformative possibilities fostered by the transitional state, Turner focused almost exclusively on the liminal by the end of his career when theorizing rites of passage. He stresses the "positive and active" qualities of the transitional phase: its ability to transcend structure through "flow," the experience of "direct, unmediated communion with one another."[39] Similarly, Frederick Jackson Turner, the historian, considers the frontier to be a margin of social renewal. For the latter, social order is inverted on the frontier as the pioneering frontiersman finds himself in "continuous touch with the simplicity of primitive society" and in the position of remaking American society. As Frederick Jackson Turner states, "American social development has been continually beginning over again on the frontier."[40] Although he does not use the terms "limen" or "transitional phase," Frederick Jackson Turner exalts its culturally creative and socially transformative properties: for him the frontier effects the "perennial rebirth, this fluidity of American life, [and] this expansion westward with its new opportunities," all of which "furnish the forces dominating American character."[41]

However, for cultural others, being in the borderlands between groups that make contact is not always reenlivening or creative. As Anzaldúa asserts, "hatred, anger and exploitation" characterize the border for Chicanos.[42] Pratt ascribes to the frontier contact zone "conditions of coercion, radical inequality, and intractable conflict."[43] Similarly, Robert Berkhofer argues that the Anglo American frontier "was perceived more as a zone of conflict than one of cooperation."[44] On the frontiers, both whites and nonwhites faced alien cultures, engaged in conflicts, and competed in the struggle for survival.

At the same time, frontiers were not simply sites of victimhood or negation; rather, they were places where cultural others mediated between groups and defined and analyzed social and cultural problems. Authors between cultures found themselves in the "pure potentiality" of the borderlands, scrutinizing the social milieu they confronted. The frontier prepared them to grapple with the problems of Americanization as they separated from their original cultures and faced a new culture that debated what to do with them. Also, existing between cultures, the authors used their writings to imagine or to revise the anticipated destinies of their societies and to reconfigure U.S. culture.

And they reconfigured culture by attempting to shape frontier intercultural relations. *From* the borderlands the authors anticipate the establishment of white dominance; *in* the borderlands the expected social order is presently becoming; hence, the authors exist in a potentially creative space. Unlike Victor Turner's initiands who separate from and return to the same tribal society in a rite of passage, writers "west of the border" separate from and return to different cultures on the American frontiers; social inversion is thus double-edged. As Frederick Jackson Turner states, the culture and customs of the Anglo American frontiersman are inverted in the wilderness when "he shouts the war cry and takes the scalp in orthodox Indian fashion."[45] In the borderlands, cultural others find their native laws and customs subverted by Anglos. But cultural others also invert the prescriptions of the dominant society in order to negotiate the frontiers, and they endeavor to shape their own historical and social fates through cross-cultural dialogues. Confronted with their cultural and social co-optation, these writers face the closing of the frontiers.

According to Turner, the historian, the frontier officially closed in 1890 when the continent had been crossed and its "free land" exhausted. However, Turner's claim was based on the authority of Patrick Porter, the superintendent of the U.S. Census, who, it is said, lacked expertise in both demographics and statistical analysis. Challenging Turner's claim that the frontier closed in 1890, Gerald D. Nash asserts that,

> as eminent geographers who were Turner's contemporaries pointed out, specifically Isaiah Bowman, the western frontiers did not disappear in 1890. Frontier-type settlement, Bowman noted, continued steadily in the United States (and western Canada) between 1890 and 1930. Indeed, between 1905 and 1915 more than 500,000 Americans participated in a land rush to the western Canadian provinces, a rush that was one of the largest of its kind. When compared to the censuses of 1900 or 1910, that of 1890 was not especially distinctive. From the perspective of 1990, therefore, 1890 may not have been as significant a watershed as contemporaries believed.[46]

If, as Nash asserts, "the western frontier did not disappear in 1890," when did the frontier close?[47] As human spaces where cultures meet, frontiers close when one group can no longer rule and define itself because another group exercises control over it.[48] The sociological factors that indicate the closing of a frontier are extermination, assimilation, exclusion, and/or expulsion, although in some cases there may be an impasse between groups.[49] On the borders where Native Americans, Mexicans, and Asians encountered Anglo Americans, specific historical contests ensued over control of the frontiers as different sides determined whether to efface the frontier by eliminating the other or brave the experience of culture contact.

Assimilation to white customs, expulsion from their land, and extermination through wars menaced Native Americans in their frontier relations with Anglo Americans. Tribes confronted land-hungry settlers and missionaries who sought to convert them to Christianity. The U.S. government removed Native Americans from their land and totally dispersed the tribes or placed them on reservations where they were unable to consolidate their power and retaliate effectively. On reservations, government agents acculturated the tribes by giving them European-style clothing, offering them an Anglo education, and training them in agricultural methods. Opponents of the reservation system argued that Native Americans would more quickly become assimilated if they were individual property owners and U.S. citizens. The Dawes Act of 1887 sought to make them independent farmers by allotting 160 acres of land to each head of a household. However, a consequence of the Dawes Act was that the government also appropriated for white settlers large tracts of land allegedly not being used by tribes. Ironically, allotment divested the Plains tribes of 60 percent of 138 million acres of their land. Further, their farming ventures failed to profit them because the most effective uses of Plains land—that is, ranching or large-scale farming—required tracts of land larger than 160 acres.

While allotment and reservationism threatened tribal cultures, Native Americans resisted the closing of the frontiers. They exploited religious factionalism among Anglo Americans to achieve their own ends. Among their various acts of resistance were "religious revitalization movements . . . last-ditch stands, passive resistance through factional splits, and antagonistic acculturation as time went on."[50] Ultimately, as Native Americans were displaced from their lands and stripped of their tribal customs, the frontier was closed to them. However, in the early twentieth century, the Indian Reorganization Act under the liberal auspices of the Commissioner of Indian Affairs John Collier, proposed to abolish allotment, reestablish Native American government, and effect the cultural and aesthetic revival of aboriginal traditions. Collier, it seems, desired to right the wrongs done to Native Americans, although some tribal groups (for example, the Navajos) criticized the Indian Reorganization Act for employing a liberal guise to justify once again controlling Native American life.[51]

While Mexicans, like Native Americans, were perceived as an obstacle to Manifest Destiny, they, unlike the aboriginal tribes, were not considered assimilable by nineteenth-century Anglo Americans. In the nineteenth century, the Mexican-American War erupted over the issue of U.S. expansion: the United States annexation of Texas in 1845 fueled Mexican aggression as did the feud over whether the border of Texas was the Rio Grande or the Nueces River.

During the 1820s, as the cotton kingdom expanded in the South, U.S. planters migrated to the Mexican territory of Texas. Consequently, Mexico outlawed slavery in 1829 and U.S. immigration to Texas in 1830, but since U.S. citizens outnumbered Mexicans in Texas by this time, they defied the antislavery law. In 1836, an armed insurrection of 187 U.S. rebels in Texas was defeated at the Alamo by the Mexican army, led by General Antonio Lopez de Santa Anna. A few days later, the Mexican army captured another Texas detachment of 350 men and executed them all in the town of Goliad. In retaliation for these acts, Sam Houston surprised Santa Anna's forces near the San Jacinto River, killed 630 Mexicans, forcing Mexico to cede Texas to the Americans.

After the official annexation of Texas in 1845, Mexico broke off diplomatic relations with the United States. The two countries continued to fight over the border of Texas: the United States declared the border to be the Rio Grande, whereas Mexico insisted it was the Nueces River, 150 miles north. Soon after President James Polk ordered General Zachary Taylor to occupy the disputed area with his troops, a skirmish broke out that served as a pretext for war. At the same time, in the Mexican territory of California, the illegal immigration of Americans increased because California proved to be an excellent source of raw materials. In 1846, these immigrants, under the aegis of the "Bear Flag Republic," revolted against Mexico and declared their independence in California. In addition, Commander John D. Sloat of the U.S. Navy sailed into Monterey Bay and took possession of California.

The Mexican-American War ended in 1848 with the signing of the Treaty of Guadalupe-Hidalgo. Mexico accepted the Rio Grande as its border and ceded California, New Mexico, Nevada, and parts of Colorado, Arizona, and Utah to the United States in exchange for $15 million. Following the Mexican-American War, that frontier stayed painfully open for many displaced Mexicans who remained in contact with their conquerors. Those living in areas annexed to the United States suffered the alienation of being foreigners in their own land.[52] Nine days after Mexico relinquished California to the United

States, gold was found there. The Foreign Miners' Tax, which targeted Spanish-speaking miners, was a reminder to the displaced Mexicans of their national alienation.

Unlike the Native Americans and Mexicans who were the conquered subjects of westering Anglo invaders, Asians, coming from further west, forged a counter frontier and were feared as potential colonizers. To Americans, Asians represented the Yellow Peril: military invasion, racial intermixing, and the moral degeneracy of America through Asian influence. There is no evidence, however, that Asian immigrants espoused any ideology akin to Manifest Destiny. They migrated to the western United States to mine the "Gold Mountain" and to work as laborers on the railroad. At first, Anglo Americans encouraged Asians to immigrate because they were a much needed source of cheap labor, but when they started to compete with whites for jobs, they became the objects of discriminatory legislation. Chapters 3 and 4 develop the historical context in which Americans sought to close the Asian frontier through anti-immigration, exclusion, and anti-miscegenation laws. While the frequently unjust legislative and social practices of Anglos often inform the historical perspectives of writers west of the border, the emphasis is on their efforts to seek inclusion in American life.

If closed frontiers bolster the power and supremacy of the dominant culture, then open frontiers are ambiguous, contradictory, subversive, pluralistic, and resistant. Closed frontiers denote the termination of intercultural relations and the institution of Anglo dominance; open frontiers indicate the continuation of intercultural relations and resistance to Anglo dominance. However, open and closed frontiers are abstract and ideal categories since states of openness and closure are never absolute. Rather, American identity and culture involve a constant negotiation between open- and closed-frontier politics, and frontier politics emerge from the tension between the possibility inherent in the transitional phase and the order prescribed by the dominant Anglo culture. Writers west of the border position themselves in relation to potential (if unrealized) closed frontiers. Both Beckwourth and Ridge seek to close the frontier through their writings. Ridge closes the frontier when he loses faith in Trickster's mediating abilities; Beckwourth does so when, seeking renown as a white hero, he uses his insider position in Crow society to instruct Anglo Americans in extermination techniques. Both Beckwourth and Joaquin Murieta (Ridge's bandit) exist between cultures but also identify with Anglo American culture and accept its inevitable dominance. Conversely, Sarah Winnemucca Hopkins, Sui Sin Far, and many of the authors of the trickster tales employ their writings to wedge open the frontier that is closing upon them. Caught in the time period in which Japanese people went from being viewed as fascinating exotics to potential conquerors, Onoto Watanna betrays an ambiguous position to frontier politics. Finally, writing after Turner claimed that the frontier was closed, Mary Austin attempts to reopen it by rejecting assimilation and emphasizing the art, spirituality, and customs of the aboriginal people.[53]

Through the frontier autobiographies of James P. Beckwourth (1856) and Sarah Winnemucca Hopkins (1883), chapter 1 examines how "double consciousness" affects their social rite of passage. Double consciousness results from Beckwourth's and Hopkins's existence between cultures: Beckwourth juggles black, white, and Crow identities; Hopkins, as translator, mediates between Paiutes and whites on the frontier. In addition, double consciousness is a function of Beckwourth's and Hopkins's bicultural collaboration with white editors, their rhetorical relationship to a white audience, and the texts' autoethnographic form as the writers "engage with the colonizer's own terms."[54] They do this through such double-voiced strategies as parody and hidden polemic.

Beckwourth's double consciousness is manifested in the dual, paradoxical structure of the autobiography, which couples a conventional, heroic frontier saga with his insights about Crow humanism and ingenuity. While simultaneous narratives that both bolster and subvert Anglo rule create a schism in Beckwourth's autobiographical self, he attempts to heal the rift in his divided self and to close the frontier when he concludes his narrative with an essay on how to exterminate the Plains tribes. Unlike Beckwourth, who is controlled by his double consciousness, Hopkins employs hers rhetorically to persuade her audience. Working in the historical period between reservationism and allotment, she dismantles Anglo stereotypes of Native Americans to modify and rebuild their image. Ultimately, Hopkins seeks to pry open the frontiers by preventing the unjust agency system from destroying the Paiutes and by reimagining assimilation as an open-frontier policy.

Similarly, trickster border narratives, examined in chapter 2, respond to frontier politics. Native American trickster border narratives, created after first contact with whites, reimagine relations between colonizers and natives. Like the Trickster of precontact myths, the Trickster of postcontact tales is a mediator, but the newer figure takes on the auxiliary function of cultural intercessor. In Native

American mythology, Trickster was a figure who ordered the world for humans soon after it was created and then disappeared when his work was complete. Trickster border narratives portray the second coming of Trickster, who returns with the potential to reorder the chaos of the frontier for Native Americans.

Through Trickster's performance as cultural mediator, authors and raconteurs test Trickster's ability to respond to culture contact. Some tales simply lament the negation of Trickster's work by whites; others suggest behaviors that tribes must practice in order to survive the frontier. In *Coyote Stories* (1933), Mourning Dove practices assimilation by rewriting Trickster for a white audience. The variable success of her revisions speaks to the uneven outcome of assimilation. Through Trickster, Mourning Dove discovers a position of intercultural synthesis and of cultural critique from which to write. As opposed to Mourning Dove, John Rollin Ridge, in his 1854 dime novel about the trickster-bandit Joaquin Murieta, doubts the mediating ability of his Trickster. In an allegory, Ridge links injustice toward Mexicans during the Gold Rush with the abuses inflicted on Cherokees during removal, but he dismantles the allegory as he creates trickster writing. Masquerading as social critique, his novel performs a "ritual of status reversal" that "reaffirm[s] the order of structure".[55] In the end, the rangers murder the rebel Murieta and quash the Mexican resistance. Whereas Beckwourth closes the frontier and reinforces his assumed identity as a white hero, Ridge closes it believing that the trickster-bandit is impotent to reorder the frontier.

At the turn of the nineteenth century, Chinese people became the objects of exclusion and antimiscegenation legislation that sought to maintain a Chinese "bachelor society," prevent Asians and whites from intermarrying, and stay the spread of the "Yellow Peril." Chapter 3 focuses on the cultural work of Sui Sin Far, who uses her fiction to counteract both the restrictions of the Asian frontier and the mainstream representations of Chinese life that link marriage to bride bartering and evince miscegenation phobia. Born of an English father and a Chinese mother, Sui Sin Far embraced her Asian identity when she could have passed as white. A bold activist who agitated against racism toward the Chinese, she exploits her mixed identity in her fiction. Her collection of short stories *Mrs. Spring Fragrance* (1912) explains Asian marriage traditions to mystified white readers and portrays intermarriage as a viable option for men and women in the United States. Within the private realm of marriage relations, Sui Sin Far seeks to maintain an open frontier.

Unlike Sui Sin Far, who shapes her fiction to answer America's stolid anti-Chinese fervor, Onoto Watanna (Sui Sin Far's biological sister and the focus of chapter 4) chose to pass as Japanese in order to exploit American interest in Japanese exoticism and secure her fame and fortune as a romance writer. In Japanese American romance novels like *Miss Nume of Japan* (1899) and *A Japanese Blossom* (1906), she idealizes Japan and envisions Japanese people as assimilable, noble, attractive marriage partners and model U.S. citizens. As anti-Japanese sentiment evolved, the concept of Japanese American romance became oxymoronic for Onoto Watanna and her interracial couples began to push against the line of social acceptability. Confronting American antipathy for the Japanese, she strives to make her characters and stories more appealing to her audience. Consequently, besides producing Oriental stereotypes, she acts as an apologist for the Japanese and deflates "Yellow Peril" paranoia. In so doing, she maintains an ambiguous position in frontier politics.

Mary Austin, the subject of chapter 5, writes after the western coast of America has been reached and Native America has been invaded by westering settlers. A white woman, Austin demonstrates—even as she raises complex concerns about the appropriation of native cultures by whites—that resistance to Anglo dominance is not wholly the domain of minority authors. By adopting native and aboriginal guises, she legitimates her work of reopening the frontier closed to Mexicans and Native Americans. Austin inverts the structure of the closed frontier by incorporating, revising, and building upon the language and concepts of conservation and anthropology in such works as *The Land of Journeys' Ending* (1924) and *One-Smoke Stories* (1934). Reopening the frontier is linked, for Austin, to her political, artistic, and literary historical projects. Nature must be conserved because it produces culture, and native cultures must be protected because they are the origins of a distinctly American aesthetic, cultural, and literary tradition.

When shaping *West of the Border,* several factors influenced my choice of subject matter. I wanted, for one thing, to contribute to the recovery of noncanonical works in American literary studies by considering marginalized writers and unfamiliar works. Since many previous books on U.S. frontier literature discuss the pioneering frontiersman, I chose writers who played diverse roles on the frontiers. Hopkins was a translator for the military, Beckwourth, a fur trader and Indian chief; Mourning Dove was an amateur folklorist, Ridge, a newspaper editor and dime novelist; Sui Sin Far was an activist for Chinese rights, Onoto Watanna, a popular romance writer; and Austin was a conservationist and anthropologist. By approaching multicultural frontier literature from several different perspectives, I explore the complexity and variety of American frontier interactions, not just the Anglo frontiersman's encounter with "free land."

In addition to examining various kinds of frontiers, I have sought writers for whom the frontier experience was truly multicultural. This criterion helps explain a choice of writers that might seem unusual.[56] All of the writers exhibit biculturality; some, like Ridge and Beckwourth, negotiate several ethnic identities, evincing "triculturality." As a result, many writers employ the narratives of other cultures: the Cherokee Anglo author Ridge tells the story of Mexicans in nineteenth-century California; Austin appropriates the lore of several Southwestern cultures; and Onoto Watanna adopts Japan and Japanese characters as the basis of her novels. All of the writers enable my exploration of the intercultural complexities of the U.S. borderlands. I hope this book might pave the way for other studies of intercultural American literature, such as that of the Canadian, Hawaiian, and Alaskan frontiers.

Still, the question must be asked: why read these works? Besides their obvious interest to scholars in American studies and cultural studies, for those interested in multicultural literature the writings raise timely and provocative issues about the relation between culture and literature, the function of stereotypes in ethnic writing, and the contributions of marginalized writers to literary history, among other things. Beckwourth and Onoto Watanna, for instance, call into question the use of stereotypes in ethnic writing. In explaining his frontier identity, Beckwourth employs several conventional, often contrasting types, like the Indian-hater and the Indian chief, only to reveal how these representations cannot effectively convey his experiences. Onoto Watanna, who both responds to and replicates Japanese stereotypes, makes her readers ponder the inherent negativity of stereotypes and reevaluate the function of the popular romance in American culture. Other writers, like Sui Sin Far and Austin, make valuable contributions to realist-regionalist fiction at the turn of the last century. Sui Sin Far, whose *Mrs. Spring Fragrance* (1912) precedes both James Joyce's *Dubliners* (1916) and Sherwood Anderson's *Winesburg, Ohio* (1919), creates a collection of short stories that are linked by character, theme, and setting. Yet in addition, she interrelates the stories dialogically, creating a point of view in one story only to qualify that point of view in another story. Austin, a self-proclaimed regionalist writer, extends the boundaries of regionalism when she produces theoretical, travel, and folkloric writings. Austin's social, political, and artistic commitment to the land and people of the Southwest enables her to broaden the theoretical and generic borders of regionalist writing. The works of all the writers in this book reveal how they shape different literary forms cross-culturally to develop a genuinely U.S. literature.

Finally, the writers and works suggest issues relevant to American society at the turn into the twenty-first century by raising critical concerns about frontier politics and ideology. They also expand the boundaries of frontier studies by giving voice to minorities who refuse to be silenced. Their texts, which embody the voices of cultural others, form a continuum of responses to the Anglo American frontier migration. Some writers capitulate (often uneasily) to the inevitability of Manifest Destiny; others protest the hegemony of white Americans or seek to undo the ruling majority's course in the West. While *West of the Border* illustrates the historical dialectic between open- and closed-frontier politics, such tension is inherent in U.S. pluralism to this day. Throughout history, the United States defines and redefines itself as it struggles to establish not only its geographical borders but the boundaries of its national identity.

1 Double Consciousness in the Borderlands

The Frontier Autobiographies of James P. Beckwourth and Sarah Winnemucca Hopkins

In *Life among the Piutes,* Sarah Winnemucca Hopkins recalls the Paiutes' initial contact with whites, when her Grandfather Truckee introduced the tribe to written language, his "rag-friend."[1] As Hopkins relates, her grandfather "then showed us a more wonderful thing than all the others that he had brought. It was a paper, which he said could talk to him. He took it out and he would talk to it, and talk with it. He said, 'This can talk to all our white brothers, and our white sisters, and their children. . . . He also said the paper can travel like the wind, and it can go and talk with their fathers and brothers and sisters, and come back to tell what they are doing, and whether they are well or sick.' "[2] To Grandfather Truckee, the "rag-friend"—a letter of commendation signed by General John Fremont, documenting Chief Truckee's service in the war against Mexico—is the means to achieve his dream of community and cooperation with whites. It represents within his oral community the possibility for open communication that defies time, space, and cultural prejudice. Like the "rag-friend," the autobiographies of Hopkins and James P. Beckwourth intercede between whites and Native Americans on the frontiers.

The Life and Adventures of James P. Beckwourth, as told to T. D. Bonner (1856), and *Life among the Piutes: Their Wrongs and Claims* (1883) portray lives situated on the frontier between Native Americans and encroaching Anglos.

In his narrative, the biracial Beckwourth—he was both black and white—portrays himself as a white hero and relates his adventures as a fur trapper and chief of the Crow tribe. According to his editor, Beckwourth's autobiographical text is of ethnographic value in that it provides "more interesting particulars than were ever before given of the aborigines."[3] The Hopkins account, on the other hand—she is a Paiute woman who worked as a translator and interpreter for military personnel and reservation agents and as a scout for the U.S. Army during the Bannock War—is an autobiography written for political purposes: Hopkins wrote it to tell her white audience about the injustices of the reservation system and to raise money for the impoverished Paiutes. There is a difference in the significance that writing has for these two autobiographers: ultimately, Beckwourth rejects the mediating capacity of frontier autobiography, while Hopkins discovers that the survival of the Paiutes depends on her literacy skills.

Like Grandfather Truckee's "rag-friend," Beckwourth's and Hopkins's autobiographies talk to their white brothers and sisters. Hence, from a rhetorical perspective, the autobiographies mediate between white audiences and nonwhite narrators. As Arnold Krupat observes, most nineteenth-century Native American autobiographies are "bicultural composite compositions." This is true in both of these cases: the autobiographies of Hopkins and Beckwourth are produced by nonwhite authors with white collaborators. Mirroring in their origins the meeting of cultures, the narratives are "the textual equivalent of the frontier."[4] In other words, historically, both Beckwourth and Hopkins migrate between the often contrasting Native and Anglo cultures on the frontiers; formally, their autobiographies are the products of collaboration between whites and nonwhites; and rhetorically, the narratives exist between the nonwhite culture from where they are written and the white culture for which they are written. These multiple liminal situations, or instances in which the writers are between cultures, create a context that gives rise to the double consciousness of the narrators.

Analyzing the psychic predicament of African descendants in America, W. E. B. Du Bois develops the concept of double consciousness—a concept also applicable to Native Americans. Double consciousness, he asserts, is the African American's legacy from the "American world,—a world which yields him no true self-consciousness, but only lets him see himself through the revelation of the other world." Given the multiple liminal contexts of their autobiographies,

Beckwourth and Hopkins, far from experiencing "true self-consciousness," constantly confront the "revelation[s]" of two (or more) worlds. For Du Bois, double consciousness is both a state of psychosocial oppression or the experience of "two warring ideals in one dark body"; and a "gift" of "second-sight in this American world."[5] In allowing the African American to "see himself through the revelation of the other world," double consciousness necessarily provides access to the dominant white consciousness. As a result, double consciousness may occasion manipulating, conversing with, or subverting the dominant culture. For example, the genre of autoethnography presupposes double consciousness since "autoethnographic texts are those the others construct in response to or in dialogue with" European ethnographic representations of subjugated others.[6]

This brings us to the ideas of parody and hidden polemic. Henry Louis Gates's theory of signifyin(g) suggests strategies of response or dialogue, ways in which "double-voicedness" can be an empowering exploitation of double consciousness. Building on Bakhtin's theory of double-voiced texts, Gates defines the two forms of signifyin(g) mentioned above, parody and hidden polemic. In parody, an author strips another person's text of its original intention and invests that text with an opposite meaning so that it serves different aims. Hidden polemic involves indirection, as a writer's text alludes to and is crafted into an attack against some outside text.[7] Viewing themselves through "the revelation of the other world," Beckwourth and Hopkins employ parody and hidden polemic to transform double consciousness into empowered double-voicedness.

Beckwourth, anticipating the interpretive practices of audience groups who know he is black, crafts an indirect attack on the atavistic belief that race and character are inextricably entwined. Yet, for the most part, double consciousness in his text is exhibited in the creation of narratives that simultaneously threaten Crow survival and praise Crow humanity and ingenuity. Double consciousness complicates Beckwourth's identity, whereas Hopkins manipulates double consciousness to critique Anglo and Native American frontier relations. As Karl Kroeber states, "The overwhelming attention to problems of African Americans in our society, moreover, has obscured the very different situation of Indians, who are not necessarily afflicted with that 'double consciousness' so famously formulated by W. E. B. Du Bois. . . . For some Indians at least, indigenous and European cultures could be complexly reinforcing rather than simply divisive."[8] Hopkins uses parody and hidden polemic politically to persuade her audience by delineating the "complexly reinforcing" affinities, rather than the differences, between whites and Paiutes.

Through double consciousness, these writers confront the tension between open and closed frontiers—the struggle to continue or to terminate culture contact. Beckwourth apprehends this tension and writes concurrent narratives that bolster and undermine Crow survival. Ironically, given his biracial identity, he seeks to end culture contact, to close the frontier, with his concluding chapter on how to exterminate the Native Americans. Hopkins, however, never abandons the creative and constructive potential of the frontier. Working in the historical gap between reservationism and allotment, she wrests open the frontier that is fast closing upon her people.

The Life and Adventures of James P. Beckwourth realizes a cultural enigma: Beckwourth, though of biracial, black and white, parentage, passes as white in his autobiography, which recounts his adventures as a Crow chief. From which ethnic tradition, then, should his autobiography be approached? In whose canon does it belong? In the preface to his autobiography, Beckwourth's collaborator T. D. Bonner directs the audience to regard Beckwourth "as an Indian" who "speaks of [Crow] customs, and describes their characteristics" (iv). Historian William Loren Katz finds that Beckwourth was traditionally thought to be a white culture hero and cites as evidence the 1951 movie *Tomahawk*, in which his character is played by a white actor. However, as his book's title suggests, Katz reclaims Beckwourth as a "black Indian."[9] Assigning his autobiography to any one tradition over another is done at the expense of its many frontiers. Instead, in approaching it as a *frontier* narrative, the reader refuses to accept his wholesale "passing" and in so doing is challenged both to investigate the cultural layers of Beckwourth's autobiographical self and to examine the connection between Beckwourth's position between cultures and double consciousness on the frontier.

At the heart of his autobiography, Beckwourth recalls his sojourn with the Crows and his heroic rise to chief of the Crow tribe. A Siouan tribe, and part of the Hidatsa group, the Crows met the whites for the first time in 1802. They occupied the vast and valuable territory from the North Platte River to the

Yellowstone River, along the eastern base of the Rocky Mountains. They were mainly a hunting tribe that participated in communal buffalo hunts, but cultivated some land to grow the tobacco they used in their tobacco ceremony. The Crows were also known to possess "more and better horses than any other tribe in the Missouri Valley."[10] Beckwourth's narrative relates how he sojourned with the Crows, learned their language and customs, married many wives, and eventually became a chief.

Beckwourth also recounts his entry into fur trading following his fight with the Saint Louis blacksmith to whom he was apprenticed. The autobiography depicts his fur-trading adventures with William H. Ashley's company; his expedition with Ashley's successors Jedediah Smith, David Jackson, and William Sublette; and his work as agent among the Crows for the American Fur Company. Further, he chronicles his experiences as a soldier in the Seminole War, various travels in the West, and discovery of Beckwourth Pass—a new emigrant route to California. Throughout his life, Beckwourth wandered between Crow and Anglo cultures.

In 1853, at his hotel near the Beckwourth Pass, Beckwourth, seeking to secure his renown, solicited the aid of Bonner—a con man and "itinerant justice of the peace" in the gold camps—in writing his life story.[11] The text they produced contains thirty-seven chapters of rather stylized prose, detailing with occasional passages of introspection Beckwourth's "heroic" and often bloody endeavors. The result is a hybrid narrative of Western and Native American literary forms. Krupat places this autobiography in the Western American tradition, which shares similarities with the Native American. For instance, both traditions borrow formal models from war and captivity narratives.[12] In addition, the function and the origin of Western and Native American autobiographies are the same in that both celebrate the triumph of civilization over savagery and both issue from a collaborative process.[13] On the former account, Beckwourth's autobiography focuses on Native American warfare and celebrates the frontier victory of the white man; on the latter, as part of the tradition of cross-cultural frontier narratives, Beckwourth's story dramatizes the autobiographical subject's excursions between cultures.

Beckwourth's "as-told-to" autobiography is produced by an editor who is white and a narrator who exists in black, white, and Native American worlds. Writing about his editorial intrusions, Bonner claims: "In prosecuting the task, the author has in no instance departed from the story of the narrator, but it was taken down literally as it was from day to day related. Beckwourth kept no journal, and, of course, relied upon his memory alone; consequently dates are often wanting" (iv). As David Murray suggests, while it was conventional for white collaborators in the bicultural composition process to downplay their editorial intrusions in order that the narrator might "appear in his own right," they consequently proffered an inexact view of the narrative's production.[14] In Bonner's case, despite his outrageous claims to fidelity to Beckwourth's every word as he orally composes a 537-page text, there is evidence of his creative incursions in the text. The last sentence of the narrative flows without stopping into the poem "Pine Leaf, The Indian Heroine" as if Beckwourth had spontaneously composed it. However, Elinor Wilson attributes the laudatory poem to Bonner, noting that it mimics "full Temperance-Society style"—and Bonner, at one time, was involved in the Temperance Society and wrote temperance poetry. Also, accepting that the entire autobiography is a mere transcription of Beckwourth's speech would entail believing Beckwourth spoke the following sentence:

> I would break my narrative for a while to afford some explanation in regard to the different bands of the Pawnee tribe; a subject which at the present day is but imperfectly understood by the general reader—the knowledge being confined to those alone who, by living among them, have learned their language, and hence become acquainted with the nature of their divisional lands. (26)

This sixty-six-word sentence, which winds around like a ball of yarn, sounds more like highly stylized writing than informal speech. Complex sentences such as this one raise suspicions that Bonner was, at times, more than simply Beckwourth's scribe.

The perfect chronology of incidents and the narrative's organization into thirty-seven chapters further indicate that Bonner shaped Beckwourth's autobiography—a genre that, by definition, is supposed to be penned by the narrator. However, this is not to dismiss Beckwourth's autobiographical identity as corrupt. Bicultural collaborations, Murray maintains, are simply "not the voice" of the subject regardless of what white editors assert; rather, the multiple voices in the narrative raise critical issues about how the voices conjoin or struggle against each other, and how they are "implicated in cross-cultural complicities and contradictions."[15] For instance, the illiterate Beckwourth in his autobiography appeals to a reviewer through conventions that mirror those of the frontier romance. We do well to ask to what extent the literary crafting of Bonner is complicit in the creation of these conventions. Although it is not possible to chart with certainty where Beckwourth's voice ends and Bonner's begins, the bicultural collaboration intrinsically affects the formation of the autobiographical subject's double consciousness.[16]

In addition to Bonner's intrusions, Beckwourth's presentation of himself as a member of Anglo and Crow cultures contributes to the formation of a double-voiced text.[17] Helen Carr finds that with as-told-to Native American autobiographies there is difficulty interpreting the narrative because the Native American subject uses the "dominant discourse" to tell his or her story.[18] In as-told-to accounts, then, the socially marginalized narrator is isolated from the language in which the writer tells the subject's story. It then becomes "naive and treacherous realism" to accept wholesale the expression in the autobiography because it is proffered in the language of the dominant group, the language through which the speaker is marginalized.

In Beckwourth's case, the distance between the narrator and his story is even more confounding. Krupat remarks that in as-told-to autobiographies the sender of the narrative and the "cultural code" implicit in the story are doubled.[19] Beckwourth's account quadruples the sender and cultural code since Beckwourth's tale is shaped by Bonner who is Anglo and Beckwourth who poses as a "black Indian," as a "white Indian," and at times as an "Indian hater." As the narrative subject, then, he not only adopts both dominant and marginalized roles but also ranges between those competing positions.

Mediating between marginalized Crow and dominant Anglo cultures, Beckwourth manifests double consciousness. In reality Beckwourth was the son of a slave mother and an overseer father; in the autobiography he passes as white and speaks as a Native American. He slights his black background when he absents his mother from his life story. Double consciousness, then, involves Beckwourth's awareness of himself as biologically black and narratively white. To readers who know he is black he directs a hidden polemic, while hoaxing the readers who accept his passing as white. Both hidden polemic and hoax respond to white society's fear of atavism—the belief that in biracial persons race and character are so interwoven that no matter how convincingly one "passes," ultimately "black blood . . . always tells."[20] Responding to atavism, Beckwourth challenges the rationale that people of color are morally inferior and, therefore, in need of subjugation by a "superior" race. Hence, he questions a basic justification for closing the frontier through assimilation or, worse, genocide.

Many of Beckwourth's contemporaries, privy to legends about the famous "mulatto" fur trapper, were aware of his racial background and, consequently, unadmiring of his character and suspicious of his tale. Like many nineteenth-century slave narratives considered beyond the ability of a slave, Beckwourth's autobiography was caught in a debate about its authenticity, but not until after its second publication. As Robert B. Stepto observes, authenticating documents are intended to establish the existence of the author and the truth of the tale.[21] Although Beckwourth's existence was never contested, his credibility preoccupies scholars to this day. The original edition of the autobiography published in 1856 contains only the narrative and a brief preface by Bonner. The farthest Bonner goes in attempting to authenticate the teller is when he states: "Beckwourth is personally known to thousands of people 'living on both sides of the mountains,' and also, from his service under the United States government, has enjoyed the acquaintance of many officers of the United States Army, who have been stationed in Florida, Mexico, and California" (iv). He offers no authenticating letters from these officers and not a word defending the veracity of the tale.

However, in the 1892 English edition of the autobiography, Charles Godfrey Leland undertakes the task of authentication in his preface. He states, "I incline to think that Beckwourth has been too severely judged as regards veracity." He offers tales from other sources about Beckwourth and uses them to verify the autobiography by concluding that both have the same manner and style. He also collects "anecdotes" that "abundantly prove" that the autobiography "reflects very truly the real spirit of life as it was among those aborigines with whom he lived."[22] Leland reasons that because the stories he collects are as spirited and adventurous as Beckwourth's, Beckwourth's tale must be true. Perhaps Leland attempted to authenticate Beckwourth's autobiography for his British readers, who could neither fathom nor relate to the wildness and violence of the American frontier experience. Yet as recently as 1972, Beckwourth's veracity was the central critical issue for Delmont R. Oswald in his new edition of the text for the University of Nebraska Press. Oswald states that the goal of his heavily annotated version is "to show as comprehensively as possible what parts of Beckwourth's story are authentic, what parts are questionable or at least not susceptible to proof, and what parts are unreliable or deliberate lies."[23]

Beckwourth undoubtedly evoked the tall-tale tradition as he articulated his life story. However, Katz finds that black frontiersmen were even more severely indicted than whites for blotting out the truth of their tales. In addition, Katz states that the "black Indian" Edward Rose was degraded by a "more modern scholar" as a "morose, moody misfit of mixed blood and lawless disposition."[24] Similarly, some of Beckwourth's contemporaries linked negative character traits to his racial background. Bernard DeVoto observes that historian Francis Parkman scrawled in the margin of the preface to Beckwourth's autobiography: "Beckwith [*sic*] is a fellow of bad character—a compound of white and black blood, though he represents otherwise."[25] Other contemporaries of Beckwourth's, like Charles Christy and James H. White, conscious of his black blood, deem him morally degenerate and an outrageous liar.[26]

Beckwourth responds to those who, capitulating to the myth of atavism, might connect his bloodthirsty behavior to his mixed race. After many chapters relating his facility and expertise in Native American warfare, Beckwourth accounts for his ferocious conduct:

> Many of my readers will doubtless wonder how a man who had been reared in civilized life could ever participate in such scenes of carnage and rapine. . . . I hardly ever struck down an Indian but my mind reverted to the mangled bodies of my childish play-fellows. . . . When I fought with the Crow nation, I fought in their behalf against the most relentless enemies of the white man . . . I saved more life and property for the white man than a whole regiment of United States regulars could have done in the same time. (232–33)

On the one hand, Beckwourth patriotically proclaims his loyalty to the United States and his revenge upon her behalf. On the other hand, he indirectly implicates whites in atavistic behavior. Rather than allowing the possibility that his black blood incited his "jungle behavior," he likens his actions to those of the U.S. Army. Also, he imputes his massacring and scalping of so many Native Americans to the vengefulness he feels on behalf of whites who have been murdered in unforeseen "Indian" attacks. If black blood tells for Beckwourth, it tells in the name of white culture and its frontier interests.

Many of his contemporaries, however, believed Beckwourth to be white. His biographer Elinor Wilson reports "several . . . did not remark that he was a mulatto (unless they wrote their memoirs years after they had already absorbed the legendary tales about him)."[27] In his double-voiced narrative, Beckwourth hoaxes those who believed he was white. The anonymous author of "Story of James P. Beckwourth," a review article of the autobiography published in 1856 in *Harper's New Monthly Magazine*, shows how those who accept Beckwourth's passing-for-white might interpret his character.

With this audience of peers and contemporaries, Beckwourth partakes in a farce that pivots on his creation of himself as a white hero. *Harper's* was neither an abolitionist nor a racially liberal periodical.[28] It is ironic, then, that the reviewer depicts the biracial Beckwourth as a representative man who "displays traits of character that are not inherent in ordinary men." According to the reviewer, Beckwourth is a man "possessed of high moral qualities," exhibiting a "divinity that stirred within him," and enjoying a "delicate sense of honor."[29] The writer connects Beckwourth's superior traits to his supposed heritage when he declares: "He combines the superior intelligence of the white man (and that of a high order) with the cunning of the aborigines" (458). He also describes him as "unsurpassed in the exhibition of the superior sagacity of the white when combating with the savage foe" (459). Beckwourth is so successful in passing as a white person in his narrative that the *Harper's* reviewer predictably reads the text for indications of white heroism. Had he known Beckwourth was biracial, no doubt he would have read it differently. Because of Beckwourth's hoax, the anonymous reviewer, in disclosing the arbitrary connection between race and character, unwittingly subverts the myth that marries blackness to mental and moral degeneracy, and whiteness to intelligence and sagacity.

Beckwourth also enjoys a private extratextual laugh at peers and readers like the *Harper's* reviewer to whom he passes. One scene whose purpose seems to be to bash the "naive" Crows is injected with new meaning in the context of Beckwourth's masquerade as a white man. When the amicable Crows visit the camp of Beckwourth and his companion Greenwood, Greenwood convinces them that Beckwourth is a long-lost Crow who had been captured by the Cheyenne as a child. Beckwourth admits he "was greatly edified at the inordinate gullibility of the red man, and when they had gone to spread their tale of wonderment, we had a hearty laugh at their expense" (140–41). Undoubtedly, he has a "hearty laugh" not only at the "gullible" Crows but also at the expense of readers who believe he is a white man.

Yet Beckwourth's stance toward atavism is riddled with ambiguity. While never admitting he is biracial, he peoples his text with morally degenerate "half-breed" characters. For instance, the "half-breed" Garro ambushes a group of white traders and steals their horses (255). Beckwourth also describes a "mulatto" who "induced eleven of Mr. Adams's party to desert him, when, with the participation of High Lance and other bad Indians, they stripped [a white man] of all his goods" (251). Although this may be a strategy to sustain his masquerade, implicit in this stereotypical depiction of the half-breed is the same belief—that race and character are intrinsically related—that infuses the myth of atavism.

Beckwourth exhibits his position between cultures in consistently and simultaneously writing from the perspective of several ethnicities. Beckwourth's narrative is analogous to a positive and negative "ambiguous object"—a black-and-white visual composition that creates an optical illusion. By focusing alternately on the black and then the white space, the viewer perceives two different images; for instance, the black space may appear to be two profiles facing each other, and the white space a chalice. In the autobiography different ideologies emerge depending on whether one visualizes a white or black foreground. About midway through the narrative, Beckwourth addresses the reader: "I learned this one truth while I was with the Indians, namely, that a white man can easily become an Indian, but that an Indian could never become a white man" (323). From one perspective, this is an affront to the Native Americans whom Beckwourth ridicules for their inability to become "civilized." But, switching perspectives, this is also a critique of atavism: if the white man can easily become an "Indian," is it because "savagism" is intrinsic to white culture and, therefore, reversion to it is readily possible? Critiquing atavism even as he capitulates to it in his text, Beckwourth sustains the tension between open and closed frontiers.

While Beckwourth toys with his audience through perspective switching, he creates a central rhetorical problem: how to shape himself as a white hero even as he narrates the story of his appropriation of "savage" manners. *Harper's* published *The Life and Adventures of James P. Beckwourth* to answer the demand for more literature about Western America.[30] As he writes to a mainstream U.S. audience, Beckwourth shapes a narrative that formally mimics a coup tale—an account of feats of bravery, such as scalping the enemy and stealing his horses.[31] Also, his sojourn with the Crows is completely voluntary, and so to a white audience he might appear a renegade. In making himself heroic, Beckwourth celebrates his martial and political triumphs for an audience who would view many of his actions as "uncivilized." Because he exists between Anglo and Crow cultures, and as he contends with this rhetorical problem, Beckwourth evinces double consciousness in which his inherent attraction to Crow culture is in conflict with how mainstream culture imagines the western hero.

On the one hand, Beckwourth is a conqueror who "transculturates": he makes an individual choice to join a marginalized culture.[32] Though engorged with the bloodshed of Native Americans, at times he is compelled by Crow values and tribal humanism. On the other hand, as a "white" western hero, he exploits the Crows by infiltrating their culture for his own economic gain. Double consciousness is manifested in his double-voiced autobiography, composed of narratives that bolster Crow culture and threaten its survival. Drawing on the assertions of Paula Gunn Allen and Henry Louis Gates, Elizabeth Ammons states: "If subversion is the sole purpose of a narrative or of an author's choices, then the whole project of that narrative or author remains totally defined in terms of the dominant culture's power and presence."[33] In Beckwourth's case, both of his narratives reinforce his depiction of himself as a white hero who defines himself in terms of Anglo culture.

Double consciousness is reflected in the reasons Beckwourth offers the reader for not disabusing his Crow captors of the illusion that he is "the lost Crow" (145). He betrays an attraction for the Crows when he states: "I could not find it in my heart to undeceive these unsuspecting people and tear myself away from their untutored caresses" (150). At the same time, he discloses a greater mercenary scheme: as a Crow he can "trap in their streams unmolested, and derive more profit under their protection than if among my own men, exposed incessantly to assassination and alarm" (150). Economic self-interest is an integral part of Beckwourth's attitude and interaction with the Crows, and it justifies to whites his self-adoption into the tribe.

Historically, blacks were major figures in the fur trade, and effective mediators with Native Americans. Blacks operated in the fur trade as "entrepreneurs, voyageurs, and hunters." In 1888, Colonel James Stevenson of the Bureau of American Ethnology stated that he preferred sending blacks to negotiate with Native Americans because blacks had a "pacifying effect" on tribal negotiators and caused "less friction" with them than did whites.[34] The Crow tribe, in particular, was socially receptive to outsiders, usually from the fur industries, sojourning with them. In 1805, the French fur trader François Antoine Larocque of the Northwest Fur Company spent the summer wandering with the Crows around the Big Horn Mountains. Edward Rose, a fur trader of Cherokee, African, and European descent, joined the Crows in 1807, eventually—like Beckwourth—became a chief, and lived with them until 1823 as a tribe member.[35]

Of the fur companies originating from Saint Louis (Beckwourth's hometown), most operated along the Yellowstone River in peaceful Crow territory, rather than along the Missouri River in the hostile Blackfoot region. In 1808, Manuel Lisa, organizer of the Missouri Fur Company, conducted business in Crow territory because of Blackfoot enmity toward outsiders. Around 1825, William H. Ashley's Rocky Mountain Fur Company, Beckwourth's early employer, engaged trappers and held rendezvous (bartering sessions between company leaders and fur trappers) on Crow lands. When Ashley sold the company to Smith, Sublette, and Jackson, they relocated the company but still employed trappers in Crow territory from 1829 to 1830. In 1832, the American Fur Company built Fort Cass on the Crow Reservation, but the post was soon abandoned for lack of employees willing to work in Native American territory. Eventually, the American Fur Company, with whom Beckwourth was an agent among the Crows, indirectly aided in pushing the Crows from their land. Because the Sioux had more fur to sell, they were able to purchase from the traders more guns, powder, and ammunition than the Crows. With the advantage of these firearms, the Sioux vanquished the Crows.[36]

As a fur trader, Beckwourth's marriage of convenience to the Crow tribe is "antagonistic," to borrow a concept from ethnologists George Devereux and Edwin M. Loeb, because rather than adopting the culture and its goals, he assimilates only to support his already existing economic goals.[37] His "antagonistic" stance toward the Native Americans on the frontier resounds in his justification for his brief sojourn with the Blackfoot: "Experience has revealed to me that civilized man can accustom himself to any mode of life when pelf is the governing principle—that power which dominates through all the ramifications of social life, and gives expression to the universal instinct of self-interest" (120). The "instinct of self-interest" is not universal, at least not to Native Americans, who stress the communal over the individual. Although he superficially assimilates to Crow life, "speaking nothing but Crow language, dressed like a Crow, my hair as long as a Crow's, and myself as black as a crow" (177), he retains Anglo habits and values. As he rises politically, eventually becoming chief, he disseminates white cultural practices by exploiting the tribe's beliefs.

Weaving a narrative that reveals his efforts to undermine the Crow tribe's stability, Beckwourth depicts how he manipulates the tribe through both his powerful political position and their reverence for his martial powers. He overtly states his antagonistic agenda to his readers: "to induce the Crows to devote their undivided attention to trapping, not alone for their own benefit, but for the interest of the [fur] company in whose service I was engaged" (220). His intentions, he indicates, are less to "benefit" the Crows than to increase the fur company's wealth at their expense. To ensure their cooperation, he exploits their sacred belief in "medicine." The Crows consider Beckwourth's medicine extremely powerful, given his success as a warrior and immense collection of coup. Realizing this, he informs them that his medicine instructs that they not go to war. He further consolidates his scheme after he becomes chief upon the death of A-ra-poo-ash. When a chief dies, as Beckwourth states, "all his plans die with him" (270). With the help of allies on the tribal council, Beckwourth soon turns the Crows' attention "to trapping and killing buffalo" (271). By capitalizing on his political power and preventing their constant warring, he maintains their interest in fur trapping.

Besides compromising the cultural integrity of the Crows by aiding the fur industry in its economic exploitation of them, Beckwourth closes the frontier on the Snake tribe by undermining their culture in the interest of his financial agenda. Having secured the industry of the Crows to advance his economic goals, he enlarges his wealth through additional political maneuvering. Throughout the narrative, the Snake and Crow tribes are constantly at war with each other. Since their friction is economically disadvantageous to Beckwourth, he mediates peace between them. He allows both the Crows and the Snakes to believe that a nearby trading post is Crow property and that they enjoy an alliance with whites. The Snakes are "so impressed with the idea of [Crow] superiority" that they join them, intermarry, and renounce their own culture. The obliteration of Snake culture is the consequence of Beckwourth's formation of an alliance to gain the Snakes' business at the trading post.

Yet despite his exploitation of the Crows, the autobiography contains a narrative that expresses his admiration of Crow culture. He often includes sentimental scenes depicting the humanity of the Crow. For example, when he is accepted into the tribe, he is granted a wife, whom he honors as "affectionate, obedient, gentle, cheerful." In addition, Beckwourth describes his tender "reunion" with the tribe: "the cordial welcome, the rapturous embraces of those who hailed me as a son and a brother, the exuberant joy of the whole nation for the return of a long-lost Crow" (149–50).

Besides marveling at the demeanor of the Crows, Beckwourth also esteems them for their communal values and behavior. He wonders at his tribal blood brother who grants him four animal skins after Beckwourth has an unsuccessful day hunting, declaring: "Take them . . . you are my friend: your traps have been unlucky to-day" (155). Even more admiringly, he directly lectures his audience: "There is one trait in Indian character which civilized society would derive much profit by imitating. Envy is a quality unknown to the savages" (161). Moments like these throughout his narrative question Anglo dominance by according the Crows a position of superiority in relation to whites.

Beckwourth challenges the belief that sanctions the inevitable progress of white over aboriginal cultures and deems the two intellectually, morally, and technologically realms apart. Historian Roy Harvey Pearce has shown that these categories were essential to nineteenth-century ideology, which sought to "prove savagism, progress, and the manifest destiny of American civilization." According to Pearce, 1851 marked the demise of savagism as scientists began to view the Native American as having "a tolerably respectable civilization of his own"; yet "they continued to try to comprehend that way of life historically, in its relation to the long evolution of man toward high civilization."[38] In dismantling the opposition between "savage" and "civilized," Beckwourth's irony is unconscious, even inadvertent. Should Beckwourth consciously destroy the differences between the two, he would ultimately humanize the Crows and, in turn, place his entire capitalist enterprise in an even less savory light.

As he levels the hierarchy that places Anglos above Native Americans, Beckwourth challenges the frontier myth that Native Americans were to blame for problems on the frontier, and that consequently their extermination was necessary. In regard to the hardships early pioneers suffered—namely, the widescale loss of cattle—"the Indians came in for their full share of blame," he comments (52). Yet he simultaneously acknowledges that "through extreme carelessness" of white frontiersmen, "so many [cattle] were lost" (52). This undermines his justification for helping the government to annihilate the Native Americans—one of the purposes of his narrative. If the Native Americans are not solely responsible for the havoc and chaos on the frontier, then it becomes more difficult to rationalize their extermination and to close the frontier.

Although Beckwourth appears to reinforce Native American stereotypes, he actually challenges them. For example, Beckwourth vows never to send a deputation of Crows to Washington to negotiate a treaty, fearing "they would return home dejected and humiliated . . . feeling their own comparative insignificance" after witnessing "the predominance and magnificence of the whites" (349). His ostensible empathy for the Crows thinly masks an assertion of white cultural superiority. Later, a white passenger, when traveling in a storm with Beckwourth, "astonished" by his "Indian fire-striker," exclaims: "If you can strike a fire . . . in such a storm as this, I do not fear perishing" (379). That a white man who probably knows the splendors of Washington can marvel at a Native American tool suggests that the excellence of a culture is relative to one's immediate circumstances. In his counternarrative, Beckwourth erases the frontier line that keeps "savage" and "civilized" separate, contradictory, and opposite.

Yet Beckwourth does not seem to be in control of the irony of his representations. Instead, his final chapter reemphasizes Anglo dominance and attempts to resolve the tension between open and closed frontiers by offering advice to his readers on how effectively to exterminate the Native Americans. At first, he gushes, "My heart turns naturally to my adopted people" (535). However, he proceeds to advise the military to cease sending troops to make war since Native Americans are far more mobile and use "robes and mirrors" to telegraph spies (530). He explains that treaties are futile because to Native Americans they symbolize the white man's fear (531). Instead, he ruthlessly instructs the government to supply "whisky among the Red Men," starve them by depriving them of buffalo, and employ mountaineers who are familiar with Native American habits to fight them (533–34). That is, Beckwourth now poses as an Indian-hater, a role that clashes with his moments of appreciation of Crow culture and threatens his mercenary scheme.

A conventional historical and literary character, the "Indian-hater" figures in James Hall's *Sketches of History, Life, and Manners, in the West*, the source of Herman Melville's sketch of John Moredock in *The Confidence-Man*

(1857).[39] As Hall explains, hatred develops in the Indian-hater "in consequence of some personal wrong"; John Moredock becomes an Indian-hater when his entire family is killed in a massacre.[40] Similarly, Beckwourth rationalizes his murderous endeavors earlier in the narrative through a tale recounting the mass homicide of his neighbors by vicious Indians. According to Hall, "the ruling passion of [Moredock's] life" was to kill Indians.[41] Beckwourth also expresses enjoyment in slaughtering tribal enemies although he admits at one point that the constant bloodshed sickens him. Louise K. Barnett describes the "Indian hater" as abiding "like metaphoric half-breeds between the white and Indian communities, isolated from ordinary men of either race by the intensity of their hatred and the single-mindedness of their commitment."[42] Like the Indian-hater, Beckwourth is a "metaphoric half-breed" between white and Native American cultures. Unlike the Indian-hater, Beckwourth betrays not single-mindedness but double consciousness: he portrays himself with varying degrees of intensity as a genocidal conqueror, a conventional fur trader exploiting the Crows, and a tribal member steeped in the culture and loyal to its members.

While Beckwourth mimics the conventional Indian-hater, especially in the last chapter, that self-representation is not consistent throughout his story. Hall's and Melville's sketches of the Indian-hater illustrate that Indian-haters are "by nature absolutists" in unequivocally and myopically pursuing the destruction of Native Americans.[43] Yet any race hatred Beckwourth harbors is diluted by his yearning for economic gain; he cannot afford to destroy them since he needs them to increase his wealth. Further, his passion for warfare is directed toward Crow enemies. Only in the final chapter does he suggest without discrimination how to kill Native Americans for the "benefit" of the United States. Also, as Hall asserts, the frontier child "learns to hate an Indian" by hearing "horrid tales of savage violence" and "narratives of aboriginal cunning and ferocity."[44] However, Beckwourth expresses several insights which delineate his unlearning of race hatred. Finally, Barnett explains the quandary of the Indian-hater who, paradoxically, to achieve his goals assimilates superficially to Native American culture by utilizing its weapons. If the Indian-hater overly emulates Native Americans, he is considered a renegade white Indian. If he becomes too revengeful and passionate about murder, he is alienated from the white community and loses his white identity.[45] Beckwourth walks this frontier boundary between renegade and conqueror like a tightrope.

Beckwourth's tale, despite its ambiguity and double consciousness, most likely reinforced stereotypical and conventional beliefs concerning Native Americans for his audience. While a close reading of the autobiography reveals Beckwourth's grappling at the borders as he occasionally sees beyond stereotypes of the "savage Indian," to a nineteenth-century audience who accepted his narrative passing, the autobiography confirms conventional representations of Native American life. As Jane Tompkins argues in *Sensational Designs*, external context, not some intrinsic property, makes a text "visible" to a reader.[46] Beckwourth's autobiography, published in 1856, was written when "frontier romances," or tales by whites incorporating Native American characters, flourished. These tales are comprised of stock conventions including "a standard plotting device, stereotyped characters, and a racist-nationalistic philosophy of white-Indian relations."[47] Besides external context, Forrest G. Robinson finds audiences sometimes deny "departures from leading public ideals"; he terms "bad faith" an audience's "retreat from unbearable truth."[48] The *Harper's* review ironically illustrates how to a nineteenth-century reader Beckwourth's autobiography speaks to traditional Native American stereotypes, like those in the frontier romances.

The *Harper's* reviewer invites the reader to anticipate a new (American) aesthetic in Beckwourth's autobiography. To echo Tompkins, the context of the periodical, *Harper's New Monthly Magazine*, creates conditions that control the reader's perceptions of Beckwourth's narrative. From its origination, *Harper's* was known (and by some criticized) for providing its American audience with the works of British writers like Charles Dickens, William Makepeace Thackeray, and George Eliot. However, feeling competition from *Putnam's*, in 1853 *Harper's* scrambled to include more American writers in their issues.[49] Given this context of renewed interest in American art, the *Harper's* reviewer considers Beckwourth's text innovative. He recalls the aborigines of "Chateaubriand" and "the harmonies of Hiawatha," but dismisses both as products of "civilized" minds, declaring that "the characters illustrated are artificialities, having no existence but in the poet's brain" (455). In opposition to the romantic, he asserts, Beckwourth provides

> at last something really genuine about the privations of the mountaineer; something to be relied upon relating to the inner life of the savage; the vail [*sic*] has been lifted, and although somewhat rudely done, the scene is before us in its deformity and its beauty—the ideal and the actual struggle for mas-

tery—the poetry we meet is full of originality—its gold is genuine—and though mixed with the dull earth, it is more brilliant from the crudeness of its associations. (455)

Although the reviewer claims that for him "the vail has been lifted" on the "inner life of the savage"—a claim that carries with it the possibility of open frontiers, of continued culture contact—he offers no evidence of the new motives he anticipates but reads the texts as the locus of "predictable motives."[50] In his review, a seventeen-page synopsis of a 537-page book, he consistently emphasizes for his reader traditional, artificial, romantic images of Native Americans that correspond to conventional stereotypes.

For example, he highlights two noble savages Beckwourth creates. The first is Beckwourth's blood brother, a Crow with no living relatives, who engages Beckwourth in a ceremony that makes them family. The reviewer refers to him as "a melancholy and sentimental Indian." Later, the reviewer describes the death of the great Chief A-ra-poo-ash: "It would be difficult to imagine a more poetical rendering of the last moments of a great warrior" (465). Far from relating the "inner life of the savage," the reviewer summons from current American frontier romance the noble savage, a stereotype of the Native American that derives in part from the romantic movement in England and Europe.[51]

Besides the romantic, the reviewer records and describes Native American types that are resoundingly puritanical. The writer reports the pivotal scene in Beckwourth's autobiography—the one also conventional to Indian-hater narratives—when the Indians massacre his playmates and he discovers "their bodies mangled, their scalps torn off" (456). In addition, the reviewer refers to "the most providential appearance" of the two Native Americans who rescue Beckwourth from death by starvation. This phrase is an echo from the captivity narrative of Mary Rowlandson, who views all humane acts toward her and other whites by their Native American captors as works of providence.[52]

Finally, the *Harper's* reviewer derives very conventional depictions of the Native American woman from Beckwourth's autobiography. Rayna Green finds that the Native American woman in U.S. culture is burdened by a virgin/whore (or more aptly, "princess/squaw") complex.[53] The reviewer bases his characterizations of Pine Leaf and Beckwourth's "little wife" on the more romantic princess archetype. Although Pine Leaf is the tribe's only female warrior and is bent on collecting one hundred enemy scalps to avenge her brother's death, the *Harper's* reviewer emphasizes her role as Beckwourth's unrequiting lover. He records a dialogue between her and Beckwourth from the autobiography in which she repels his advances and explains: "You have too many wives already." The reviewer portrays Pine Leaf as a coy mistress; she is much like the "sacrosanct" Indian princess whose "sexuality can be hinted at but never realized."[54] On the other hand, in the "little wife" the reviewer depicts the princess as "Mother Goddess," "exotic, powerful, dangerous."[55] The little wife is in fact the mother of Beckwourth's only recognized Native American child. Her power and danger are exhibited when she performs the medicine lodge ritual to become initiated into the tribe as a virtuous woman. Proving her virtue and passing the test, she is extolled by both the tribe and the reviewer, who deems her "a naturally noble nature in an untutored Indian girl" (470). In merging the noble with the untutored, the reviewer fashions the little wife into a female version of the noble savage; her integrity arises from the chastity of the "Indian princess."

For the *Harper's* writer, living historically in the midst of frontier contact, the veil remains drawn on Native American life—the status quo intact. Given Beckwourth's Anglo audience and his passing narrative, at least some, as is evidenced by the *Harper's* reviewer, read his autobiography as reinforcing Anglo beliefs about and representations of Native American culture. Functioning to close the frontier, the autobiography, like frontier romances, keeps intact the conventional images of Native American life and the "racist-nationalistic philosophy of white-Indian relations." In *The Life and Adventures*, Beckwourth glimpses the creative and constructive potential of the frontier contact zone. The autobiography in part asks what is the role of the Crows in U.S. society and trade relations? What is the future of Native and Anglo American relations? While Beckwourth's one voice answers for the exploitation and eventual extermination of the Native Americans, his other voice justifies their continuation. Ultimately, the autobiographical narrator, situated between cultures on the frontier, struggles with his own double consciousness.

If Beckwourth is ultimately controlled by his double consciousness, Sarah Winnemucca Hopkins is more in control of hers in *Life among the Piutes:*

Their Wrongs and Claims. Like Beckwourth, Hopkins exists between cultures on the frontier as a negotiator, but unlike Beckwourth, whose loyalties lie with the dominant group, Hopkins agitates strongly for tribal rights. As a translator on the frontier, she mediates between the military, reservation agents, and Paiutes; as an author she grapples with her white audience over the fate of her tribe. In addition, her autobiography is historically on the borderline between the end of reservationism and the advent of allotment. Hopkins's double consciousness is exhibited in her simultaneous cultural attraction to whites and her moral quest to help the beleaguered Paiutes. Yet she is also aware of the ways in which whites view Native Americans, and she uses that insight into the white psyche rhetorically, to persuade her audience. Through hidden polemic and parody, she deftly creates a double-voiced text to attract her audience to her cause. In manipulating her double consciousness, Hopkins critiques Anglo and Native American frontier relations and suggests alternatives to the tragic social order under reservationism. More than Beckwourth, she capitalizes on the subversive potential of the border and pries open the frontier for the Paiutes. Although assimilation usually heralds the closing of the frontier by anticipating the conquest of "savagery" by "civilization," Hopkins reconceptualizes assimilation to open the frontier.

For the Paiutes, the decline of traditional tribal life began in 1857 when U.S. Agent Frederick Dodge held a council meeting with tribal chiefs to determine which of their lands would be designated reservations.[56] On reservations, Native Americans were segregated from whites but also from other tribes, to prevent their consolidating forces. Although assimilation was forced on reservations, Native Americans were still able to preserve their tribal cultures. In the 1880s, opponents of the segregationist reservation system proposed allotting Native Americans individual plots of land. Those favoring allotment held that the answer to the "Indian Problem" was assimilation to white ways via integration into American society and the detribalization of Native America.[57] Because the Paiutes were physically threatened with starvation and poverty on the reservation, Hopkins advocates allowing the military control of allocating government rations to the Paiutes, granting the tribe allotment in severalty, and bestowing on them rights as citizens.

Hopkins's narrative of Paiute "wrongs and claims" influenced Senator Henry L. Dawes in the creation of the General Allotment Act, which was passed only four years after the publication of *Life among the Piutes: Their Wrongs and Claims*. The Dawes Act, or General Allotment Act, of 1887 effected the disintegration of reservations by awarding 160 acres of land to each head of a Native American family. The act states that recipients must work their land for twenty-five years; they then would be given title to the land and rights as citizens. The "surplus" land not allotted to Native Americans was reserved for purchase by whites, and the money from the sales went into a fund for the education and "civilization" of Native Americans.[58] Prior to the passage of the act, Senator Dawes invited Hopkins—with her publisher, the Transcendentalist and liberal educator Elizabeth Palmer Peabody—to lecture in his home. Hopkins knew that Dawes held ideas about allotment similar to hers, and Dawes, in turn, was inspired by her narrative. Yet Hopkins neither anticipated nor sanctioned two dire consequences of the Dawes Act: the detribalization of Native America as the reservation system was dismantled, and the selling of "surplus" lands to whites.[59]

Undoubtedly, Dawes was moved by her account of the Paiutes' poverty and oppression on the reservation. The autobiography is centered more on depicting tribal life than on rendering Hopkins's personal and individual life. In part, the communal focus of the narrative is a function of Hopkins's political agenda. But also, as Murray states, "the concept of an individual life as an unfolding story which can be isolated, recalled and retold, made into a product for contemplation, is not one necessarily shared by other cultures, and in particular not by oral cultures."[60] In her eight chapters of narrative, Hopkins unfolds the story of a communal life.

The autobiography begins with Sarah, as a fearful and comprehending child, recounting the initial contact between Paiutes and whites. In the rest of the book, the adult Hopkins describes aspects of Paiute culture: she calls it a civilization, discusses the difficulties and wasted possibilities of the reservation system, and details the climactic Bannock War and its aftermath, including the transfer of some of her people away from tribal lands and onto the Yakima Reservation. In addition, the autobiography contains an editor's preface and appendix of valorizing letters.

Both the content and the context of the autobiography reveal Hopkins's difficulty finding a voice with which to write and to speak. Although Hopkins's narrative is mainly a "self-written" autobiography,[61] like Beckwourth she is assisted in her writing—in her case by an editor, Mary Peabody Mann,

Elizabeth Palmer Peabody's sister. Elizabeth served not only as Hopkins's publisher but also as benefactor and fund-raiser. She was a writer, lecturer, and associate of the Concord Transcendentalists, and publisher of their books. One of her major social works was to establish German kindergartens in America. Her sister Mary, herself a skilled writer, was organizer of Elizabeth's humanitarian crusades and the wife of education pioneer Horace Mann.[62] Hopkins's narrative, because of the collaboration with Mary Mann, is like Beckwourth's in that it exists between Anglo and Native American cultures; however, given Hopkins's controversial political activism, it took patronage such as that of the Peabody sisters to assure the very existence of the Hopkins autobiography.

Mann, editor of the manuscript, was also personally moved by the plight of the Paiutes. One Christmas she sent clothing and used goods for the impoverished people on the reservation.[63] Her elder sister, Elizabeth Peabody, encouraged Hopkins to lecture on the history, traditions, and tribulations of the Paiutes. When Hopkins realized she had more to say than could be contained in a lecture, Peabody encouraged her to write and agreed to publish her book. The sisters introduced Hopkins to their select circle of friends, including John Greenleaf Whittier, Ralph Waldo Emerson, and Oliver Wendell Holmes. Through Peabody, Hopkins spoke at Vassar, as the guest of the wife of musician Ole Bull.[64] Peabody expressed admiration for Paiute culture; it was, she stated after hearing Hopkins lecture, based on "natural religion and family moralities."[65] Hopkins sold autographed copies of her book to members of the audiences at her lectures, the money going to support her and her husband Lewis Hopkins and to aid in establishing a school for Paiutes.

As Mann understood it, the true purpose of the book was "to influence the public mind by the details of the Indian wrongs she can give so as to induce Congress to give them their farms in severalty and give them rights to defend them in the courts." To accomplish these purposes, Hopkins circulated a petition to her audiences and eventually collected five thousand signatures.[66] Peabody supported Hopkins not only by collecting subscriptions to underwrite the cost of the book, but also by procuring letters on Hopkins's behalf from influential friends and congressmen. Eventually, Hopkins opened the Peabody Indian School, unique among boarding schools because it was initiated and largely run by Native Americans; it fostered in its students habits of self-education; and it employed a bilingual curriculum. The government refused to recognize the school; Elizabeth Peabody raised $1,000 in funds for its up-keep in the summer of 1885.[67] Needless to say, neither Hopkins nor Peabody supported the article in the Dawes Act that required Native American children to attend white, English-centered schools that consequently stripped them of their language, culture, and self-esteem.[68]

Mann, like Bonner in the Beckwourth book, downplays her editorial role in preparing Hopkins's manuscript. In the editor's preface, Mann asserts that the extent of her editing has been "copying the original manuscript in correct orthography and punctuation, with occasional emendations by the author." She is more specific about those emendations in a letter to a friend:

> I wish you could see her manuscript as a matter of curiosity. I don't think the English language ever got such a treatment before. I have to recur to her sometimes to know what a word is, as spelling is an unknown quantity to her, as you mathematicians would express it. She often takes syllables off of words & adds them or rather prefixes them to other words, but the story is heart-breaking, and told with a simplicity & eloquence that cannot be described, for it is not high-faluting eloquence, tho' sometimes it lapses into verse (and quite poetical verse too).[69]

Mann justifies her lack of editorial intrusion in the name of preserving authenticity: "In fighting with her literary deficiencies [Hopkins] loses some of the fervid eloquence which her extraordinary colloquial command of the English language enables her to utter, but I am confident that no one would desire that her own original words should be altered." Ironically, that the text is Hopkins's "own original words" is moot even before one considers Mann's assistance. If the writer of autobiography fashions "her life and its cultural context through language,"[70] Hopkins, in writing about Paiute life in English, already loses much of the cultural context that her own words, her native language, would embody.

Whereas one can only speculate about the specific manifestations of Bonner's interference in Beckwourth's text, we know that Mann and Peabody are responsible for the appendix of valorizing letters in Hopkins's autobiography.[71] These letters, written by various military personnel, both attest to her good character and verify and compliment her performance as scout, guide, interpreter, and mediator during the Bannock War. Also, in order to prove her identity, she includes the letter appointing her interpreter for the Paiutes at Malheur Reservation, one from a person requesting descriptions of Paiute ceremonies, and another congratulating her on her marriage. A number of letters document the Paiutes' escape from Yakima Reservation and issue orders for the military to bring them back. The appendix ends with editorials from the *Boston Transcript* and the *Silver State* defending Hopkins's character in light of the libelous accusations made against her by *The Council Fire and Arbitrator,* the newspaper of the Bureau of Indian Affairs.

Hopkins incited a quarrel with *The Council Fire and Arbitrator* when she traveled to Washington to complain about reservation oppression and to argue for the transfer of power on the reservation from the agents to the military. In 1871, after he dismantled the treaty system, President Ulysses S. Grant wanted to place the army in charge of reservations: he reasoned that commissioned army agents, being bound by military honor, which places the good of the nation foremost in their minds, would not be swayed by politics; military agents, then, would create peace and restore integrity to dealings with the Native Americans. In 1870, Congress had prohibited the employment of army officers as agents and, instead, supported the "Quaker Policy," which advocated having Christian sects nominate good men for the posts as agents.[72] Hence, Hopkins explains with irony that her nemesis, the self-serving W. V. Rinehart, replaced the benevolent Sam Parrish as reservation agent for the Paiutes because Rinehart was a "Christian."

After Hopkins argued for a military reservation agency, *The Council Fire and Arbitrator* attacked her by publishing affidavits that Rinehart had collected against her when she complained about his treatment of the Paiutes in Washington. These documents accused her of dishonesty and wanton conduct with officers.[73] As a defense against the Indian Bureau's libelous "rag-friend," Mann and Peabody encouraged Hopkins to include an appendix of valorizing letters in her book. While *The Council Fire and Arbitrator* stereotypes Hopkins as a lascivious "squaw," Mann and Peabody recuperate her character (and, undoubtedly, shield themselves from social reproach) by using the letters—written mainly by military personnel—to refilter Hopkins's tarnished image through the prism of polite, white society. As a result, those who want to validate and those who seek to discredit Hopkins shape her autobiographical identity.

The difficulty in finding a voice with which to write mirrors Hopkins's dramatized struggle as translator to reclaim her personal and individual voice.

Her bilingual utterance itself embraces the frontier because in and with her voice she mediates between Native and Anglo American cultures. Unfortunately, to her people she assumes the role of "half-breed" mediator and becomes more a destroyer than a facilitator of communication.

In the nineteenth century, whites responded to the biracial or "half-breed" person mainly with ambivalence. Some viewed the half-breed "as a tragic figure, a marginal person caught between two cultures and often rejected by both." The more liberal minded saw in the half-breed the possibility for an "integrated society."[74] To many, half-breeds were outsiders, receiving neither social position nor respect from either of the nations to which they belonged.[75] One of the myths about them is that because of biological intermixing, half-breeds suffer from "blood poisoning," which manifests itself in "physical deterioration ... mental inferiority ... immorality and cultural degeneracy."[76] Hopkins echoes this belief when she comments about half-breed interpreters in general who "easily get corrupted, and can be hired by the agents to do or say anything. ... My people are very reasonable and want to understand everything, and be sure that there is fair play" (91). As the narrative progresses, Hopkins, much like Beckwourth, is shaped by her people into the image of the half-breed interpreter, whose words cannot be trusted and who threatens standards of fair play.

The Paiutes perceive Hopkins as a half-breed interpreter because the U.S. government uses her voice to transmit lies to them. After the Bannock War, the soldiers renege on an agreement to return her people to Malheur Reservation and they direct Hopkins to inform the Paiutes that they must move away from their sacred homeland to Yakima Reservation. However, she has already assured them that the soldiers would prevent their being sent away. Hopkins then worries that the Paiutes "will say [she and her cousin Mattie] are working against them and are getting money for all this" (204). In another instance, Hopkins guides her people to Lovelocks to collect tents promised them by the government only to learn that instead they must journey to Malheur Reservation in waist-high snow. Again she fears that rather than viewing her as the government's pawn, her people will accuse her of deception and trickery.

Eventually, the Paiutes denounce her for earning money by betraying them. Her reply articulates the dilemma of the linguistic "half-breed": "You have a right to say I have sold you. It looks so. I have told you many things which are not my own words, but the words of the agents and the soldiers. I know I have told you more lies than I have hair on my head. I tell you, my dear children, I have never told you my own words; they were the words of the white people, not mine" (236). Although she is paid by the U.S. government to speak on its behalf to Paiutes, her purpose as author of the autobiography and actor in its plot is to agitate for Paiute tribal rights. However, because she is linguistically of both nations, her people are suspicious of her supposed loyalty to them. Hopkins struggles to dissociate "the words of the white people" from her own and extricate herself from the Anglo power structure. Her repetition of "I have told you" (as opposed to "I said") suggests that she is relating tales to them rather than partaking in genuine self-expression. Her people, however, consider any incongruity between her words and government actions as corruption on her part. Moral degeneracy, then, is implied of the bilingual as it is of the biological half-breed. The consequence of her role as translator is the distortion of her voice: Hopkins cannot disengage herself from the false language forced upon her by the white government.

As a translator of the Paiute language to whites, on the other hand, Hopkins uses her bilingualism to resist white exploitation. The requirement that she speak *for* whites and not *to* them is implicit in her role as interpreter for the U.S. government. When she accompanies Chief Egan and Chief Oytes to Camp Harney to report to the soldiers the physical and economic abuses suffered by the Paiutes at the hands of Agent Rinehart, Rinehart quickly dismisses her from her duties as interpreter (142). In another instance, she travels to Washington to state her complaints to Secretary of the Interior Carl Schurz (Schurz was a liberal reformer who rejected reservation concentration and supported allotment and assimilation for Native Americans).[77] When Hopkins alerts Schurz about the oppressive Agent Rinehart and the displaced Paiutes' desire to return to their homeland, Malheur Reservation, he promises: "The government is going to do right by your people now. Don't lecture now; go home and get your people on the reservation—get them located properly; and then, if you want to come back, write to us, and tell us you want to come back and lecture, and we will pay your way here and back again" (221). Schurz fails to fulfill his promise to remove Agent Rinehart from Malheur Reservation. Unlike Grandfather Truckee, who envisions the communicative potential of written language, Hopkins learns the limitations of the "rag friend": Schurz offers "in writing, promises which, like the wind, we heard no more" (221). In turn, Schurz evinces his fear of Hopkins's voice of resistance and his dire need to silence it.[78] As a bilingual, Hopkins is a threat to both nations for whom she translates. In the context of frontier intercultural relations, Hopkins unfolds her growing awareness that language, rather than being concrete and binding, is malleable, insubstantial, and as transitory as the "idle wind."

Hopkins continued to lecture on Native American abuses and rights. Because her voice of resistance could not be silenced, *The Council Fire and Arbitrator* disparaged and attacked her character. One article charged that Hopkins "is so notorious for her untruthfulness as to be wholly unreliable. She is known . . . to have been a common camp follower, consorting with common soldiers. It is a great outrage on the respectable people of Boston for General Howard or any other officer of the army to foist such a woman of any race upon them."[79] There is some irony here: not only as a translator to Paiutes is Hopkins accused of lying to and deceiving her audience, but also as a speaker to whites. Both her image as a linguistic "half-breed" and as a lascivious "squaw" threaten to render Hopkins silent by discrediting her words as falsehoods. Robert Stepto observes that silence and self-effacement are also the fate of the slave narrator who is removed from the "primary authenticating documents and strategy" within his own text. Such a removal "weakens his control of the narrative and . . . relegates him to a posture of partial literacy."[80] However, Hopkins's voice intercedes in the appendix to control the reader's perceptions of the validating documents. In the midst of all the letters, Hopkins interjects a personal statement in which she laments: "Every one knows what a woman must suffer who undertakes to act against bad men. My reputation has been assailed, and it is done so cunningly that I cannot prove it to be unjust" (258). She maintains, "It is true that my people sometimes distrust me, but that is because words have been put into my mouth which have turned out to be nothing but idle wind" (258). There is a risk that the authenticating mechanism will weaken her control of her voice and assign her to partial literacy; in this case, however, the letters seek to reverse the damage done by extraliterary sources and political enemies.

That Hopkins's work on behalf of the Paiutes was threatened by her character assassins is illustrated cogently in Louise Hall Tharp's biography, *The Peabody Sisters of Salem* (1950).[81] Tharp devotes two pages to the Peabody sisters' relationship with Hopkins, dismissing Hopkins as a swindler and depicting the Peabody sisters as naive victims of a Hopkins scam. According to Tharp, Hopkins, the self-styled Indian princess, was an impostor who "won over the susceptible Elizabeth" and her "usually more cautious" sister.[82] Tharp asserts that Mann gave Hopkins all the credit for writing *Life among the Piutes: Their Wrongs and Claims,* when in reality Hopkins told her story to Mann, who then wrote it. (Tharp does not, however, pursue the implications of Mann's involvement in Hopkins's deceptions.) Tharp concludes that Hopkins put on "a good show" and then "returned to her people with a good-sized haul."[83] As I will explain, Hopkins posed as an Indian princess to appeal to the romantic and conventional expectations of her white audience; further, no evidence suggests that Mann and Peabody catered to her presumption of royalty, and she does not portray herself as a princess in her narrative. Tharp's depiction of Hopkins indicates the extent to which Hopkins's reputation was debased. Mann's and Peabody's suggestion that she create an appendix of vindicating letters in her book represents their effort to reempower her voice by validating it. While Hopkins struggles to be heard even as her voice is compromised, the letters reclaim and consolidate that voice.

Though variously mediated, the voice Hopkins attains is politically and rhetorically astute within a complex cultural context. As Hopkins writes to an audience who is neither herself nor of her tribe, she translates her Native American culture to accommodate the understanding of a non-Native audience.[84] As a Paiute activist, she must petition an audience not always sympathetic to her cause, harboring their own fears and prejudices about Native Americans. In addition, her purpose is not benignly to inform; rather, in an effort to rescue her tribe from destruction, she seeks to persuade her white audience that Paiutes are abused and mistreated by corrupt whites on the frontier. Her autobiography ends with a note from Mann asking patrons to sign a petition to Congress on behalf of the Paiutes; she asks that people reproduce and disseminate the petition to others "in the hope that it will help to shape aright the new Indian policy" (247). The petition foreshadows General Allotment in requesting that the displaced Paiutes be returned to their homeland, that the head of each family be given individual parcels of tribal land to cultivate, and that the annuities granted to the tribe by the government be disbursed by the military.[85]

Rhetorically, the politically conflicted and volatile Hopkins is faced with the challenge of finessing the prejudices of her audience and obtaining their support for her cause. In order to accomplish both these aims, she employs double consciousness as a tool. In an interview from 1870, she makes a personal disclosure:

"I like the Indian life tolerably well; however, my only object in staying with these people is that I may do them good. I would rather be with my people, but not to live with them as they live. I was not raised so; . . . my happiest life has been spent in Santa Clara while at school and living among the whites."[86] The double consciousness that pervades *Life among the Piutes: Their Wrongs and Claims* reverberates in this quote: morally and politically, Hopkins sides with her people as she advocates their cause; culturally, however, she prefers many Anglo customs.[87] She tempers her radicalism by affirming Anglo culture and espousing an assimilationist, rather than a nationalist, philosophy.

For instance, Hopkins draws on a Paiute origin story as a tribal precedent to sanction her attraction to white culture. Subverting the stereotype of Native Americans as bloodthirsty savages reveling in the massacre of whites, Hopkins describes her Grandfather Truckee's excitement about the first contact with Anglos. Chief Truckee communicates his hopes to the tribe by recounting an origin story about the first woman and man and their four children—a dark boy and girl, and a light boy and girl. The four children quarrel incessantly and their parents finally send the light children across the sea. Believing the whites have come to "heal all the old trouble" (7), Truckee trusts that the frontier meeting will rectify the tragedy in the origin story. He declares to his people, "I want to love them as I love all of you" (7).

Perhaps this is an example of what Jarold Ramsey calls "conservatism": "the tendency of myth, when it is still an active mediating force in peoples' lives, to imaginatively transform 'real events,' no matter how strange, according to its system, so that the people can assimilate such events, and 'believe' in them."[88] The tale prescribes, early in the autobiography, the tribe's commitment—one deeply embedded in the mythic structure of their culture—to reunion and cooperation with their long-lost white brothers and sisters. Ironically, what instead occurs in the narrative is another enforced separation of whites and Native Americans by the reservation system, whose administrators, like the first man and woman, hold that segregation is the means of ending interracial violence between Paiutes and whites.[89]

Hopkins's double consciousness is exhibited not only in her concomitant attraction and repulsion to Anglo culture but also in her ability to see herself "through the revelation of the other world." The Hopkins family—Sarah, her father, and her sister Elma—exploited their double consciousness in the performance of tableaux vivants for white audiences. After one of these performances in San Francisco, a female acquaintance of the Paiutes wrote an editorial revealing the troupe's purpose. The Paiutes were impoverished; "For this reason [Chief Winnemucca] had condescended to make a show of their habits, their pastimes, and among them, their time honored dances: and his object in so doing is to raise money to buy food and blankets for his people."[90] However, the stage show was shaped to entertain, not to depict the reality of Paiute life.[91] The tableaux vivants indicate that the Winnemuccas knew of their white audience's expectations regarding Native Americans and used that knowledge to create profitable entertainments.

Prior to the performance of the tableaux vivants, the Winnemuccas would appear on the street as "Indian royalty." Chief Winnemucca wore a "crown of feathers and on his shoulders brass epaulets," symbols of his martial and ruling powers. Sarah rode beside him, with Elma behind on his horse. His entourage of braves held a red-white-and-blue crescent over his head. Under the crescent, he delivered a patriotic speech, interpreted by Sarah, in which he declared he was a friend of whites and had no desire to fight them. He would then pass the hat, seeking contributions from the onlookers.[92] The stage performance itself, in a theater hall, began with the grand entrance of the royal family and their braves. Next, a man dressed in black would "read a lecture on Piutes 'and any other Indians'" which ended with a eulogy for the Great Chief. After an intermission, the tableaux vivants proceeded: "The Indian Camp," "The Message of War," "The War Council," "The War Dance," "The Capture of a Bannock Spy," "Scalping the Prisoner," "Grand Scalp Dance," "Scalping of an Emmigrant [*sic*] Girl by a Bannock Scout," "The Wounded Warrior," "The Coyote Dance," and five scenarios portraying Pocahontas saving John Smith's life. The show ended with a speech by Chief Winnemucca, delivered in his native tongue, and translated by Sarah.[93]

The tableaux vivants of the Winnemucca troupe reproduce the images of the "primitive" and "noble" savages inherent in nineteenth-century racial ideology. On the one hand, they portray warfare and scalping as definitive cultural activities. On the other hand, they replicate the noble savage in the royal Winnemuccas and in their dramatization of the story of the most legendary American "noble savage," Pocahontas. Of course, Pocahontas was not a Paiute, and so the inclusion of her story in the performance betrays some overt rhetorical and ideological purpose. Pocahontas, John Smith relates, when he, Smith, was being attacked, laid her head over his to prevent her father's men from smashing his skull. As the legend goes, she then took Smith under her wing and taught him the secrets of the wilderness. When he rejected her love, she converted to Christianity and married John Rolfe. We no longer know how much of the legend the Winnemucca troupe dramatized, but this synopsis from the *San Francisco Daily Alta California* does depict, consistent with Hopkins's agenda, the assimilability of the Native Americans and their peaceful coexistence with Anglos in the new world.

The tableaux vivants illustrate how the Winnemuccas—in order to earn money to sustain their dying tribe—exploited the very racial ideologies that threatened the extinction of Native Americans. Later, in her autobiography, Hopkins again taps into those Anglo images of Native America, but this time she revises them through hidden polemic and parody.[94] Whereas Beckwourth's narrative appeals to the *Harper's* reviewer's conventional tastes, Hopkins's text revises conventional representations of Native America. Both cases indicate that while audiences claimed to be interested in "authentic" Native Americans, they were receptive predominantly to romantic and unrealistic representations of them. Hopkins's goal in revising such representations is to undermine the current reservation system—ironically, a system intended, at its origin, to prevent the extinction of tribes—and impede the closing of the frontier through the impoverishment and physical devastation of tribes on the reservations.

For example, by evoking the stereotypes of white "civilizers" versus Native American "cannibals," Hopkins dismantles the opposition between Anglos and Native Americans. As Grandfather Truckee makes the origin story of the light and dark races speak to Paiutes, Hopkins makes the Paiute historical narrative speak to whites. Through hidden polemic, Hopkins justifies Native Americans' assimilation to white culture and institutes guidelines for managing interracial violence. As Hopkins relates, "many hundred years ago" when a group of barbarians lived near them along the Humboldt River, Paiutes were forced to become "Say-do-carah," "conqueror," or "enemy" (73, 75). The barbarians would capture, kill, and eat their foes, as well as exhume and then eat their own dead. The Paiutes, on the other hand, intolerant of these barbarous cultural practices, instead of immediately attacking the enemy, "took some of them into their own families, but they could not make them like themselves" (73–74). Consequently, for three years the Paiutes made war on the cannibal tribe and killed many of them. Hopkins explains, "My people would ask them if they would be like us, and not eat people like coyotes or beasts . . . but they would not give up" (74). Ultimately, the Paiutes conquered and killed the entire tribe.

Hopkins's critique is shaped as she echoes, though with qualifications, the imperialist ideology of European colonizers. First, the "civilized" conquerors demand cultural assimilation by the "barbarous" tribe. Should they refuse to accommodate to more "civilized" ways, then tribal genocide, the story suggests, is both necessary and justified. The implied difference between Paiute and Anglo conquerors is that Paiutes offered the barbarian tribe an opportunity to assimilate before killing them. Insinuating that the Anglo conquerors should offer the Paiutes the same opportunity, Hopkins seeks the continuance of culture contact on the frontiers; however, while Paiutes continually accept white cultural practices, they are systematically denied the opportunity to assimilate. At one time, they are managed by an ethical reservation agent, Sam Parrish, who teaches farming, carpentry, and blacksmithing to the adults, and educates the youth in a white school. Parrish professes to the tribe, "I want to teach you all to do like white people" (107). Hopkins describes how the tribe (all but the belligerent villain Oytes) cooperates with Parrish and, as a result, enjoys communal productivity and material plenty. To the reader, Hopkins insists that it will not take "two or three generations to civilize my people" (89). She advises her audience to "take interest in teaching us" and not send "agents . . . who do nothing but fill their pockets" (89). On behalf of her people, she invites whites to "teach" and "civilize" her tribe. Using Agent Parrish as a model of the ideal "civilizer," she supports the institution of an agency system that is administered justly.

Conversely, Hopkins's central political critique is that most agents deny the naturally cooperative Paiutes fair and just chances to accommodate to white culture. Instead, they are victims of the laissez-faire ideals of the U.S. government and the self-interest of the reservation agents. Historically, through the reservation system, the U.S. government nominally enjoined the assimilation of Native Americans by offering them an Anglo education, issuing the clothing of white culture, and instructing them in industries like farming.[95] However, situated emotionally and geographically distant from the frontier, the government did little to enforce, through its reservation agents, the administration of these goals. Hopkins intimates that, in guaranteeing the physical survival of her people, enforced assimilation is less pernicious than the treatment the Paiutes suffer from hostile white frontier groups—groups whose interests preclude the "civilization" of tribes. Many frontiersmen, for example, regarded Native Americans as enemies and competitors for desired land and wished to see them vanquished.[96]

Hopkins incisively depicts in her autobiography how the self-interest of government agents will inevitably result in the extermination of the Paiutes. Agent Parrish's successor on Malheur Reservation, Agent Rinehart, is a tyrannous master who seeks to exploit rather than assimilate the Paiutes. Under his administration, the Paiutes' relationship to the land is radically altered. Rinehart informs them: "This land which you are living on is government land. If you do well and are willing to work for government, government will give you work. Yes, government will do more than that. It will pay you one dollar per day; both men and women will get the same" (124). Officially, the policy concerning land ownership on reservations was ambiguous at the time of Hopkins's writing. In the Trade and Intercourse Acts passed between 1790 and 1834, the government set aside for tribes certain lands that were off limits to whites, shaped a detailed definition of "Indian country," and granted the president powers to prohibit when necessary the sale of liquor on reservations.[97] Yet the various tribes were not given title to reservation lands. Agent Parrish liberally accords the Paiutes "ownership" of the reservation. He tells them, "The reservation is all yours. The government has given it all to you and your children" (106). Through Agent Parrish's successful governing of the reservation, Hopkins illustrates the potential triumphs of allotment. In contrast, under Rinehart's rule, the Paiutes are no longer landowners but dispossessed, underpaid government "wards." Rinehart not only controls the yield of the land but the cash flow on the reservation. He reneges on his agreement to pay them a dollar a day and, instead, offers them their salary in overpriced government rations that he is supposed to issue freely. Further, he thwarts the Paiutes' plan to buy rations at cheaper prices from the soldiers' store by refusing to grant them any cash. In this way, Rinehart contains the wealth on the reservation and financially prospers while the Paiutes are deprived of clothing, food, and blankets.

Given the mercenary behavior of reservation agents, the belief in racial differences implicit in whites' conception of the "savage, red man," and the greed for land on the part of frontiersmen, any efforts to convert tribes to white culture and values were doomed to failure. However, contrary to Hopkins's account, Paiutes may have actively resisted assimilation to white culture. Two contemporary ethnohistorians, Martha C. Knack and Omer C. Stewart, maintain that the Paiutes "refused to accept wholesale the values which Anglos sought to impose upon them," and explain how they circumvented the intrusions of whites into their culture. Paiutes were gatherers who traveled widely in the northwest region of the United States, searching for fish, wild game, and plants. Their mobility threatened whites, who consequently instituted the agency system to contain threats of violence by converting them to Anglo ways—educating them in white schools, teaching them how to farm, and so forth. Paiutes, however, used cash not to make purchases at white trading posts, but for gambling, which had been a part of their culture for thousands of years. Also, when whites tried to enforce individualism as a value by instructing Paiutes to work for personal gain, they resorted instead to their communal economy.[98]

Whether the Paiutes, as a tribe, supported assimilation or not, Hopkins did. Krupat asserts that Hopkins's autobiography is synecdochic because through the "collective experience" of the tribe the reader comes to understand her life.[99] However, through the narrator in her autobiography, Hopkins filters tribal and frontier politics, and although Hopkins emerges as an empowered spokesperson for her tribe, the apparent ease with which she relinquishes her culture is disconcerting. It must be remembered, on the other hand, that for Hopkins, the physical survival of the Paiutes is of immediate importance.

A case in point illustrating the importance of physical survival for Hopkins is her explanation of the Bannock War. Current historical accounts attribute the war to Native Americans' growing frustration over white encroachment.[100] Supposedly, Native American tensions rose when U.S. settlers allowed their livestock to feed on camas roots, a major staple of local tribes' diets. An implication, then, is that the war originated over issues of cultural power: Native Americans, refusing to adopt white food customs, incited the war.

Although this explanation speaks to the ethnocentrism of whites, Hopkins ascribes the Bannock War to a far more insidious cause. She narrates that two Bannocks "got drunk and went and shot two white men. One of the Indians had a sister out digging some roots, and these white men went to the women who were digging, and caught this poor girl, and used her shamefully.

The other women ran away and left this girl to the mercy of those white men, and it was on her account that her brother went and shot them" (139). By inverting cause and effect in this passage, Hopkins first presents the reader with a familiar stereotype—the image of an uncontrollable, drunken "Indian" killing two white men. She then jolts the reader when she assigns a cause to this behavior—the two Bannocks were avenging the rape of a tribeswoman. To Hopkins, then, the real drama of the frontier for Native Americans is the struggle, not for cultural integrity, but for physical survival.

But to what extent did Hopkins perceive assimilation to be a threat to Paiute cultural integrity? Did assimilation connote detribalization, the closing of the frontier, for Hopkins? On the one hand, she is seemingly resigned to the conventional theme of western autobiography, the conquest of the "savage" by the "civilized."[101] On the other, she is extremely ambivalent as she disparages and critiques the white civilization to which she seeks admission. Double consciousness reveals to Hopkins the image of "Indians" as "savages," but rather than accepting such representations, she revises them through parody. By investing the terms "savage" and "civilized" with her own meaning, Hopkins dismantles the argument that "savage life and civilized life are realms apart."[102] For example, she states: "It is the way we savages do when we meet each other; we cry with joy and gladness" (101); and "Although we are savages, we love one another as well as the fairest of the land" (129). Hopkins deems her people "savage," but then defies conventional notions of savage behavior when she imbues *savage* with another meaning—joyful, humane, and loving. In so doing, she calls into question cultural stereotypes that replace individuals with stock characters.

Another rhetorical strategy Hopkins uses to parody the concept of "civilized" is the irony of repetition. She relates to the reader her complaint to the soldiers about Agent Rinehart, who confiscates Paiute land, starves them, and withholds government rations.

> We told the commanding officer everything about our *Christian* agent's doings, and he told me to write to Washington, and he would do the same. I did as I was told; and when I had written it all the head men of my people signed it, and then our *Christian* agent discharged me from my office of interpreter.... My cousin, Jarry, had not spoken to me all that time, and I too went away, and had to leave my stove, for which I had given fifty dollars. Mr.

Reinhard [*sic*] used it all the time, for which I tried to get paid; but I had to lose it, because he was a *Christian* man. (134–35)

Three times, Hopkins repeats "Christian" to describe the vile Rinehart; each time the word becomes more ludicrous, more distant from the character of Rinehart. As with *savage,* the term *civilized* is emptied of its standard meaning and, instead, signifies its antithesis—thieving, self-serving, abusive, dishonest. Given conventional beliefs that link white culture with civilization, it is ironic that Hopkins anticipates the triumph of white over Native American cultures but does not envision the victory of civilization over savagery.

As Hopkins closes the space between savagery and civilization, she opens the frontier. If *savage* and *civilized* are not opposites, then assimilation to white customs does not necessarily demand the destruction of tribal ways. Ultimately, Hopkins is not a radical assimilationist seeking detribalization in an effort to catalyze cultural melting. The second chapter of her autobiography extols Paiute traditions, offering parallels between Paiute and Anglo culture: "We have a republic as well as you. The council-tent is our Congress" (53). Hopkins also fought to send the displaced Paiutes back to their ancestral lands from the Yakima Reservation, and she opposed white-administrated, Native American boarding schools. Her language implies that assimilation would not necessarily obliterate Native American culture because Native and Anglo America share commonalities. Further, in dismantling the opposition between "savage" and "civilized," she opens the frontier by carving out a safe haven for her people; if her white audience can cease viewing her people as savage, they can empathize with the abuses they suffer. From the position of mutual empathy, constructive intercultural contact may occur.

If a reading of Beckwourth offers any insight into Hopkins's audience, it is that constructive intercultural contact may be unattainable. Rather than discovering mutual empathy with the Crows, Beckwourth evinces a divided self that he attempts to synthesize by closing the frontier. Hopkins, however, uses parody and hidden polemic to critique the reservation system and to propose a brand of assimilation amenable to open-frontier politics. In his theory of African American criticism, Gates attributes acts of signification like parody and hidden polemic to Esu and the Signifying Monkey, the Tricksters of the black literary tradition; rhetorically, Hopkins and Beckwourth function as Tricksters in their texts.[103] Like Native American trickster tales, Beckwourth's narrative demonstrates that "there can be no logically final form to any literary word, phrase, sentence, or entire text, but, instead, only active self-dismantling, self-reformulating processes."[104] As scribe and translator, Hopkins imitates Trickster, the consummate liminal, double-voiced being.[105] But while the traditional Trickster mediates between humans and animals, nature and culture, the individual and the community, Hopkins functions as an intercultural negotiator. Chapter 2 explores the Tricksters situated on various Native American and Anglo frontiers in both oral and written tales. In postcontact trickster border narratives, Trickster reemerges as an intercultural mediator to order the chaos produced by the advancement of the American frontier.

2 The Second Coming of Trickster

Culture Contact and Trickster Border Narratives

Trickster is the consummate, liminal frontier figure; as Victor Turner states, trickster tales throw "into sharp relief many aspects of liminality."[1] Drawing on Turner, Barbara Babcock-Abrahams states that Native American Tricksters exhibit an "ability to live interstitially, to confuse and to escape the structures of society and the order of cultural things."[2] The traditional mythological Trickster mediates between humans and animals, nature and culture, the individual and the communal. Trickster's existence betwixt and between things is presupposed by the ambiguity of his character,[3] for in the fullness of his being, to quote Mac Linscott Ricketts's famous formulation, he is "trickster–transformer–culture hero." As Trickster, he is alternately agent and dupe of mischief; as transformer, he establishes existing patterns in the world; and as culture hero, he improves the quality of life by bringing culture to the people.[4] Similarly, he is at once an "absolute fool" who has a "high sense of mission" yet is "deceitful, vain, and selfish."[5]

According to Ake Hultkrantz, a scholar of Native American religions, the culture hero in Native American mythology is "often regarded as a trickster" who disappears upon completing his work of refashioning the world.[6] The Winnebago trickster cycles, created prior to contact with whites, portray Trickster's emergence into the world, his transformations of it, and his disappearance when his work is complete.[7] But, according to Hultkrantz, Trickster will "return at some future time." Hultkrantz continues, "A. Van Deursen suggests that the notion of the return of the culture hero expresses the hope that the golden age of the past, in which he was engaged, will be restored, but ideas of that kind have certainly been absent in America outside the high culture before the time of the messianic movements."[8] In postcontact trickster tales—imagined after first contact with Anglo American culture— Trickster attains a new function: cultural mediator who ushers his people through the frontier rite of passage. True to his contradictory nature, Trickster often greets the hatred, anger, and exploitation of the borderlands with wit, humor, and even buffoonery. Trickster reappears during culture contact not to restore "the golden age of the past" but to witness the undoing of his transformations or to reorder life for Native Americans on the chaotic frontiers.

As Hultkrantz asserts, Native Americans anticipated the return of Trickster, but not until after the time of the messianic movements. Native American messianic movements originated in the eighteenth and nineteenth centuries as settlers threatened natives and tribes faced cultural erosion.[9] Hence, Native American prophets sought to contend with white encroachment, often by appropriating Christian elements in their religions in order to condemn Christian cultures.[10] Between 1760 and 1770, four prophets—among them Neolin and Wangoment—issued from the Delaware nation alone. Neolin influenced Handsome Lake, the Iroquois religious leader from 1799 to 1815. In the early nineteenth century, the brother of the great chief Tecumseh, Tenskwatawa, endeavored to halt white expansion through his prophecies. Later in the century, the first Ghost Dance religion (1862–72) was instituted by the Paiute Wodziwob. He affected the Wanapam Smohalla, whose Washani religion motivated Chief Joseph of the Nez Perce in 1877 to conduct an uprising against the U.S. Army. A Paiute named Wovoka, who gained knowledge of Smohalla's teachings while working in the Oregon hopfields, became the messiah of the second Ghost Dance religion (1889–92), which instigated the battle of Wounded Knee in 1890.[11]

Wovoka revealed himself at a time when the Plains tribes collectively needed a culture hero and practiced the religion of the Ghost Dance. The prophet Wovoka appeared to the people as a messiah who embraced both Anglo and Native American identities. Porcupine, a Cheyenne observer of this messiah, asserts: "I had always thought the Great Father was a white man, but this man looked like an Indian."[12] In his testimony Porcupine describes "the Christ" as dressed in white man's clothes but wearing moccasins. After hundreds of years during which Native Americans had been confronted with and stymied by Christian hypocrisy, Wovoka appropriated the Anglo Christ to turn him against whites, his original followers. Appearing to the tribespeople as a betrayed and vengeful Christ, Wovoka bewailed the wickedness of Christians and their injustices toward Native Americans. Porcupine relates:

> The circle was prepared again. The people assembled, and Christ came among us and sat down. . . . He said: "I am the man who made everything you see around you. I am not lying to you, my children. I made this earth and everything on it. . . . My father told me the earth was getting old and worn out, and the people getting bad, and that I was to renew everything as it used to be, and make it better."[13]

Endeavoring to restore precontact life, this messiah vowed not only to return the buffalo to earth and resurrect dead tribal members, but also to exterminate all the whites and reestablish the preeminence of the Native American people.[14] Yet Wovoka preached pacifism as he forbade his followers to engage in any warfare. In essence, the Ghost Dance religion was a nonviolent movement whose participants believed that if they simply continued to sing and dance as the messiah instructed, he would renew and perfect the world. Hence, although the prophets of the messianic movements did not necessarily play tricks, like the trickster-transformer they sought to order the lives of their followers who were heading toward cultural, if not physical, extinction.

Like the messiah of the Ghost Dance religion, Trickster enjoys a "second coming"; in fact, in the second Ghost Dance religion, the second coming of Christ concurs with the second coming of Trickster. According to Hultkrantz, both the Prophet Dance of the Plateau and the Ghost Dance hold the precept, inspired by Christianity, that the trickster–culture hero "will return with the dead before the high god proper."[15] Perhaps because Native Americans were overpowered in warfare, they turned to religion for mediating entities. Trickster was one such religious figure upon whom they drew. Mac Linscott Ricketts states that although Trickster is not worshiped, he is a religious "myth-being."[16] Hultkrantz finds that Trickster takes the place of the Supreme Being in origin stories and etiological tales; that is, tales that explain the causes of natural phenomena. He describes the religious function of Trickster: "He is the one who bestowed on mankind in its infancy its cultural institutions, its material and spiritual heritage. Still earlier he is, it seems to me, the one who transformed the world after its creation or assisted the high god in the act of creation. He has at times totally replaced the Supreme Being as creator in mythology."[17] Yet both Trickster and the prophets behave less as spiritual guides than as transformer–culture heroes. In the Ghost Dance religion, the messiah–culture hero, confronted with the intolerable conditions of Native American life, vowed to reverse the "progress of civilization" and annihilate the whites; in other words, he planned to efface the frontier. In trickster border narratives, the revivified trickster-fixer accepts the frontier but approaches it as "a world . . . which is chaotic and needs to be set in order."[18]

At the same time, trickster tales are like religious revitalization movements in that they are, in Kenneth Morrison's words, "efforts to utter effective stories" on the part of Native Americans. Morrison continues, "Numerous small shifts in story likewise accommodated the realities of impinging Euroamerican culture. . . . Old stories were retold by conservatives bent on constructive change" or "the survival of ethnic distinctiveness."[19] Handsome Lake's prophecies adopted Christian concepts like heaven and hell, sin and redemption, into a worldview that preached segregation and anti-assimilation.[20] Similarly, Smohalla, the nonviolent prophet of the Wanapam, taught his people to resist becoming assimilated into Anglo American culture, but also predicted that precontact Native American cultures would be revived.[21] He prophesied that if followers practiced ancient rituals, religion, and dances and abandoned "civilization," whites would eventually be relegated to subservience, if not extinction, by supernatural intervention. Then the natives would return to their precontact ways, and the land would be restored to them. Further, religious revitalization movements, like some trickster border narratives, "restructured tribal world views in ways that represented the colonizing influence of Western culture, serving as a means of criticizing colonial power."[22] In the revision and recreation of Trickster, raconteurs and writers expounded new stories that took the form of trickster border narratives— postcontact trickster tales that, in content and often in structure, reflect interactions between colonizing Europeans and Native Americans.[23]

Like the prophecies uttered by Native American messiahs, trickster border narratives confront the exigencies of culture contact and colonization.

Jarold Ramsey finds that in the wake of contact "Indian storytelling became, not surprisingly, a form of imaginative coping with a new reality indeed full of drastic change and trouble."[24] That "new reality" threatened to destroy Native American customs and territorial control in America. One of the biggest threats to tribal culture outside of genocide was the General Allotment Act of 1887, which sought to prevent the extermination of the natives by integrating them into U.S. society. However, prior to the establishment of legislated assimilation, some tribes faced organized and institutionalized Americanization efforts—for instance, on the part of missionaries who forced conversion to Christianity, or traders, who instituted among them the cash system and individualist economics. Culture contact also resulted in territorial disputes between invading settlers and aboriginal inhabitants. Within the context of colonization, postcontact Trickster is especially suited to the task of contending with this "new reality." As Barbara Babcock and Jay Cox explain, conquest and colonization created in Native American consciousness "a sense of discomfort": "This discomfort is the perfect proscenium for the persona of Trickster and all his/her revolutionary subversion, inversion, and reflexivity. The liminal space where cultures clash is simply the best place to command power, to confuse the 'enemy,' and to spin out a good story."[25] In the border narratives Trickster emerges from a religious-political context with the potential to teach natives how to survive on the margins of Anglo American culture and how to establish tribal patterns for relations with whites.

But to what extent is Trickster capable of ordering the frontier? Has the power of the returning culture hero been compromised in the postcontact milieu? In *Coyote Stories* (1933) Mourning Dove, mediating between the Okanogan culture she will not relinquish and the white culture to which she has accommodated, ponders Trickster's function, asking whether it be to attain intercultural synthesis or to resist Anglo values and customs. Undoubtedly, in some cases, as when Trickster faces the problems of physical, cultural, and religious encroachment on the tribes, his power to order these frontier events for Native Americans *is* compromised. Through Coyote, the Comanche and Apache tales seek to order trade relations with whites, especially the practices of cheating and swindling that accompanied bartering. Yet in other cases, Trickster is much less a figure of mediation, resistance, or critique. The Paiute "White Men Are Snakes" records the negation of Coyote's transformations by Christianity, although the speaker rejects Christianity and the white man.

Finally, John Rollin Ridge, in *The Life and Adventures of Joaquin Murieta* (1854), finds his trickster-bandit impotent to reorder the frontier thrown into tumult by culture contact. Ridge himself acts the trickster when he seems to subvert Anglo authority but in the end endorses it. Trickster fails to reconcile frontier tensions as Ridge's trickster techniques sabotage his trickster-bandit's subversive function. Ultimately, through Trickster, these speakers and writers variously deal with the tensions between open and closed frontiers.

Within the Southwestern contact zone between Native Americans and Anglos, postcontact Trickster becomes a more openly subversive figure than the traditional Trickster. As Barbara Babcock-Abrahams maintains, Trickster's mythic function as the "chaotic Everything," the "tolerated margin of mess," is to reflect inversely an image of order in Native American society and indicate areas in which change is possible.[26] The precontact Native American Trickster levels social distinctions, for instance, by parodying the tribal shaman; the chaos he creates implies the existence of the actual structure of society in which the shaman is a revered, vital member. However, in postcontact trickster tales when, for example, Trickster cheats soldiers into buying a tree that supposedly grows money, the chaos he creates in mocking the soldiers is an attractive alternative to living under Anglo military control. Hence, whereas traditional, precontact Native American trickster tales subvert only to reaffirm cultural values, some postcontact trickster border narratives are more like African American trickster tales, which provide audiences with a model for manipulating the slave system.[27] The Comanche and Apache Tricksters cheat the white man and thus wreak havoc on mercantile capitalism.

In the Comanche trickster narrative, Coyote tricks soldiers into trading two horses for a magical kettle that boils water without fire. I quote it in its entirety (it carries no formal title):

> Coyote was thinking how he might get some money. A great many soldiers were following his trail. Coyote took his kettle and dug out a place in the bank. There he made a fire and placed the kettle over it. He put in water, which began to boil. The soldiers were coming near. Their captain ap-

proached Coyote, asking him how he was. Coyote just continued cooking. The captain said, "You have a mighty good kettle!"—"Yes, it is a good one."—"Can't I buy it from you?"—"Oh, I think a great deal of it." The captain said, "Well, I will give you my horse for it."—"Oh, no! You must offer something I care for very much."—"Well, I will give you two horses."— "My kettle is a mighty good one."—"Well, select whatever two horses you wish for it." Coyote then picked out two very fine horses, and departed. The soldiers left with their kettle. When they camped, they set the kettle down, poured in water, and sat watching to see it boil. They had to wait a very long time. "Evidently Coyote has got the better of us," they said. From that time on, the whites have always traded with the Indians. Coyote taught us to do so.[28]

Coyote is revived by the Comanches and Apaches in order to create chaos and mess in trade relations with whites. With the introduction of Anglo American goods into their economies, many Native Americans found their modes of living, warfare, and industry altered. The Comanche and Apache subsistence pattern changed in the sixteenth century when Spanish invaders introduced the horse to them. As the horse was adopted into their cultures, raiding and trading horses and goods became central to their economy. On the one hand, Comanches were shrewd in playing the French and Spanish off against each other as they struggled for control of Comanche trade. The Comanches would raid Spanish settlements in Texas for horses and captives and trade them to the French and British for weapons. In addition, they were wise to border politics. After Texas and New Mexico seceded from Mexico, Comanches would raid Mexico and flee to U.S. territory, where they would not be pursued by Mexicans. Apaches also engaged in this practice of raiding and trading across the border.[29]

On the other hand, Comanches often found themselves to be dupes in their trading with whites. The Comanches in the eighteenth century discovered the value of the horse as a marketable commodity.[30] With the help of ethical and honest reservation agents, they learned to manage money and protect themselves in trade relations.[31] Authorities from the Indian Bureau tried regulating prices at trading posts; nevertheless, many Anglos were able to "wheedle, cajole, or threaten" the Comanches into spending money, at times for items they did not need.[32]

The Comanche tale reverses the historical reality in which Southwestern natives were duped by white traders. Galen Buller argues of Comanche trickster border tales that their purpose is to integrate whites into the Comanche worldview, although not necessarily "at an equal level."[33] Wiget finds that trickster border narratives are a "medium for attacking the institutions of invading peoples."[34] These readings suggest that postcontact tales differed from the precontact model; they suggest that postcontact tales on the whole are more preoccupied with Anglo than with Native American society and values. The story in which the Trickster dupes the white soldier can be interpreted by Comanches as signifying that "trading with Whites can be both entertaining and advantageous."[35] Coyote is a culture hero, or rather, antihero, who ordains the white/Comanche trade union when he brings cheating into the world by robbing and swindling whites.

The Comanche Coyote, then, functions like a bandit; interestingly, on the Southwestern frontier where Mexicans and Native Americans intermingled, the Trickster and bandit are interchangeable characters. The figure in Mexican folklore who merges the Trickster and bandit traditions of the Native American and Mexican borderlands is Pedro de Urdemalas, or Pedro of Mischief, the social bandit who is also a Trickster. Pedro de Urdemalas dates from the sixteenth-century Spanish *picaresco* tradition. Much like Trickster, the picaro is a rogue who lives by his wits, travels about experiencing different adventures, and exhibits very little character development. The occurrence of identical tale types (such as the stories of the tree that grows money, the self-burning kettle, and the mule that excretes gold) in Comanche, Apache, and Mexican folklore underscores the connection between bandit and Trickster. In other words, some of the antics involving Trickster's swindling of Europeans attributed to Coyote by Comanche and Apache storytellers are also credited to the bandit Pedro de Urdemalas by Mexican raconteurs.[36] Coyote and Pedro de Urdemalas are connected through the dissemination of similar tales along the Southwestern frontier.

Despite the tale's endorsement of cheating as an effective way to retaliate against white soldiers, the closing lines are enigmatic in their explanation that whites have traded with Comanches ever since the Comanche Trickster first cheated whites. Viewing Coyote as the hero of the story presupposes that the entire Comanche audience, homogeneously, identifies with and validates Trickster and his cheating behaviors. But as Wiget has shown of traditional trickster tales, a tale's significance resides with the individual hearer. In this case, some may laugh at Coyote at the end when the status quo is reaffirmed, whereas for others the crucial laugh occurs when Trickster defies constraints.[37] As a cheater, Coyote's heroism is compromised; hence, some of the audience might not identify with Coyote at all, or if they do, might see in him their own foibles reflected. If Coyote often functions as the "margin of mess" who mirrors inversely an image of order in society, then the tale may actually work in the culture to affirm the values of honesty and fair play. In fact, the resolution to the story distances Comanches from Coyote and links whites to him because Coyote taught them to cheat. Cheating, then, is both a frontier survival skill and a Coyote-like behavior.

It is not coincidental, considering that Apache was adjacent to Comanche territory in the Southwest, that cheating is also a theme in the Apache story "Coyote Gets Rich Off the White Men."[38] The tale is composed of four interconnected episodes; in the first, foolish Coyote steals liquor, gets drunk and rowdy, and fails to escape the white men, who jail him. As Wiget states, some trickster tales are moral, especially those in which Coyote does not achieve any goals and is punished.[39] In the Apache story, Coyote is punished for his lack of restraint and indulgence in alcohol—a vice that led to the extermination of scores of Native Americans. Also, Coyote's actions ironically suggest that the white man's introduction of whiskey to Native Americans and his desire to cultivate their addiction to it result in his being the victim of theft and the disorderly conduct of drunkards. The other three episodes that structure the narrative all depict, in different ways, Coyote swindling the white man. Given that Coyote eludes his dupes and is never punished for his dishonesty, the story, again like the Comanche, depicts Coyote manipulating trade relations with whites.

While Coyote is both buffoon and Trickster, his heroism is again ambiguous since, like the Comanche story, this Apache version links Coyote's foolishness and cheating to white behavior. When Coyote trades the money tree to soldiers, in exchange they give him a pack of mules. Annoyed by their constant braying, Coyote kills the mules and decides to buy another burro from another man. Coyote then again meets some soldiers, and they pay him money for the burro, which he claims excretes gold. When the burro fails to produce, they mutilate it, searching for the gold inside. Thus Coyote has foolishly slaughtered his mules for doing what comes naturally to them, and the soldiers have

stupidly dissected the burro for not unnaturally excreting gold. Soldiers and
Coyote are implicated in similar foolish behavior. Like the Comanche, this
Apache tale simultaneously proffers an aggressive model of behavior for dealing with whites on the frontier, links cheating to white culture, and characterizes that behavior as Coyote-like.

In the Comanche and Apache tales, the borderland Trickster exhibits
subversive and manipulative behaviors designed to get the better of whites in
trade relations. At the same time, Trickster is a subversive figure in a social order thrown into chaos by colonialism. As the "chaotic Everything" in precontact tales, Trickster creates a "margin of mess" to define the structure of society
by its antithesis. However, the postcontact frontier that the revivified Trickster encounters is already, from the perspective of Native Americans, disor-
dered; the chaos created by Trickster is therefore an inversion of an already
subverted state. We thus see that Comanche and Apache stories reveal cheating to be a socially vindicating form of resistance to contact with Anglo culture
and institutions.

The Comanche and Apache tales, which were published in *The Journal of
American Folk-Lore* in 1909, are interesting examples of postcontact trickster
border narratives; however, Paula Gunn Allen suggests adopting a cautious
stance to traditional, translated tales because, she argues, "the cultural bias of
the translator inevitably shapes his or her perception of the materials being
translated, often in ways that he or she is unaware of." As a result, Anglo trans-
lators may impose their "unidimensional, monolithic, excluding, and chronological" ways of perceiving the world onto traditional tribal literature which is
inherently "multidimensional, achronological, and including."[40] Translating
and reading traditional Native American literature, then, become contact-
zone issues: in the translated tale, Anglo cultural and literary perceptions meet
those of traditional tribal people, and a contest for authority ensues. In many
cases, the result is what Allen refers to as "the colonizing process of story-
changing."[41] Or it may result in the co-optation of the traditional story by the
collector or reader who transforms the tribal story into a liminal work.

Mourning Dove and Ridge purposely create liminal, mediating works in
which they marry Native and Anglo American cultural perceptions. *Coyote
Stories* is a product of Mourning Dove's double consciousness; it is her attempt
to build a bridge between Anglo and Okanogan cultures. As Mourning Dove
details in her autobiography, she grew up experiencing a simultaneous attrac-

tion and revulsion to white and Okanogan cultures. *Coyote Stories*, the result of her bicultural collaboration between her and her white editors, seeks to reconcile narrative authenticity in the interest of Okanogan cultural continuity with the demands and expectations of her white readership. The tales themselves rehearse Trickster's mediating capacity in a multicultural, colonized society by practicing various ways in which Anglo and Okanogan cultures can mingle and merge.

Like the postcontact Trickster, Mourning Dove was born in the midst of the struggle between Christianizing missionaries and anti-assimilation prophets. To counter the efforts of missionaries who forced natives to adopt Anglo customs and the Christian religion, many of the Salishan tribes turned to nativist prophets. Although Mourning Dove was enrolled as a Lake Indian on the Colville Reservation, she always identified herself as an Okanogan, a Northwest tribe that lived in close proximity to the Colville, Sanpoil, and Nespelem tribes. Many prophets surfaced among these people as a consequence of Roman Catholic and Protestant missionary activity. One of the most famous was Skolaskin, a Sanpoil whom the Okanogans claimed as one of their own.[42] Skolaskin came to power around 1872 and preached a nonviolent message of escape and salvation from whites. Although he merged Native American, Catholic, and Protestant elements into his religion, he rejected Roman Catholic encroachment and governmental control of his people. Similarly, in the mid-nineteenth century, the Nespelem evangelist Slaybebtkud spread the Roman Catholic mass and rituals to the people while prophesying that the white man would bring evil to their world; encouraging tribes to live good lives, he urged them not to surrender themselves to that evil.[43]

Mourning Dove and her trickster tales thus emerge from a culture experiencing a messianic movement. However, Mourning Dove sought to contend with whites, rather than to escape or avoid them. She was open to Anglo cultural customs and Christianity. Born somewhere between 1882 and 1888 (her exact birth date is unknown), she was affected by General Allotment (1887), which (as noted in chapter 1) advocated the assimilation of Native Americans to the dominant culture by allotting 160 acres of land to each head of a family. It also instituted mandatory Anglo education at government boarding schools, dismantled communal culture, and prohibited various forms of cultural expression (boarding schools, for example, disallowed the making of tribal crafts and the speaking of native languages).

Mourning Dove received about eight years of Anglo education throughout her lifetime. As a young child, she attended the Goodwin Missionary School, a Roman Catholic institution. When the government reneged on funding for Catholic schools, she enrolled in the Fort Spokane School. She pursued her education as a young adult by serving as a matron in exchange for classes at the Fort Shaw School in Montana. Finally, in order to advance her writing career, she honed her language skills at a business college in Calgary, Canada. In her memoirs, Mourning Dove describes being "anxious to learn more English and read" as a child. Moreover, unlike Skolaskin's followers, Mourning Dove's mother was a "fanatically religious Catholic." Mourning Dove recalls how in growing up she "had to adapt to the modern world and the sacred teachings of the Catholic church."[44] She portrays herself in her childhood recollections as readily adopting Catholicism and anxious to receive an Anglo education.

Yet at least at one point in her life, Mourning Dove renounced her accommodation to white culture. In a letter dated February 9, 1915—her first letter to her collaborator Lucullus V. McWhorter—she declared:

My blood has called to me, I have lived the Whiteman's traits of life for years, and at last I heard the voice, which seemed but a whisper at first till it sounded so loud to me till it reached the mountaintops. Than, I could not resist. And I threw all civilized life, to the four winds, and I roamed back to my own kind, to live among the golden Race, who I would lay my life for, to endure the teepee smoke and smell the roasted Mowwich deer over the bon fire again. Than than [sic] the memory of my past childhood days, seem to all come back to me again. A life that I have cherish in my bosom, among all my travels with my "put on life." A life that no real Indian dare lead and leave his dear life of nature which God gave him, as his own.[45]

Perceiving a division between her native self and her "put on life," Mourning Dove threw away "civilized life." Yet nowhere in her autobiography does she so strongly reject white culture. She does not categorically indict Anglos but distinguishes between those who help and those who exploit the natives: "Gradually whites moved in, but they were there as traders, missionaries, and agents working for the benefit of the people. Then others arrived and began to take instead of give" (180). Further, seeming not to bemoan the abolition of native traditions, she states that through the "influence and encourage-ment" of Father Etienne De Rouge, "the Indians gradually discontinued their ancient customs" and sent their children to the Goodwin Missionary School (26). Because she was open to Anglo culture, Mourning Dove accepted the encroachment of "helpful" whites.

Mourning Dove wrote her memoirs sometime before *Coyote Stories* went to print (they were published posthumously).[46] In her memoirs, as a re-sult of her vacillation between the Okanogan and Anglo world, she mediates between the two cultures. Although she expresses enthusiasm for her board-ing school education, she also speaks of having "the opportunity to learn the legends, religion, customs, and theories of my people thoroughly" (12). At one point, she even proclaims: "I was now more sure than ever that our ancient Indian wisdom and knowledge was the surest source of safety, sal-vation, and success in life" (90). She accords Roman Catholicism and sha-manism equal influence in her life, claiming that they had "made me resolve to help my people record their traditions and gain all the rights they are en-titled to" (32). Mourning Dove's explanation of the intermingling of tribal and Christian religions sums up her own position toward assimilation: "Yet to some extent we have tried to live in both worlds. An Indian knew he could be faithful to his native creed and still pray every day to the God of the whites" (141).

Like Mourning Dove herself, her *Coyote Stories* reveals a tug-of-war be-tween two worlds, a consequence, in part, of the text's bicultural collabora-tion. In creating the text, Mourning Dove enlisted the aid of two white editors: Hester Dean Guie, who illustrated and edited her stories, and McWhorter, who initially suggested she collect "authentic" Okanogan tales and who provided the explanatory notes for them. Guie inspired the cre-ation of bicultural narratives when he suggested she write the tales for chil-dren of other cultures. Guie continually entreated her to be consistent and accurate with pattern numbers and Anglicized spellings of Okanogan words.[47] But both he and Mourning Dove agreed on her making specific changes to the tales. As Jay Miller observes, she removed elements that she considered "an objection to printing and reading," like references to feces and bodily fluids as well as to infanticide and incest. As a result, the complex-ity of Coyote's character is diminished and he is treated somewhat su-perficially in *Coyote Stories*.[48] Miller finds she also excised from the tales some "just so" explanations and general aspects that her white audience may have considered superstitious. Consequently, many of the tales were unrecognizable to her fellow Okanogans.[49]

From its initiation, *Coyote Stories* was subject to split purposes. In a letter to Mourning Dove, McWhorter attempted to persuade her to undertake the task of collecting folktales, insisting "it is a duty she owes to her poor people, whose only history has been written by the destroyers of their race."[50] As an alternative to cultural genocide, he metaphorically describes this scenario:

> I see old people open their bundles [of tradition and history] and take from them many beautiful stories, which glint in the sunshine like silver and gold, and see them give these to the young woman who eagerly places them in her bundle, which daily grows larger. I see the old people take her by the hand and bless her as she passes on. I note the happy look that radiates from the face of the young woman as she receives these gifts from the many old people, and I see her bundle growing larger and more valuable as she travels towards the parting of the trails.[51]

McWhorter, "a blue-eyed 'Indian' . . . whom the Yakimas adopted," presents himself in this letter as the recipient of a dream vision in which he visualizes Mourning Dove's collaboration with the elders in the interest of tribal, cultural persistence.[52]

However, in her folkloric efforts Mourning Dove never fully realized McWhorter's imagined ideals. Rather than sharing openly with the elders, Mourning Dove admits acting the Trickster in a letter to McWhorter: "The 'poor dears' did not know I was going to write stories for printing purposes while [sic] they told me in every day 'talk.' Of course, it looks sneaky, but it was the only means I could be able to collect datas, otherwise it would have been hard for me to get the material which should be preserved for the coming generation of Indians."[53] Ironically, she does not view the compromises she makes with the material as in conflict with the goal of preserving the lore of her people, as she indicates to McWhorter. She explains to him: "You will see that in my *recastings* I have purposely ommitted [sic] a lot of things, that is an objection to printing and reading, but an Indian knows the story and can read between the lines just the same."[54] While Mourning Dove purports to collect Salishan folklore to be "preserved for the coming generations of Indians," it is unclear how future Native Americans would be able to "read between the lines" of these stories that she "recasts" in a style and manner suitable for a white audience.

These cross-purposes—preserving authentic Okanogan folklore and presenting it to a white readership—are also apparent in the prefatory writings to *Coyote Stories*. In the foreword, Chief Standing Bear praises Mourning Dove for "fulfilling a duty to her forefathers, and at the same time ... performing a service to posterity" in preserving Salishan folklore (6).[55] Mourning Dove, conversely, declares in the preface a different purpose: these legends, she states, "have been set down by me for the children of another race to read" (12).

Just as Mourning Dove found herself between cultures on the frontier and just as *Coyote Stories* became a negotiation between different cultural agendas, Mourning Dove employs her Tricksters to mediate frontier relations. Through her recastings, she merges Okanogan and Anglo worldviews as she ponders how to heal the division between her native self and "put on life." In "Chipmunk and Owl-Woman," she retains the substance of the Native American tale but appends to it a Judeo-Christian moral ending. Traditionally, the trickster tale is not "followed, Aesop-like, with a set of moral truisms"; instead, "the story carried its own meaning; its action dramatically confirmed, without direct moralistic commentary, the values of the audience."[56] Given that trickster tales in general are not overtly didactic, Mourning Dove's "Chipmunk and Owl-Woman" is atypical of the genre since it ends with a moral. Owl is a typical "bogey man" character among Native American tribes.[57] In both Mourning Dove's tale and the Comanche tale "The Deserted Children," Owl kidnaps and eats children.[58] But the purpose of these tales is not to reinforce vulnerability and frighten children into submission. Jarold Ramsey explains the psychological function of trickster tales that mediate between "children and their unverbalized fears and preoccupations about themselves ... and render such anxieties harmless or at least subject to normative laughter, and not a furtive amusement, either, but shared openly with the adults of the tribe."[59] These Owl stories reflect children's fears of being abandoned by or separated from their parents and protectors—of being left to fend for themselves in a hostile environment. Their anxieties are rendered harmless in "The Deserted Children" when the children, abandoned by the tribe, escape the murderous claws of Owl with the help of Coyote, Frog, Crane, and Buffalo-Calf. Through the story, young listeners are given the reassuring message that all of nature sustains them and will come to their assistance in a crisis. In "Owl and Ntsaa'.z," a Salishan version of the tale, the crying boy, in accordance with his parents' threats, is kidnapped by Owl, but he eventually kills Owl, reunites with his family, and matures into a great hero. However, the reassuring resolution in Mourning Dove's version is undercut by her plot structure and moralistic ending.

"Chipmunk and Owl-Woman" is structured around the deceits of three separate characters acting as tricksters. Owl-Woman, claiming various family members are looking for Chipmunk, tries to dupe Chipmunk into accompanying her so that she might devour her. When Chipmunk escapes to her grandmother's, grandmother tries to deceive Owl-Woman into believing Chipmunk is not home until Meadowlark, for a bribe, reveals Chipmunk's hiding place. Finally, acting as hero, Coyote convinces Owl-Woman to do the Sundance and then pushes her into the fire and frees from her basket all the children she plans to roast. The story ends with the moral "Bad persons always must pay for the evil workings of their minds," (59) instead of the traditional etiological one in which Owl-Woman's bottom jaw is ripped off and thrown into the water where it becomes a breed of fish known as coots that swim in a distinctive jawbone pattern.[60] Mourning Dove replaces the traditional Native American ending in which positive natural phenomena result from a character's evil deeds with a traditional Western ending in which the story teaches the audience a lesson.

As a result of this particular recasting, the story is less authentically Native American and more disconcerting to listeners. The moral opposes traditional Native American values. Throughout Native American mythologies, Trickster commits bad acts for which he is killed, only to be later reanimated, and performs misdeeds for which he is never punished. In "Coyote Meets Wind and Some Others" in *Coyote Stories*, Coyote lies, steals, and disobeys ritual orders, but in the end safely returns home to his wife and children. Also, in "The Spirit Chief Names the Animal People," Coyote refuses to provide for Mole and his children yet is rewarded by the Spirit Chief with special magical powers and a sacred mission. Contrary to the Roman Catholic religion in which Mourning Dove was raised, there is no well-defined pattern of sin and retribution in Native American trickster tales. "Chipmunk and Owl-Woman," then, creates anxiety in the audience when it proclaims that evil will be punished. This moral is certainly borne out in the fiery fate of Owl-Woman, yet it also implicates Chipmunk. The audience, no doubt, identifies with the innocent and guileless Chipmunk, who is pursued and killed by Owl-Woman, later to be revived when grandmother replaces Chipmunk's missing heart with a berry. The clash of worldviews in this tale indicates that cultural mediation involves more than simple merger: cultures will collide as often as (or perhaps more often than) they will cooperate. Observing the workings of the frontier, Mourning Dove understood culture contact to result not in the dominance of one culture but the reconciliation of different cultures. In "Chipmunk and Owl Woman," Mourning Dove puzzles over how to unite distinct cultures comprised of persons with divergent values and ways of perceiving the world around them.

Encountering frontier politics head on, Mourning Dove exploits a trickster voice in "Why the Flint-Rock Cannot Fight Back." According to Mary V. Dearborn, "the trickster/author can rebel without seeming to, writing, for instance, within a genteel literary tradition and with the express purpose of mediating between her culture and the dominant one, but maintaining a posture of rebellion by weaving subversion into her text."[61] Mourning Dove shapes a trickster-fixer tale about how the people obtained rock into a story that confronts the Anglo value system and comments on specific frontier issues; namely, whether anyone has the right to claim ownership of the land. Not only does she play a trick in this story, but the tale turns the trick of weaving resistance to Anglo values into the polite, conciliating *Coyote Stories*.

In shaping "Why the Flint-Rock Cannot Fight Back," Mourning Dove took some creative liberties. Jay Miller notes that in her "recastings" she invents military traits for the Okanogans to appeal to white stereotypes of Native Americans as warriors.[62] Actually, the Okanogans and other Salishan tribes were known for their pacifism. As Verne F. Ray states, "peace generally prevailed among all the Salishan tribes of the American Plateau prior to the coming of the horse." He continues: there were "no wars even after that time by the Sanpoil, Colville, Southern Okanogan, Okanogan, or Lakes, against any other Salishan group of the American Plateau."[63] Yet in "Why the Flint-Rock Cannot Fight Back," Coyote functions as the trickster–transformer–culture hero who provides flint rock "for warriors and hunters to use" (77). Further, Mourning Dove reworks the conventional precontact narrative form in which Trickster subverts Native American customs and beliefs in order to reaffirm them later. Instead, in "Why the Flint-Rock Cannot Fight Back" Coyote shapes the world for humans by undermining Anglo cultural values and giving the lie to the myth that whites are the carriers of civilization and progress.

Mourning Dove's version of the flint-rock legend is a postcontact trickster border narrative that resists colonizing values, especially those relating to economic survival on the frontier. A brief comparison with the precontact Shasta tale "How the People Got Arrowheads" reveals how Mourning Dove revised her rendering into a trickster border narrative that criticizes the colonizing society.[64] In both tales, Trickster plans to acquire rock for humans so that they can make durable arrowheads. Ground Squirrel's success in the Shasta version is based on his special knowledge of Obsidian Old Man's whereabouts, while the people, who lacked that knowledge, "did not know where to get obsidian, or they would have used it."[65] However, the people know about Flint-Rock's existence in Mourning Dove's tale because he runs a trading post: "There was an open flat in front of the lodge. Flint met all his visitors there. Warriors and hunters came and bought flint for arrow-points and spear-heads. They paid Flint big prices for the privilege of chipping off the hard stone. Some who needed flint for their weapons were poor and could not buy. These poor persons Flint turned away" (73). That Flint runs a trading post is historically consistent, since the fur trade was a major source of flint for Native Americans.[66] Also, Mourning Dove's experience of the breakup of the reservation in 1896, or secondary encroachment, provides a backdrop for this tale. In her autobiography, she discusses the Mineral Law that opened the reservation to white miners. As Mourning Dove relates, despite the protests of her people, "it seemed that every projecting rock that showed any promise of a mining lode was claimed by . . . fanatical men" (177). Flint represents the "fanatical men" who ravaged the Okanogan reservation in search of the mother lode after the Mineral Law was passed. Since precontact Native American society practiced communalism, Mourning Dove creates an Anglo economic allegory in this scene. Flint, to whom the people "paid . . . big prices," operates a monetary system based on his claim to individual ownership of the land. In opposition to Native American communal philosophy, Flint's system of individual enterprise results in his perpetuating a class of poor persons "turned away" because they "could not buy."

Coyote negates the value Anglo civilization places on individualism and ownership of the land. He tricks Flint into running a race in which the prize is a beautiful woman—Coyote's wife and accomplice, Mole. Instead of racing, Coyote pelts Flint with rocks until he is a pile of chips and then spreads them "all over the earth for warriors and hunters to use" (77). This tale suggests, in opposition to the miners' and settlers' rapacious advancement onto the Okanogan reservation, that progress occurs as people shift from individual to communal living, from owning to sharing the land.

"Why the Flint-Rock Cannot Fight Back" is a trickster border narrative in which Mourning Dove equates frontier chaos with the conflicts wrought by culture contact as she seeks to order the chaos brought about by encroachment on Okanogan lands. Through this particular trickster tale, Mourning Dove discovers a way to distance herself from and interrogate the white culture to which she has accommodated. On the one hand, on the border between Native American "traditionalism" and Anglo American "modernism," Mourning Dove acts the mediator in *Coyote Stories*, envisaging cultural accretion, not effacement, as the result of culture contact. On the other hand, as her own vacillations concerning her "put on life" reveal, it is as necessary for her to develop a position of critique as it is to discover points of synthesis. Through the second coming of Trickster in *Coyote Stories*, Mourning Dove tests the range of Trickster's power to organize Native American relations with whites.

Yet in many narratives, Trickster's power to order the frontier is greatly limited. Contact with whites resulted in the resurrection of the Trickster, but postcontact Trickster does not always prove to be an effective and potent culture hero. Whereas Coyote in Mourning Dove's "Why the Flint-Rock Cannot Fight Back" subverts white values to reestablish Native American cultural patterns, in the northern Paiute tale "White Men Are Snakes," chaos follows the undoing of Trickster's machinations by Christian intruders. Coyote is a defeated culture hero rather than a sportive Trickster in this "border" narrative. Two forms—European biblical and Native American Trickster tales— fight it out as native religion confronts Christian religion: trickster-fixer meets biblical snake. The date when "White Men Are Snakes" was first "published" (or made public) is unknown, but it echoes some of the concerns of the religious revitalization prophets: it is an effective story that critiques the intersection of Christianity and colonization, censures the white invasion and removal policies, and ultimately resists accommodation to white ways. The following is the tale in its entirety:

> Almost everything was Coyote's way. The Indian planted the apple. When
> he planted it, he said for all the Indians to come and eat. When he told them
> that, all the people came.

The white man was a rattlesnake then, and he was on that tree. The white people have eyes just like the rattlesnake. When the Indians tried to come to eat the apples, that snake tried to bite them. That's why the white people took everything away from the Indian; because they were snakes. If that snake hadn't been on the tree, everything would have belonged to the Indian. Just because they were snakes and came here, the white people took everything away. They asked these Indians where they had come from. That's why they took everything and told the Indians to go way out in the mountains and live.[67]

Named only in the first line of the tale, Coyote, as culture hero, ordains the planting of the apple seed for the future sustenance of the Paiutes, and in so doing subverts the biblical analogue in which the "apple" is forbidden fruit, outside the culture's grasp. The qualifier, *almost,* suggests a vulnerability to Coyote's transformer power—one he does not usually manifest in precontact tales and that is developed more in the second part of the myth. This tale begins in the way many precontact trickster tales end, with Coyote establishing a cultural pattern for the people. The second part of the narrative, the biblical addendum, serves as a coda to the tale and reverses Coyote's creative transformations in the first half.

What is tragic about the tale is that the rattlesnake/white man converts the fruits of sustenance into forbidden fruit, symbolizing denied access to material and social culture for Native Americans due to Anglo encroachment.[68] As the snake reverses Coyote's cultural work, the biblical coda negates the spiritual function of the trickster tale. Yet the coda also implicitly subverts the white man's religion. Conflating God, Satan, and the white man into a single character, the teller rejects white culture, its claims on the Paiutes (even as the teller is oppressed by those claims), and its religion. The Ghost Dance Christ, Wovoka, was a Paiute who appropriated Christianity only to use it against whites and prophesy their extermination. "White Men Are Snakes" simultaneously comments on the extermination of Paiute culture and religion and, like the nativist prophecies, adopts Christianity only to resist it.

Just as Coyote is a defeated Trickster in "White Men Are Snakes," John Rollin Ridge in *The Life and Adventures of Joaquin Murieta* imagines a second coming of the trickster-transformer-culture hero only to concede the hero's impotence. Realizing the need for a more aggressive savior, Ridge creates a trickster who is a Mexican outlaw bandit. By retaliating against white aggressors, this trickster-bandit attempts to order the world of the frontier oppressed. Yet Ridge himself, like Mourning Dove, also acts like a trickster in his novel. Mourning Dove exploits trickster techniques by subverting while seeming to mediate; Ridge mimics Trickster in the way that he shapes his novel. Critics posit that there is an allegorical relationship between this story about the treatment of the Mexicans during the California Gold Rush, Ridge's vengeance against his father's assassins, and the Cherokee experience of removal. However, acting as Trickster, Ridge dismantles the allegory of his trickster-bandit and sabotages the trickster-bandit's ability to organize the emotional and psychological life of Ridge and the cultural milieu for Mexicans and Native Americans.

Given that the novel poses as an allegory, it speaks to both Mexican and Cherokee frontier ordeals. First, Joaquin Murieta's outlawry is the effect not only of the personal injustices heaped upon him, but also of the social inequities suffered by Mexicans because of the U.S. government's failure to fulfill the terms of the Treaty of Guadalupe Hidalgo. Also, gold was found in California just nine days after the signing of the treaty in which Mexico relinquished its ownership of the state. While both whites and Mexicans clambered to get rich during the gold rush, the U.S. government enacted the Foreign Miners' Tax. The outrageous tax imposed on "foreign miners" made it almost impossible for any but "native or natural-born citizens of the United States" to mine for gold.[69] Throughout the story, in retribution, Murieta and his band rob whites of their purses of gold.

Revenge was the lifelong preoccupation of Joaquin Murieta, and of John Rollin Ridge. For Ridge, the assassination of his family members for their role in Cherokee Removal motivated his thirst for revenge. Around 1835, the conflict reached a climax between Cherokees and whites for the fertile land in Georgia where gold had been found in the early nineteenth century. In an effort to force Cherokees from their land, Georgians made life unbearable for them—harassing, arresting, jailing them on suspicion, and hanging them for little or no reason.[70] Ridge's family members—wealthy slaveholders who led the Treaty Party of the Cherokee nation—believed that since the harassment was increasing it was in the best interest of the tribe to choose the path of least resistance and move West. In 1835, John Ridge, Major Ridge, and Elias Boudinot, among others, signed the New Echota Treaty and agreed to the removal of the Cherokees west of the Mississippi River. The signing of the treaty made the Ridges and Boudinot either outlaws or martyrs, depending on one's position, since they broke a Cherokee law that, ironically, John Ridge himself had helped draft in October 1829. The law stated that any Cherokee entering into a treaty with the United States was guilty of treason, which was punishable by death.

From 1838 to 1839, the Cherokees were forced by U.S. soldiers off their eastern lands to travel what is now called "The Trail of Tears." On that trail, approximately four thousand Cherokees died of exposure, disease, and starvation. In 1839, the death sentence was executed upon the Ridges and Boudinot by assassins from the anti-removal faction led by John Ross. Young John Rollin Ridge watched as his father was dragged from his bed early one Saturday morning and, in front of his horrified wife and children, stabbed twenty-five times.[71] The Ross faction Cherokees became the objects of John Rollin Ridge's lasting desire for revenge. As Ridge writes to his cousin Stand Watie in 1849: "There is a deep-seated principle of revenge in me which will never be satisfied until it reaches its object."[72]

Ridge chooses as his novel's main character Joaquin Murieta, a revenge-seeking trickster-bandit. The Trickster of precontact oral literature often acts as a thief who steals to acquire necessities for humans, and some precontact Cherokee trickster tales, as well as *The Life and Adventures of Joaquin Murieta*, portray Trickster stealing to benefit society.[73] Although Murieta most often uses violence to steal from victims, theft is for Murieta, as it is for Trickster, his response to unequal social conditions. Murieta's campaign to steal from whites is partly in response to Anglo Californians' attempts to block Mexicans from taking part in the Gold Rush. Murieta and Trickster both forcibly undo discrimination; both level distinctions between people.

There is a kind of symbiotic relationship between Tricksters and bandits. While Tricksters often act as thieves, bandits often perform tricks to outwit opponents or to escape from danger. In his study of African American folklore, John Roberts views "the badman tradition as a transformation of the trickster tradition or the trickster as proto-outlaw."[74] A similar cross-characterization is evident in the character of Pedro de Urdemalas, the bandit of Mexican folklore who plays tricks like the Comanche and Apache Coyote. The black badman, like Murieta, operates under socially oppressive conditions: the law is against him and he acts in order to secure his interests and help the people.[75] Murieta is further like the Native American Trickster in that both tend to occupy "crossroads," "thresholds," "doorways."[76] Murieta physically inhabits the border territory between California and Mexico, and in his character he embodies both the plight of the Mexicans during the California Gold Rush and that of the Cherokees during removal.

While Joaquin Murieta is a trickster who inhabits border territory, Ridge —an author who exists between Mexican, Cherokee, and Anglo cultures— uses trickster language and techniques in *The Life and Adventures of Joaquin Murieta*. For example, as in some trickster border narratives, the language of Ridge's novel embodies "contradictoriness, complexity, deceptiveness, and trickery," especially in regard to his critique of racism.[77] He appears to fashion an allegorical protest novel, but ends up rejecting any consistent political position and, ultimately, suggesting that the trickster–culture hero is impotent for Ridge.

Ridge's critique of racism in the novel unravels as his tricksterism emerges. Louis Owens asserts: "Ridge paradoxically both embraces the racist values of his fellow Californians and protests social and racial injustice at the same time."[78] On the one hand, the character of Murieta illustrates that criminal conduct is socially, not racially, determined; "dark" behavior is the response of the victimized race to their victimizers, not the result of being born with dark skin. In the beginning of the story, Murieta is depicted as both pure in character and "colorless." He is described as having "a very mild and peaceable disposition"; physically, "his complexion was neither very dark or very light, but clear and brilliant."[79] While spiritually he transcends race classification, politically he is a Mexican and an object of contempt to Americans, who in the aftermath of the Mexican War viewed Mexicans as "conquered subjects of the United States" (9). As a Mexican, he suffers major indignities: he is driven from gold mining by greedy Americans who beat him and rape his wife; he is forced from another home by white settlers who covet his land; and when he is found riding a suspected stolen horse given him by his brother, he is unjustly lashed and his brother hanged without a trial.[80]

Only after experiencing violence does Murieta psychically "darken." As the narrator explains, when Murieta's wife is raped, "the soul of the young man was from that moment darkened" (10). Following the murder of his brother, "he walked forth into the future a dark, determined criminal" (14). The violent circumstances of his life prescribe for him the path of banditry.

Racism debases Murieta's character and perpetuates itself: prior to the assaults on his family, Murieta has "the most favorable opinion" (8) of Americans, but subsequent to his violent experiences, he "contracted a hatred to [sic] the whole American race" and vowed "to shed their blood, whenever and wherever an opportunity occurred" (14). By the end of the novel, Ridge extends his critique of racial and social injustice, addressing his readers. He preaches "that there is nothing so dangerous in its consequences as *injustice to individuals*—whether it arise from prejudice of color or from any other source; that a wrong done to one man is a wrong to society and to the world" (158).

Despite his censure of racism and its destruction, the characters in the novel evince both "prejudice of color" and "injustice to individuals." Ridge mimics Trickster, a figure who is outside the bounds of logic and resists fixed interpretation, according to Karl Kroeber.[81] In the preface to the novel, Ridge's editor claims Ridge's purpose is "to hold up a manifest contradiction" to the postwar image of Mexicans as cowards (4). However, throughout the narrative Ridge stereotypes and caricatures other nonwhite characters. For instance, the narrator explains that "cowardice" is "a quality that particularly distinguishes the California Indians" (37). He mockingly describes the Tejon chief, Old Sapatarra, as "seated upon his haunches in all the grandeur of 'naked majesty,' enjoying a very luxurious repast of roasted acorns and dried angle-worms" (36). The Chinese are portrayed as cowering in their pacifism and are routinely murdered by the sinophobic Three-Fingered Jack.

Not only does the overt prejudice of the narrator and other characters contradict the novel's critique of racism, but inadvertently so does Murieta's outlawry. One night, during the height of Murieta's career, a young man travels from door to door seeking shelter in a rainstorm, and no one dares to offer him hospitality. The narrator explains, "It seems that the young fellow was dark-skinned and, unfortunately, not a very amiable-looking fellow at the best, and he was, accordingly, taken for Joaquin or some one of his band traveling around as a spy" (145). Mexican resistance against oppression thus only perpetuates continued color prejudice. Although the novel critiques racial and social injustice, almost every character is implicated in unjust acts, and so Ridge, in the end, refuses to offer any solutions to this social problem. By sincerely censuring racism while simultaneously reproducing it and ultimately refusing to offer any solutions to the problem of racial injustice, Ridge exploits the ambiguity and mystery of Tricksterism.

Another trickster technique Ridge uses in the Murieta story is alternately encoding and rejecting external reference to his own life. After Murieta and his family have been victimized by whites, he organizes a rampage through southern California to rob and kill white people. Given the violent assassination of Ridge's family members because of their participation in Cherokee Removal and its obvious emotional parallels with the plot of the novel, critics have come to agree on two major points. First, most assert that Ridge infuses the narrative with his desire for vengeance against the Ross faction Cherokees.[82] Second, they also hold that in this story about whites' oppression of the Mexicans, he vents his distress and frustration over the treatment of his people during removal.[83] The implication of these two points is that one can interpret Ridge's Trickster as a subversive character used by Ridge to turn an allegorical trick.

However, Ridge's trick is that his allegory breaks down; surface and allegorical meanings do not always correspond. Kroeber's view of Trickster accounts for why the allegory disintegrates: the Trickster, Kroeber declares, "transforms, or deconstructs, any definition of him even as he provokes one into making a definition. He functions both as man and as animal because he is neither by being both. Neither man nor animal is ground for the figure of the other but each is alternately figure and ground."[84] Ridge continually alternates figure and ground, dismantling each allegorical reference as it is articulated, deflecting his Trickster's function with trickster language. Are whites heroic pursuers or abusive oppressors of Mexicans? Are Native Americans unworthy victims of removal policies or inherently degraded beings? Is resistance or assimilation the answer for Native Americans to the cultural war waged by whites?

Ridge links the revenge of politically oppressed Mexicans against whites to that which he harbors against his family members' assassins. In the autobiographical essay that prefaces his *Poems*, Ridge describes the effect of his father's murder on him: "It has darkened my mind with an eternal shadow."[85] In the narrative, Ridge uses similar light/dark imagery to depict Murieta's darkening emotions after each incident of abuse by whites. Also, in a letter to Stand Watie, Ridge excitedly writes of Tom Starr, who murdered a member of the Ross faction: "He is a second Rinaldo Rinaldini." In the novel, Murieta is referred to as "the Rinaldo Rinaldini of California" (7).[86] Both of these allusions link Cherokees of the Ross faction and whites as victimizers and objects of Starr's and Murieta's outlaw revenge. Historically, however, whites and Ross faction Cherokees were politically opposed: Ross's band fought to resist white encroachment and removal policies. It was the Treaty Party, led by Ridge's family members, that politically sided with whites. Although Ridge's family chose not to fight for their homeland but to sign the New Echota Treaty, Ridge creates a hero who ferociously resists oppressive whites.

In his political life, Ridge supported his father's assimilationist politics and shared his attitude of cooperation with whites. Much like Sarah Winnemucca Hopkins, Ridge petitioned for the civil rights of assimilated Native American members of white civilization. In an autobiographical essay, he bitterly laments the oppression and removal of the Cherokees: "Oppression became intolerable, and forced by extreme necessity, they at last gave up their homes, yielded their beloved country to the rapacity of the Georgians, and wended their way in silence and in sorrow to the forests of the far west."[87] At the same time, throughout his life, Ridge persuaded Native Americans to adopt Anglo lifestyles and education, and advocated the admission of a Native American state into the union.[88] In regard to his revenge quest, he considered whites to be his, not Ross's, allies. He writes to Watie of whites who "say, if [the] Government would only hint to them to go in, they'd slaughter 'that damned Ross set' like beeves." In particular, he mentions Weaver, a white man who "is very anxious to induce me to raise a company of some twenty-five or thirty white men to go and kill John Ross."[89] Although he enjoys a personal attraction to Anglo civilization and views Anglos as allies, he nevertheless connects them to Ross faction Cherokees in the story.

Critics also hold that, in a story of Mexican oppression, Ridge turns white abuses of Native Americans into allegory, but no correspondence between Mexicans and Native Americans exists in the novel. The Tejon Indians are depicted as dirty and cowardly, Digger Indians as servile and degraded. Further, in one scene after Murieta's band falls into the clutches of the Tejons, the Tejons betray them and report the capture to apathetic Americans. Owens accounts for these portrayals by postulating that Ridge viewed the Cherokees, one of the five "civilized" tribes, as highly cultured and superior to other Native American nations.[90] But there is yet more Tricksterism. Ridge also denigrates Cherokee "half-breeds," a group to which he belongs: his father was Cherokee and his mother, Sarah Bird Northrup, was white. Cherokee "half-breeds" assist whites in capturing Mexicans and ruthlessly slay the wounded Mexican captives left in their care. Ridge, then, dissociates Mexicans and Native Americans. Ultimately, Ridge rejects or subverts any allegorical reference to historical and biographical events in the interest of creating a trickster narrative that defies fixed interpretation.

A trickster technique Ridge uses to bolster the contradictoriness of the narrative is to create separate and distinct points of view for Murieta and the narrator. In her reading of Winnebago trickster narratives, Anne Doueihi observes that "by dividing himself, so to speak, into narrator and character, [Trickster] both tells the story and is 'in' the story."[91] On the one hand, Ridge attributes to Murieta "a hatred to the whole American race" and a determination "to shed their blood, whenever and wherever an opportunity occurred" (14). On the other hand, the narrator himself, when directly addressing the reader, depicts both Murieta and the whites who pursue him as heroes. While General Bean's murder is excused as "an act of self-preservation on the part of Joaquin," Bean is lauded as "a generous, noble-hearted, and brave man" (49). Of another murdered posse member, Peter Woodbeck, the narrator declares: "The brave fellow had fought like a true American, long and well, but who can prevail against a league of men and devils in an evil hour?" (123). Finally, Murieta's captors and murderers, Captain Love and his Rangers, were historically "as disreputable a group of thugs as ever killed under the law"; Love's own life ended when he was shot while abusing his own wife.[92] Nevertheless, from the narrator's point of view he is a hero: "a leader . . . whose soul was as rugged and severe as the discipline through which it had passed, whose brain was as strong and clear in the midst of dangers as that of the daring robber against whom he was sent, and who possessed a glance as quick and a hand as sudden in the execution of a deadly purpose" (146). By distinguishing the narrator from Murieta, Ridge turns the trick of sustaining simultaneously the heroism and antiheroism of both whites and Mexicans.

The first novel written in English by a Native American, *The Life and Adventures of Joaquin Murieta* follows in the tradition of trickster border narratives. While seeming to encode personal history and border politics into his work, Ridge systematically frustrates, through his trickster narrative, any attempts to make the story an allegory. In the end, the novel rejects all political positions to signify Trickster. Perhaps because Ridge subscribed to assimilation, Trickster refuses to take sides, and the Rangers ultimately kill Murieta and quash the resistance. Trickster in his second coming dies powerless to transform border injustices or mediate between cultures, just as Ridge, no doubt, felt powerless in his quest to exact revenge on his father's murderers.

In the context of frontier relations, Native Americans enacted a second coming of Trickster to resurrect a culture hero for what seemed to be a border apocalypse. The messianic movements provided the impulse for revivifying Trickster. On the border between cultures, both Trickster and the prophets confront the chaos produced by culture contact. The prophets Smohalla and Wovoka solved the "Anglo Problem" by prophesying the extermination of whites in order to eliminate the frontier before it closed down on them. However, the postcontact Trickster's purpose is not so indisputably ordained; instead, only in some cases does he bring order to the frontiers. The Comanche and Apache tales open the frontier to natives by using a resistant trickster-bandit who cheats Anglos—the people who brought the Comanches and Apaches mercantile-capitalism and along with it the practice of cheating. Pondering Trickster's mediating capacity, Mourning Dove desires to keep the frontiers open but considers, in *Coyote Stories,* whether Trickster should act as a bridge between cultures or as an agent for overturning Anglo values and customs. In other postcontact border narratives, Trickster succumbs to the inevitable closing of the frontier. Christianity undoes the transformations of the trickster–culture hero in "White Men Are Snakes." As Ridge shapes *The Life and Adventures of Joaquin Murieta,* he employs trickster techniques that render his trickster-bandit powerless, sabotage the resistance, and close the frontier. Postcontact Trickster is a pliable character who enables Native Americans to rehearse various ways to negotiate the frontier rite of passage.

Similarly, two Anglo Chinese sisters who negotiate the Asian American frontiers—Sui Sin Far and Onoto Watanna—adopt different stances toward white culture in their fiction. As we will see in the next two chapters, both write stories about the Asian American immigrant experience in which marriage is a prevalent theme. Sui Sin Far identifies herself as Chinese and writes as an activist against sinophobia. According to Annette White-Parks, her character Mrs. Spring Fragrance adopts a "border position—between cultures and individuals, as matchmaker and trickster."[93] Her sister, Onoto Watanna, plays the trickster and passes as a Japanese writer of Japanese American romances, inventing techniques to promote her popular novels as anti-Japanese sentiment evolves.

3 Bartered Brides and Compulsory Bachelors on the Chinese American Frontier

The Short Stories of Sui Sin Far

As Asians undertook their rite of passage into American society, many U.S. citizens feared this new contact zone would threaten national security, economic control, and racial purity. In the eighteenth century, the goal of frontier Manifest Destiny was for Americans to expand west, discover a passage to India, and eventually dominate trade in Asia.[1] When Asians in the late nineteenth century forged a counterfrontier, crossing the Pacific Ocean and pushing toward the eastern coast of the continent, Americans, fearful of being conquered, reacted anxiously to the influx of Asian immigrants. The manifestation of their anxiety was "Yellow Peril" paranoia: the American fear of "possible military invasion from Asia, perceived competition to the white labor force from Asian workers, the alleged moral degeneracy of Asian people, and the potential genetic mixing of Anglo-Saxons with Asians, who were considered a biologically inferior race by some intellectuals of the nineteenth century."[2] As a result, legislators sought, through staunch exclusion and antimiscegenation laws, to close the frontier by preventing the proliferation of Asian families.

In the literary arena, many writers at the turn into the twentieth century adopted a border position and attempted to explain Asian customs to a U.S. audience. Asian marriage customs and family life were of particular interest to writers at the time, many of whom perpetuated sinophobia by linking arranged marriage to bride bartering and rejecting the idea of intermarriage. In response to Yellow Peril propaganda and in an effort to open the frontier to Chinese immigrants, Sui Sin Far (Edith Eaton), a self-proclaimed activist, wrote short stories that depict the immigrant experience of being between cultures, critique unjust U.S. policies against the Chinese, demystify Chinese marriage, and analyze the obstacles created by Anglo society for the formation of Asian American families.

Yellow Peril signifies fear of Asian conquest, which need not only be a military phenomenon but can also be achieved through the propagation of Asian families and population growth in America. As the U.S. government created laws that preserved Chinatown "bachelor societies," anti-Chinese writers perpetuated culture clash by mystifying Chinese matrimony and misrepresenting customs like arranged marriage. In "Chinese Slavery in America," an 1897 article in the *North American Review*, Charles Frederick Holder, anxious about the state of U.S. "law, order, and morality," describes the trafficking of Chinese women to the United States by the "criminal or slave-dealing class." An agent in China, he explains, seduces a "country girl" with promises of a "rich husband at Canton." Arriving in Canton, the girl is informed that the husband has been detained on business but wishes her to meet him at another destination. Once on board a ship departing China, the girl is forced to obey her kidnappers, who terrorize her with threats that U.S. Customs officials will throw her into jail and torture her if she is discovered. In the United States, she is taken to the "Queen's Room," where she is bartered for by single men and brothel owners and sold to the highest bidder. Holder concludes: "Unfortunately the Chinese law and custom of marriage aids the kidnapper. A wife rarely sees her husband before marriage; the affair being a business arrangement, pure and simple, and the girl bargained for by the agent of the prospective husband."[3]

Holder equates arranged marriage with the kidnapping and selling of Chinese women despite the fact that Anglo culture practiced arranged marriage, the subject of many eighteenth-century British and American novels. True, the proliferation of anti-Chinese laws resulted in the emergence in Chinatowns of *tongs*—Chinese societies that rebelled against U.S. social "order." Dealing in illegal immigration, they also managed the sale of Chinese women as prostitutes and brides for Chinese bachelors.[4] But contrary to Holder's assertion, arranged marriage was not analogous to kidnapping women into prostitution. Legitimate Chinese betrothals were negotiated by the parents of both the prospective wife and the husband, and both the bride and the groom lacked a say in the arrangement.[5] For many couples, arranged marriage was a valued custom, not an abuse of power by the "criminal or slave-dealing class." As Sui Sin Far observes, "The Chinese firmly believe that heaven decides who are to be husband and wife, which is one reason why the parties most concerned have little, if anything to say, concerning the event, and why it is left so much in the hands of the fortune tellers and go-betweens."[6] Although the practice of arranged marriage runs counter to democratic ideals, Holder's conflation of it with female slavery distorts the traditional Chinese values and contributes to the stereotypes and false knowledge of Chinese culture that pervaded America at the turn of the century.

Anxiety about the so-called Yellow Peril also infuses the views of Chinese marriage presented in the *Overland Monthly*—a journal published in San Francisco, the site of the largest Chinatown population. The *Overland Monthly* is a significant voice because in the sixty-one years of its publication (1868–75; 1883–1936), it produced two hundred critical articles or notes, thirty-three poems, eighty-one short stories, and hundreds of references to the Chinese in various other selections.[7] Limin Chu finds "fairly consistent" the journal's stance toward immigration: "The journal sees the problem of the immigrant as one of mental assimilation with the characteristic citizens of the nation and holds that assimilation can be achieved only through education which molds the mind."[8] The *Overland Monthly*'s anti-Chinese stories bring about "mental assimilation with the characteristic citizens of the nation" when they devalue Chinese beliefs and traditions. Instigating culture clash, many of the stories mystify Asian marriage customs and denounce interracial marriage. In so doing, they perpetuate the need for a Chinese bachelor society and concede to Yellow Peril paranoia.

Within and against the mystification of Chinese wedlock, Sui Sin Far performs her "cultural work" of opening the frontier from which Chinese immigrants were systematically being excluded. "Cultural work," as defined by Jane Tompkins, "is the notion of literary texts as doing work, expressing and shaping the social context that produced them."[9] Tompkins's formulation assumes the interrelation between text and context, the parallel and reciprocal association of the work of literature with the society external to it. While literary scholars traditionally have analyzed how genre influences a writer's choices,

Tompkins's concept implies that cultural events affect formal and generic structures. Sui Sin Far wrote numerous short stories illustrating the everyday lives of struggling Chinese immigrants. In *Mrs. Spring Fragrance* (1912), her collection of short stories, seeking to oppose anti-Chinese sentiment by documenting West Coast Chinese life, she devises realist techniques.

Sui Sin Far constructs her realism when, much like Sarah Winnemucca Hopkins, she exploits her double consciousness of Anglo and Chinese worlds to finesse her white audience. In "Mrs. Spring Fragrance" and "The Inferior Woman" she draws on her understanding of both cultures to show how Chinese and Anglo marriage customs intersect; and in "The Wisdom of the New" and "The Americanizing of Pau Tsu" she highlights cultural differences that breed pain and misunderstanding for newly arrived Chinese immigrants. She also dialogues with turn-of-the-century "metropolitan representations" of Asian others and invests the Chinese "other" with a "human essence."[10] As Annette White-Parks has shown, Sui Sin Far appeases her audience's appetite for "oriental" types in order to be published, but also breaks those stereotypes.[11] She endows her characters with a human essence when she challenges stereotypes and represents a variety of Asian Americans who offer a continuum of responses to Americanization. Further, the realism of *Mrs. Spring Fragrance* derives from its structure: Sui Sin Far considers several alternative viewpoints among her stories. If, as it might be said, the extreme responses to culture contact are to preserve the culture and follow orthodox Chinese ways or to assimilate and observe orthodox Anglo customs, Sui Sin Far's stories offer more alternatives than just these two. *Mrs. Spring Fragrance* investigates, often through the realm of marriage relations, the competing claims of American feminism, acculturation, and Chinese cultural traditions to countenance various, even conflicting, alternatives for Chinese immigrants as they establish families in America.

Sui Sin Far's flexible cultural attitudes about Chinese immigrants reflect her mixed cultural background. Sui Sin Far, or Edith Eaton, was one of fourteen children born to Edward Eaton, of England, and Grace Trepesis Eaton, of China. Sui Sin Far recalls that as a child she listened to stories of her mother's land and "of how she [her mother] was stolen from her home."[12] Kidnapped in her childhood, Grace Trepesis was eventually adopted by an English missionary couple and "brought up in a Presbyterian College" in London (835). She met Edward Eaton, a wealthy businessman, when he was on a business trip in Shanghai. Choosing to marry Grace and to pursue a career as an artist, he was disowned by his aristocratic family. The newlyweds traveled extensively and lived for a time in Japan, where Winnifred (the subject of chapter 4) was born.[13] They then settled in New York and finally Montreal, where they lived, the large family of a starving artist, an impoverished life.[14]

Raised by English parents, Grace did not teach her own children the Chinese culture or language. The products of an intermarriage, neither Edith (Sui Sin Far) nor Winnifred (Onoto Watanna) bore the unmistakable marks of Asian heredity; either could have passed as white.[15] Nevertheless, Sui Sin Far chose to pass as Chinese and, throughout her life, defend the Chinese community with her pen and serve as a spokesperson for them; in fact, she was the first person of Asian descent to write stories about the Chinese in America. In 1912, in a preface to *Mrs. Spring Fragrance* (her only book-length collection of short stories) she thanks twenty-four magazines for having published her work.[16] Much of Sui Sin Far's knowledge of Chinese culture came from spending most of her adulthood living in West Coast Chinatowns, particularly in Seattle. In her autobiographical essay "Leaves from the Mental Portfolio of an Eurasian" (1909), she asserts: "My heart leaps for joy when I read one day an article signed by a New York Chinese in which he declares 'The Chinese in America owe an everlasting debt of gratitude to Sui Sin Far for the bold stand she has taken in their defense'" (838). In 1914, the Chinese communities of Boston and Montreal placed on her Montreal grave a memorial that reads: "A righteous one who never forgets China and Chinese."[17]

Nevertheless, "Leaves from the Mental Portfolio of an Eurasian" reveals Sui Sin Far's rather sophisticated understanding of being between cultures and her inner struggle to adapt to that position. In fact, Sui Sin Far lived her entire life on an identity frontier. Her autobiographical essay develops her personal attack on racism as she retraces her growing Eurasian consciousness and, concomitantly, her evolving decision not to pass as white.[18] As she becomes aware of her ethnic identity, she is best likened to the "tragic mulatto" of African American literature: trapped on the frontier between cultures, she belongs to neither the Asian nor Anglo communities.

The autobiographical essay delineates a series of psychic permutations in young Sui Sin Far as she moves toward understanding the social implications of her Asian American identity. At first, she feels awkward and embarrassed by her ethnicity. By the time she is eighteen years old, Sui Sin Far claims to have a proud national consciousness. She reads books about the greatness of China and admits: "What troubles me is not that I am what I am, but that others are ignorant of my superiority" (837). However, when Sui Sin Far encounters Chinese people, she finds herself rejected by them because of her half-white status: "The Chinese merchants and people generally are inclined to regard me with suspicion" (840). Some Americanized Chinese people refuse to believe that she, who neither looks Chinese nor speaks the language, can be of Chinese ancestry. At the same time, she suffers the consequences of her Asian heredity. When a business associate at a dinner party states, "A Chinaman is, in my eyes, more repulsive than a nigger," Sui Sin Far contemplates remaining silent and not unmasking herself. She admits that she has "no longer an ambition to die at the stake for the sake of demonstrating the greatness and nobleness of the Chinese people" (839). However, she does reveal herself to be Chinese and, although the man offers a sincere apology, she leaves town. Besides alienation from friends and business associates, Sui Sin Far finds that her Asian ethnicity equates with sexual promiscuity when she is sexually propositioned by a U.S. naval officer in the West Indies; remembering the Chinese girls in Hong Kong, he assumes she is a prostitute.

At the end of her essay, Sui Sin Far vacillates between embracing ethnicity and desiring to transcend it. She professes: "After all I have no nationality and am not anxious to claim any. Individuality is more than nationality. 'You are you and I am I,' says Confucius. I give my right hand to the Occidentals and my left to the Orientals, hoping that between them they will not utterly destroy the insignificant 'connecting link.' And that's all" (843). On the one hand, her exploration of her ethnic self achieves a courageous resolution as she embraces both East and West in coming to terms with her biracial identity. Yet as one group of scholars assert: "The concept of the dual personality deprives the Chinese-American and Japanese-American of the means to develop their own terms."[19] Sui Sin Far seems to anticipate this problem when she views her identity as on the border between nationalities. If the frontier is that margin at which cultures meet, then the frontier boundary for Sui Sin Far is a neutral zone, a place of "no nationality" or of "individuality." Ultimately, she seeks to have it both ways as she recognizes her cultural identity in offering herself to the Orientals and the Occidentals, and attempts to transcend the dilemma of the "tragic Eurasian" by positing an essential self. Sui Sin Far raises an important question: is it possible to assert an American identity apart from, in her case, Chinese and Anglo cultural forms?

It is no wonder that Sui Sin Far imagined transcending nationality, given America's beliefs about and policies toward the Chinese at the turn of the century. She wrote about the Chinese in America between 1888 and 1913, during the time when Anglos sought to squelch Asian population growth in the United States. The U.S. economy was burgeoning in the late nineteenth century, and early in that period industries were in need of workers to perform menial labor. Many Chinese came to the United States to work on the railroad and to work as unskilled laborers.[20] Others, attracted to California by news of "Gold Mountain," arrived with the hope that they would make their fortune there. At first, Americans embraced these Chinese immigrants with open arms, deeming them hardworking and tractable people. But when they no longer filled a need in the economy, when jobs became scarcer and the Chinese began to compete with American laborers, Chinese immigrants became a problem to many Americans.

In an effort to reduce the threat the Chinese posed to the American frontier, Americans solved the Chinese "problem" with the Chinese Exclusion Act of 1882. This U.S. act, aimed at excluding Chinese laborers, prohibited the immigration of Chinese with the exception of teachers, students, tourists, diplomats, and merchants. By creating obstacles that prevented Asian men from (re)establishing families, the turn-of-the-century exclusion laws attempted to squelch the population growth of Asians already in America and protect the nation's racial homogeneity. The laws were further shaped to contain the already minute population of Chinese women in Chinatown; antimiscegenation laws forbade marriages between whites and Asians. Ultimately, Chinese men in the United States were forced to live in a bachelor society. Most Chinese laborers emigrated to America with the hopes of making a fortune and returning to China in a few years. Unless immigration was to be permanent and involved the relocation of the whole family, the Chinese wife did not accompany her husband to America. In cases where immigration was to be permanent, the wife did not resettle until her husband achieved economic stability.[21] Chinese men thus outnumbered Chinese women immigrants from the start.

Moreover, prostitution laws seemed designed to prevent Chinese women from immigrating. Seeking to regulate prostitution within the Asian community, California passed a law in 1870 to prevent "importing . . . for criminal and demoralizing purposes" Chinese women into the United States. This law, in part, states that Chinese women would be barred entry into the United States "without first presenting to the Commissioner of Immigration evidence satisfactory to him that such female desires voluntarily to come into this State, and is a person of correct habits and good character."[22] This law, entitled "An Act to Prevent the Kidnapping and Importation of Mongolian, Chinese, and Japanese Females, for Criminal and Demoralizing Purposes," claimed to protect young women against being kidnapped and coerced into prostitution. Yet prior to their sale to brothel owners in the United States, many of these women did not live as prostitutes. The law, in effect, only eliminated those who would proclaim themselves prostitutes; it did not defend women unknowingly lured by *tongs* into brothels. Also, the law undoubtedly offended the modesty of the Asian wife who, seeking to rejoin her husband, had to prove she was not a prostitute, that she was "a person of correct habits and good character," before being granted entry into the United States. The Page Law of 1875, which similarly barred prostitutes from immigrating, was so broad as to exclude Chinese wives as well.[23]

The attempt to prevent the reunion of husband and wife was bolstered in 1882 by the above-mentioned Chinese Exclusion Act. The passage of this act thwarted "spontaneous patterns" of immigration for Chinese women.[24] A later, final form of such legislation, in 1924, excluded from immigration all "aliens ineligible to citizenship [*sic*]": the Chinese and Japanese.[25] In fact, the Anti-Immigration Act of 1924 specifically barred the immigration of Chinese women, who were denied entry to the United States even if married to a U.S. citizen. Of course, alien Chinese men could not bring their Chinese wives to the United States. And female citizens of the United States, if married to a man ineligible for naturalization (for example, an Asian man) lost their citizenship.[26] William Wu suggests these laws sought to reduce the growth of an Asian American population. "The overall effect of [the Immigration Act of 1924]," he concludes, "was to condemn the population of Chinatown to a permanently single life."[27]

Sui Sin Far's story "In the Land of the Free" offers a social analysis of the ways in which exclusion laws enter the private sector and disrupt immigrant family life. Lae Choo arrives with her son, Little One, in the United States, where she is rejoining her husband. As the boat nears the dock, she evokes the myth of America, the land of opportunity, when she tells her baby: "[T]here is where thy father is making a fortune for thee" (162). Yet rather than the American dream, Lae Choo encounters a nightmare when immigration officials seize as an illegal alien her Chinese-born son.[28]

The central irony of the story arises from its social context. Exclusionism originated in the ranks of labor to prevent the competition between Chinese and white American men for jobs. In this story, however, public legislation infiltrates the private sphere of the family. The plot details Lae Choo's desperate struggle against governmental red tape to be reunited with her son. When Lae Choo offers her jewelry to James Clancy as payment to effect the release of her son, anti-immigration politics are no longer the sole province of men. Clancy "for one moment . . . hesitated" because "something within him arose against accepting such payment for his services" (176). The benefits of exclusion accrue not only to white laborers but also to white-collar professionals, like Clancy, who exploit the powerless and unfortunate Chinese for their own economic gain. What momentarily dismays Clancy is that this treachery is no longer between men but entangles the wife and children as well.

Consistent with social reality, Sui Sin Far depicts how exclusion laws began directly to alienate women. Contrary to her idealism, Lae Choo learns that the United States does in fact have a law "that would keep a child from its mother!" (167). When she finally reunites with the Little One, she grieves because he does not know her. The story illustrates how the anti-immigration climate breeds racial tension, for Lae Choo learns to hate whites. It also alludes to how exclusion laws deter Chinese women from immigrating by obstructing the formation of Chinese families in America.

Sui Sin Far was working against a body of writings that created confusion about Chinese marital customs and aided in sustaining culture conflict between Chinese and Anglos. Helping to disrupt Chinese family life and promoting the formation of Chinese bachelor societies, many short stories in popular magazines like the *Overland Monthly* contributed to the mystification of Chinese marriage rituals and relationships. Like Holder's observations, some of these tales conflate arranged marriage with bride bartering.

"A Little Prayer to Joss: Ah Foon Metes Out Oriental Justice" (1923), by Robert Hewes, dramatizes the repercussions of buying one's wife rather than securing her love.[29] The financially affluent but lonely Ah Foon purchases for $1,000 his wife, Ming Li, from her father, who ironically is a merchant. Not only their betrothal but their actual marriage is based on economic exchange.

Ah Foon shows his love for Ming Li by lavishing her, as his new wife, with gifts. When she protests his generosity, "he laughed and told her she was all he had ever saved money for" (10). This arrangement does not fulfill Ming Li, who has a tryst with her true love at a joss house. Discovering his wife's infidelity, Ah Foon administers a slow poison to her and then kills himself. He does so professing in death "they shall be reunited the closer as steel is the truer for the furnace" (48). The story illustrates the folly of arranged marriages; the bargaining between suitor and father does not secure the love and fidelity of the bride, who naturally will seek her own mate.

In "The Sale of Sooy Yet" (1900), Marguerite Stabler exposes what she deems the perversity of arranged marriage when she makes the Chinese bride, Sooy Yet, complicit in her own sale.[30] Sooy Yet is a woman who was "born and reared" to be sold to a husband (414). Although she is ugly, she has vanity enough to strive for a high marriage price. The perversity that Stabler finds intrinsic to arranged marriage is compounded because Sooy Yet effects her own sale. When she learns that men find her ugly and desire not to purchase her at all, she uses a poisoned lotion to blind her current suitor, Man Toy (who is, in a sense, her man toy). Unable to live without the cooling balm of her hands upon his diseased eyes, he purchases her (or more accurately, her hands) for the astounding price of $3,000.

Whereas Ming Li in "A Little Prayer to Joss" rejects her arranged marriage and commits adultery, Sooy Yet submits to arranged marriage and blinds Man Toy. The very institution of arranged marriage, these authors suggest, is unnatural and inherently demeaning. Sui Sin Far, though not always uncritical of arranged marriage, nevertheless portrays it, not as a glorified form of slavery, but as an alternative and, for some, acceptable mode of betrothal. Although arranged marriage is depicted in "A Little Prayer to Joss" and "The Sale of Sooy Yet" as an aberrant patriarchal tradition, it is not censured in the interest of the Chinese women involved. "A Little Prayer to Joss" depicts a strong heroine in dramatizing Ming Li's response to her lack of choice in her betrothal, but the author does not explore the woman's point of view. Stabler's "Sale of Sooy Yet" attacks the American girl's misplaced values by comparing her to the Chinese woman: "Perhaps the American girl's ambition to marry rich and the desire of the Sooy class to bring a good price have their origin in the same motive or sentiment" (414).

Besides criticizing American girls for seeking wealthy husbands, Stabler denigrates Chinese women:

> A yellow woman has no soul to speak of—that is, she is not supposed to have—so if she persists in going ahead and cultivating preferences and plans of her own she breaks with the traditions, and has no one to blame but herself when she gets into trouble, as of course she will. A well-brought-up Chinese girl is expected to have no more volition than a barnacle and to attach herself cheerfully and contentedly to whatever spot her fate may cast her upon, without questioning the reasonableness of destiny. (415)

Stabler's contempt for the submissive "Chinese girl" is equal to her criticism of the overly aggressive Sooy Yet, who for Stabler can gain control of her situation only by committing assault. At the expense of Chinese women, she offers to American women a lesson about sacrificing their volition and soul to tradition and convention. This story is ironic in that Stabler's prejudice toward Chinese women is undisguised, yet she chooses as her vehicle for critique a character she deems atypical of Chinese women. Also, while she censures Man Toy for desiring subservience and unintelligence in his wife, she creates in Sooy Yet an assertive and wily *anti*-heroine.

Evoking stereotypes found in stories in such magazines as the *Overland Monthly*, Sui Sin Far's *Mrs. Spring Fragrance* engages in a frontier cultural dialogue with exclusionists in order to refute the myths associated with Asian marriage and open the American frontier to Chinese immigrants. White-Parks has shown that Sui Sin Far draws on such stereotypes as the "Chinese laundryman," prostitute, and "fortune teller."[31] Xiao-Huang Yin states that Sui Sin Far's image of Chinese men is stereotypical in that she denies them "masculinity" and "passion."[32] Using these stereotypes helps Sui Sin Far "get past the censors," who would reject her portrayal of Chinese American society.[33] U.S. society created laws that hindered the union of Chinese husbands and wives and the formation of Chinese families. According to White-Parks, "By opening women's worlds to her audience and portraying women's perspectives, Sui Sin Far not only breaks stereotypes about Chinatowns as bachelor societies of 'alien others' but also depicts communities vibrant with women, children, and family life."[34]

Besides amending the conventional image of Chinese society, Sui Sin Far revises the genre of Chinatown fiction exemplified in the *Overland Monthly* stories. Her brand of realism questions and complicates the reality constructed in popular Chinatown fiction, which attempted to pass itself off as authentic. A conventional character in Chinatown fiction is the white reporter who probes Chinatown to discover its secrets.[35] Similarly, Holder uncovers the secret world of female slavery and bride bartering in "Chinese Slavery in America," which is presumably a journalistic essay. Yet Holder's nonfiction article and Hewes's and Stabler's fictional stories both inaccurately correlate arranged marriage with bride bartering. By echoing "nonfictional" accounts of Chinese marriage, Hewes and Stabler assume a reporter's authority and pass their stories off as factual and reliable.

Sui Sin Far's fiction counters such Chinatown stories. In *Mrs. Spring Fragrance*, she enables her readers to forego stereotypes and witness the complexity of Chinese American experience. In fact, not all of her stories are set in Chinatowns; some take place in a middle-class Seattle suburb where Chinese and Anglo neighbors commingle. Illustrating the diversity of Chinese American life, Sui Sin Far establishes a point of view in one story only to "turn the lens" in the next.[36] Through this dialogic technique, she not only creates a nuanced portrait of Chinese life but also refrains from promoting a particular agenda. Responding to sinophobia, Sui Sin Far's cultural work is about choice. Elizabeth Ammons contends: "The issue for Sui Sin Far . . . is choice: allowing people to be what they wish to be, or need to be, whether one wants them to be that or not."[37] By promoting choice in *Mrs. Spring Fragrance*, Sui Sin Far continually weighs her claims against her own counterclaims: she both criticizes and applauds arranged marriage, and, contrary to miscegenation phobia, she views intermarriage as a feasible choice for white women. Rather than extolling one culture's beliefs and traditions at the expense of another's, her stories represent a spectrum of characters and a complexity of human responses to life's situations.

The story "Mrs. Spring Fragrance" also challenges rigid adherence to cultural tradition and defends woman's right to choose whom she will marry. The plot revolves around Mrs. Spring Fragrance's machinations on behalf of her friend Laura, who cannot marry her true love Kai Tzu because her parents have arranged her marriage to the government schoolmaster's son. Sui Sin Far interweaves the debate about arranged versus American marriage with the depiction of fluid American identity. Through the character of Mrs. Spring Fragrance, the neighborhood matchmaker, Sui Sin Far dismantles the opposition between the American who chooses her mate and the Asian whose marriage is arranged; in other words, creating a bridge between American and Chinese cultures, she seeks to open the frontier.

Addressing the query, What is an American? "Mrs. Spring Fragrance" answers that "American"—or rather, "Americanization"—eludes fixed definition. Mr. Spring Fragrance bristles at the idea that cultural accommodation implies destructive transformation. With Mr. Chin Yuen he worries that "the old order is passing away, and the new order is taking its place, even with us who are Chinese" (16). Supplanting this destructive with a deconstructive view, Mrs. Spring Fragrance challenges the strict binaries of old versus new, Chinese versus American. Dismantling the notion that the Americanized Chinese is a monolithic type, Sui Sin Far represents in this story a variety of Asian Americans. She describes the Spring Fragrances: "Though conservatively Chinese in many respects, he [Mr. Spring Fragrance] was at the same time what is called by the Westerners, 'Americanized.' Mrs. Spring Fragrance was even more 'Americanized'" (1). Their neighbors, the Chin Yuen family, "lived in a house furnished in American style, and wore American clothes, yet they religiously observed many Chinese customs, and their ideals of life were the ideals of their Chinese forefathers" (2). Laura, their daughter, resists arranged marriage in order to marry Kai Tzu, the man of her choice, an "American-born." Hence, a spectrum of Chinese-American types is presented in "Mrs. Spring Fragrance."

The conflicts among these variable American identities—identities in process—are played out in a dual plot about marriage. In one story line, Mrs. Spring Fragrance deliberately disrupts the match between Laura and her betrothed, the government schoolmaster's son, to enable Laura's marriage to Kai Tzu. As a matchmaker, then, Mrs. Spring Fragrance ignores her responsibility to the couples' parents in order to make possible these love matches.[38] Unlike "A Little Prayer to Joss" and "The Sale of Sooy Yet," "Mrs. Spring Fragrance" portrays arranged marriage as an agreement between the couple's fathers that even the groom has no control over, for the government schoolmaster's son is in love not with Laura but with Ah Oi. Although critical of arranged marriage, Sui Sin Far does not misrepresent it as bride bartering.

In a parallel plot line, Mr. Spring Fragrance mistakenly believes that his "Americanized" wife is not in love with him (he is her husband through an arranged marriage). His misapprehension is triggered when he overhears his wife comforting the heartbroken Laura with the words of the "American poet" Tennyson: "'Tis better to have loved and lost, / Than never to have loved at all" (3). The Tennyson line, Ammons suggests, makes ironic "the very idea of separate national traditions," and it raises the question "*is* white American literature different from British if considered from an Asian American point of view?" Ammons asserts that from Mr. Spring Fragrance's misunderstanding, Tennyson's poetry "clearly emerges as the product of just one ethnic point of view."[39]

Sui Sin Far undermines the dominance of the Anglo over the Asian point of view through the use of the Tennyson lines in the story, but her ethnic distinctions are finer yet. The conflict is not just between Anglo and Asian modes of perception but also between those of different Americanized Asians. Sui Sin Far deepens and sharpens the irony when, communicated and recommunicated, the Tennyson verse takes on several different meanings as it is continuously misunderstood. Tennyson's speaker is not struggling with romantic love but grieving for a deceased friend when he utters these lines from *In Memoriam*. When spoken by Mrs. Spring Fragrance, the connotation of the Tennyson verse is ironically conservative for she initially uses it to reconcile Laura to the inevitable loss of Kai Tzu if she abides by her father's arrangement. Upon overhearing it, Mr. Spring Fragrance applies it to his Americanized wife and interprets it to mean that she now pines for the lover that she did not marry. Such a sentiment is antithetical to the custom of arranged marriage, which dictates that love should follow marriage. Tennyson's sentiment, then, questions the custom of arranged marriage, and so Mr. Spring Fragrance deems the poetry "disobedient to reason" (5).

The meaning of the Tennyson lines is further complicated when, in its second dispatch, the verse takes on symbolic significance. Mrs. Spring Fragrance travels to visit her cousin in San Francisco where she manipulates the marriage of Ah Oi to the government schoolmaster's son. When she writes to ask Mr. Spring Fragrance if she could remain at her cousin's another week, he records the Tennyson quotation at the end of his reply. Uninformed about his wife's intention to intervene on Laura's behalf, he has been misled by a relative into believing his wife is being courted by the son of the government schoolmaster. The Tennyson line is a rebuke to her from him who feels that "if his wife was becoming as an American woman, would it not be possible for her to love as an American woman—a man to whom she was not married?" (14). Conversely, misunderstanding the rebuke, Mrs. Spring Fragrance is thrilled by the poetry, which to her is a symbol of her husband's growth and his willingness to discuss Laura's plight with her. Through the theme of misunderstanding, Sui Sin Far shows the difficulties of communicating across cultural and generational borders. Further, the Tennyson lines not only emerge as the product of just one ethnic point of view, but they also ironically defy stable, fixed interpretation as they are employed by diversely Americanized persons. Since content is fluid in relation to context, the character of the Americanized Chinese can no more be pigeonholed than can the poetry of Tennyson.

Ultimately, oppositions like old and new order, Chinese and American, break down in the story as both American and traditional Chinese marriages are celebrated. Laura's betrothed, the schoolmaster's son, marries Ah Oi. As a result, Laura is free to marry Kai Tzu, and her father assents to the marriage with "affable resignation" (17).

Simultaneously, Sui Sin Far celebrates the Chinese tradition of arranged marriage. Mr. Spring Fragrance finds that his wife's Americanization does not require her to reject their marriage; rather, she reconciles her new American values with her traditional Chinese ones. For instance, in seeking his "permission" to prolong her visit to her cousin, she writes him:

GREAT AND HONORED MAN,—Greeting from your plum blossom, who is desirous of hiding herself from the sun of your presence for a week of seven days more. . . . Mrs. Samuel Smith, an American lady, known to my cousin, asked for my accompaniment to a magniloquent lecture the other evening. The subject was "America, the Protector of China!" It was most exhilarating, and the effect of so much expression of benevolence leads me to beg of you to forget to remember that the barber charges you one dollar for a shave while he humbly submits to the American man a bill of fifteen cents. And murmur no more because your honored elder brother, on a visit to this country, is detained under the roof-tree of this great Government instead of under your own humble roof. Console him with the reflection that he is protected under the wing of the Eagle, the Emblem of Liberty. What is the loss of ten hundred years or ten thousand times ten dollars compared with

the happiness of knowing oneself so securely sheltered? All of this I have
learned from Mrs. Samuel Smith, who is as brilliant and great of mind as one
of your own superior sex. (8–9)

Through her use of formal honorifics, Mrs. Spring Fragrance presents herself
as the submissive wife even as she undermines that role. In fact, far from being sheltered and submissive, Mrs. Spring Fragrance delivers a biting satire
of Mrs. Samuel Smith's speech "America, The Protector of China!" and U.S.
policies toward the Chinese. As Mrs. Spring Fragrance ironically observes,
the United States' historical exploitation of the Chinese in China extends to
the American frontier.[40] Americans pay Chinese workers lower wages than
white workers and then, like Mr. Spring Fragrance's barber, charge them
higher prices for services rendered. Further, the exclusion laws circumscribe
Chinese immigration and detain visitors "under the roof-tree of this great
Government" at the Angel Island immigrant station outside San Francisco.
Mrs. Spring Fragrance interweaves her mockery of male antifeminism and
American paternalism when she compares the minds of her husband's "own
superior sex" to that of Mrs. Samuel Smith.[41] Yet she truly loves her husband
despite contesting his authority through satire. She resists patriarchy, but
ironically and surreptitiously, so as not to unveil to her husband the illusion
of his own authority.

Moreover, Mrs. Spring Fragrance merges American and Chinese values
when she does not even characterize her marriage to Mr. Spring Fragrance as
a traditional arranged marriage. She cannot understand his support for
Laura's betrothal to the schoolmaster's son because "he had fallen in love with
her picture before *ever* he had seen her, just as she had fallen in love with his!"
(15). If arranged marriage is defined by the presence of love after the wedding,
then hers and Mr. Spring Fragrance's is not a customary arranged marriage.
Just as these two new Americans interpret Tennyson's verse differently, they
also have different conceptions of their own marriage.

Given the turn-of-the-century cultural dialogue concerning Chinese arranged marriage, "Mrs. Spring Fragrance" demystifies American myths about
the Chinese and tries to assuage frontier tensions. In both "A Little Prayer to
Joss" and "The Sale of Sooy Yet," the women are potentially disempowered
and objectified as the bartered items in a sale between father and prospective
husband. "Mrs. Spring Fragrance" demonstrates that arranged marriage does

not solely trouble women; the proposed arranged marriage distresses both
Laura and the schoolmaster's son. The story also depicts in Mr. and Mrs. Spring
Fragrance the happiness and love shared by some couples whose marriages
were arranged.

Regarding the issues of arranged marriage and U.S. feminism, Sui Sin Far
turns the lens in "The Inferior Woman." This story dramatizes Mrs. Carman's
efforts to arrange the marital future of her son Will. Will is in love with working-
class Alice Winthrop, the "Inferior Woman," but Mrs. Carman wants her son
to marry middle-class Ethel Evebrook, the "Superior Woman." Although
Will proposes to Alice, she responds: "I cannot marry you while your mother
regards me as beneath you" (29). The matchmaking Mrs. Spring Fragrance involves herself in the love triangle of Will, Alice, and Ethel when she acts as an
observer seeking to "write a book about Americans for her Chinese women
friends" (22). Echoing Americans who write about the Chinese, Mrs. Spring
Fragrance muses: "These mysterious, inscrutable, incomprehensible Americans! Had I the divine right of learning I would put them into an immortal
book!" (30). Her book, like Sui Sin Far's, enables her to mediate the borders
between traditional Chinese women, conventional American women, and
American suffragists. Her comment implies that U.S. culture is as much a
mystery to the Chinese as Chinese traditions are to Americans. It is doubly
ironic, then, that Mrs. Carman, the American parent, seeks to arrange the
marriage of her son, revealing middle-class Americans to be not unlike Chinese parents.

Through the character of Mrs. Carman, Sui Sin Far exposes the elitism of
middle-class white women's-rights activists.[42] Mrs. Carman dislikes Alice
Winthrop, whom she judges "uneducated," and whose "environment, from
childhood up," Mrs. Carman declares, "has been the sordid and demoralizing
one of extreme poverty and ignorance" (34-35). Although Alice has uplifted
herself to achieve "the position of private secretary to the most influential man
in Washington," Mrs. Carman asks: "Is it not disheartening to our woman's
cause to be compelled to realize that girls such as this one can win men over to
be their friends and lovers, when there are so many splendid young women
who have been carefully trained to be companions and comrades of educated
men?" (35). Through Mrs. Carman, Sui Sin Far questions the goals of women's-
rights activists: Is their purpose to produce hardworking, self-made individuals or trained companions for educated men? The Superior Woman, Ethel,

whom Mrs. Carman fancies a trained companion, admires the self-made woman. But she states of Mrs. Carman: "[A] woman suffragist, in the true sense, she certainly is not" (35).

Mrs. Spring Fragrance challenges Mrs. Carman's class prejudices against Alice by observing that Alice and Mr. Spring Fragrance are self-made people who suffer similar nonrecognition for all their accomplishments. Until Mrs. Spring Fragrance witnesses that Will's "heart enshrines . . . the Inferior" woman, she supports Mrs. Carman's desire to have Will marry the Superior Woman (23). A matchmaking trickster figure who subverts social conventions, Mrs. Spring Fragrance favors love matches over arranged marriage. When she seeks to persuade Mrs. Carman of Alice's worth, Mrs. Spring Fragrance compares Alice to Mr. Spring Fragrance, who Mrs. Carman highly respects. Early in the story, Mr. Spring Fragrance complains to his wife that although his merchant group had thrown a feast for newly arrived Chinese students in America, the Chinese newspaper had glorified only the students as instrumental to the future of China and had ignored the merchants' endeavors and successes, including the "school in Canton" and the "railway syndicate" Mr. Spring Fragrance's money had helped to build (32). This privileging of the scholars over the merchants parallels Mrs. Carman's admiration of the educated Superior Woman over the hardworking and experienced Inferior Woman. Later, Mrs. Spring Fragrance gently rebukes Mrs. Carman: "Mrs. Mary Carman . . . you are so good as to admire my husband because he is what the Americans call 'a man who has made himself.' Why then do you not admire the Inferior Woman who is a woman who has made herself?" (43). Like Mr. Spring Fragrance, who is made to feel beneath the Chinese students, Alice, despite her business success, is considered inferior to the well-educated Superior Woman. By paralleling the nonelite Chinese man and white woman, Sui Sin Far suggests a position of solidarity for them along class lines.

Both Alice Winthrop and Ethel Evebrook pose alternatives to the exclusive doctrine of Mrs. Carman. Alice emerges as a model of the self-made woman in this story; Ethel advocates the importance of life experience for women. Ironically, while Mrs. Carman speaks on behalf of "our woman's cause," she mistrusts and denigrates Alice, who has had to earn a living working with men rather than live a privileged and sheltered life. Ethel, however, sees women like herself as "schoolgirls in comparison" to Alice, and Ethel praises women like Alice "who, in spite of every drawback, have raised themselves to the level of those who have had every advantage." (36, 35). In turn, Ethel discounts her mother's praise of Ethel's ability to make speeches for woman's suffrage: "To stand upon a platform at woman suffrage meetings and exploit myself is certainly a great recompense to you and father for all the sacrifices you have made in my behalf" (36). Ethel mocks her own speeches, which "repeat in an original manner what was not by any means original" (37). Viewing herself as a bookish schoolgirl, she feels inferior to Alice, whose "heart and mind are better developed" (37).

Ethel is caught in a tug-of-war between the early woman's movement, middle-class femininity, and the self-made values that Alice represents. White-Parks comments: "Sui Sin Far's stories, especially 'The Inferior Woman,' indicate that she treads a border position on feminist issues."[43] For instance, Ethel learns from Alice's experience when she asks Alice to contribute examples to prove the thesis concerning "the suppression and oppression of women by men." Alice cannot, for as she states: "It may be, as you say, that men prevent women from rising to their level; but if there are such men, I have not met them" (37–38). Paradoxically, if men had not oppressed women, there would be no need for a suffrage movement, yet Alice persuades Ethel that many men do not, in fact, oppress women. Envying Alice's experience in life, Ethel declares that before she marries anyone, she will have "ten years' freedom; ten years in which to love, live, suffer, see the world, and learn about men (not schoolboys) before I choose one" (36–37). The values of freedom and self-education Ethel learns from the woman's movement and Alice's example conflict with the conventional middle-class prescriptions espoused by Mrs. Carman; namely, that women who experience the world are of questionable reputation. As a suffragist, Ethel plays it safe, giving speeches but not really "see[ing] the world," while her mother and Mrs. Carman groom her to be Will's wife. Sui Sin Far shows how the elitism of some so-called woman's-rights proponents cripples the broader goals of the movement.

Sui Sin Far may applaud the resilience and persistence of Alice Winthrop, but she does not glamorize the plight of the working-class woman. Even after Mrs. Spring Fragrance edifies Mrs. Carman by exposing her double standard regarding Alice and Mr. Spring Fragrance, and Mrs. Carman accepts Alice and offers to arrange for her "the prettiest wedding of the season" (46), Mrs. Spring Fragrance admits to her husband: "Ah, the Superior Woman! Radiantly beautiful, and gifted with the divine right of learning! I love well the Inferior Woman; but, O Great Man, when we have a daughter, may Heaven ordain that she walk in the groove of the Superior Woman" (47). Acting the trickster, Mrs. Spring Fragrance ends the story on a note of irony and ambivalence: what is the "groove of the Superior Woman"? Does Mrs. Spring Fragrance hope that her daughter will not have to work for a living but instead will enjoy the comfort of a middle-class lifestyle, or does she simply desire her daughter to escape the fate of marrying early? Does she really wish that her daughter is "gifted with the divine right of learning" despite the fact that she conciliates her merchant husband by assuring him he does not need "the 'divine right of learning' in order to accomplish things"(33)? Or does she accept Ethel's redefinition of the divine right of learning, hoping that her daughter will be gifted with knowledge accrued from books *and* experience?

Undoubtedly, Mrs. Spring Fragrance's "book about Americans for her Chinese women friends," ironically written from experience, will address the difficulties of Americanization for Chinese women: negotiating the borders where ethnicity, class, and gender intersect. If "The Inferior Woman" forewarns Chinese immigrant women about the conflicts that occur across gender borders, "The Wisdom of the New" and "The Americanizing of Pau Tsu" reveal the gendered conflicts that plague the borders between women of different cultures. Unlike "Mrs. Spring Fragrance," which democratically portrays the fluid American identity of the newly arrived immigrant, "The Wisdom of the New" and "The Americanizing of Pau Tsu" dramatize the stress the Chinese wife endures as she faces the demands of accommodating to a new culture.[44] These stories, then, form a component of Sui Sin Far's reflexive dialogue in *Mrs. Spring Fragrance.* "The Wisdom of the New" focuses on the reunion of Wou Sankwei, his wife from an arranged marriage, and little son in the United States. In "The Americanizing of Pau Tsu," Wan Lin Fo marries Pau Tsu, who is betrothed to him through arranged-marriage customs. The women in both stories, who wish to remain traditional Chinese wives, are the antithesis of Mrs. Spring Fragrance, who is animated by the possibilities of Americanization. Sui Sin Far writes sympathetically of their trials as they face American culture, Americanized husbands, and well-meaning but ethnocentric women's-rights activists. In these stories, as in "Mrs. Spring Fragrance," issues of marriage and American identity are interwoven, though with tragic outcomes.

The title "The Wisdom of the New" reflects several of the story's overlapping themes. Pau Lin evokes one meaning of "The Wisdom of the New" when she promises her little Yen, "Sooner would I, O heart of my heart, that the light of thine eyes were also quenched, than that thou shouldst be contaminated with the wisdom of the new" (68). Unlike the Americanized Mrs. Spring Fragrance, who uses honorifics to satirize the traditional, patriarchal husband-wife relationship, the newly immigrated Pau Lin and Lae Choo in "In the Land of the Free" employ ritual language to signify the sacred and custom-bound relationship between mother and child. To Pau Lin, who resists adopting a new culture, America is devoid of "wisdom," for it threatens to alienate her from her child and her husband. The title also refers to the wisdom of the New Woman, who figures prominently in the story.[45] Adah Charlton is the socially involved, self-determined, intellectual, progressive New Woman who lacks wisdom concerning the troubles of Pau Lin. Adah's wisdom evolves only after she can see through her ethnocentric bias to understand Pau Lin.

The central conflict Pau Lin suffers in the United States revolves around Adah Charlton. Their meeting is a contact-zone experience in which Pau Lin and Adah each struggle to understand the person on the other side of the border. Pau Lin desires only to serve and to please her husband, and so she is upset by the presence of Adah and Mrs. Dean, who accompany Wou Sankwei to greet her. Since Pau Lin's point of view is well developed, her growing jealousy of Adah is made both logical and understandable.[46] The women perceive Pau Lin's averted eyes at their meeting to be Oriental shyness, but her husband "understood the meaning." The narrator explains, "Adah Charlton's bright face, and the tone in her husband's voice when he spoke to the young girl, aroused a suspicion in her mind—a suspicion natural to one who had come from a land where friendship between a man and woman is almost unknown" (56). Pau Lin's jealousy of Adah is later qualified: she views polygamy as Wou Sankwei's "natural right," but only when his first wife is rightfully regarded as the superior of his second wife. She is confused by her husband's treatment of Adah as a superior. Not only does Sui Sin Far create an arranged marriage that is not wife slavery, for "Sankwei . . . was always kind and indulgent" (56) to Pau Lin, but she legitimizes the practice of polygamy for the Chinese.

Pau Lin's confusion about the role of Adah in her husband's life is even more intensified by Adah's ethnocentric blind spot. In other words, though

Adah's intentions are benevolent, her ethnic position clouds her judgment because Adah measures Chinese marriage according to American standards and views Pau Lin from the perspective of progressive American womanhood. This New Woman lacks the wisdom that would enable her to empathize with Pau Lin's struggles and understand her jealousy. Instead, Adah is bewildered that Wou Sankwei never wrote to his wife in China. And she proclaims to her aunt, Mrs. Dean: "I do not believe there is any real difference between the feelings of a Chinese wife and an American wife" (69). Adah makes gender an essential category universal to all women and so fails to recognize the cultural differences that exist between American and Chinese women. Consequently, Adah remains naive about Pau Lin: "Secure in the difference of race, in the love of many friends, and in the happiness of her chosen work, no suspicion whatever crossed her mind that the woman whose husband was her aunt's protege tasted everything bitter because of her" (66).

However, like Mrs. Carman, who overcomes her elitism with the help of Mrs. Spring Fragrance, Adah's wisdom accrues and she develops the insight that the white woman "has much to make her happy besides her husband. The Chinese woman has him only" (79). She discloses her insight to Wou Sankwei and insists that he cannot treat his wife as though she understands American women and their relationships to men. Unfortunately, this realization comes too late, for Pau Lin kills her young son to prevent his Americanization and concomitant isolation from her.

As in "Mrs. Spring Fragrance," acculturation issues permeate the relationships in the Wou Sankwei family and create conflicts. Pau Lin resists Americanization, and "Sankwei himself had not urged it," arguing that her days for learning are over. Yet Wou Sankwei, though supporting his wife's resistance to acculturation, is thoroughly Americanized. Conflict arises over their son, whom Wou Sankwei resolves to send to an American school, but whom Pau Lin punishes for speaking English and adopting American ways. The representation in "Mrs. Spring Fragrance" of Chinese American identities as multiple and existing along a continuum is qualified in "The Wisdom of the New," which deems marriage between an Americanized and a traditional Chinese partner impractical.

Pau Lin's anxiety is revealed in a conversation she has with her neighbors Sien Tau and Lae Choo, in which they consider the pitfalls of Americanization. They discuss the sexually promiscuous Ah Toy, who is no longer marriageable; Hum Wah, who trusted a white man to make his fortune and still waits for his return—while, in the meantime, his parents have died in China; and Chu Ping's mother, who was beheaded by villagers after they discovered her son converted to Christianity in the United States. For these people, as well as for Pau Lin, Americanization results in the loss of relations and the disruption of the family.

The agent behind the Americanization of Wou Sankwei is Mrs. Dean. While Adah's women's-rights activism is flawed by its ethnocentricity, Mrs. Dean's efforts to convert Wou Sankwei to American ways, though certainly ethnocentric, are further marred because they concentrate solely on Chinese men. Although Sui Sin Far is not totally averse to cultural change, as is evident in "Mrs. Spring Fragrance," she critiques Mrs. Dean's efforts. Mrs. Dean reproves as "bigotry and narrow-mindedness" Pau Lin's resistance to Yen's attending an American school. She is annoyed at Pau Lin's "opposing him [Wou Sankwei] with her ignorance and hampering him with her unreasonable jealousy" (68–69). Mrs. Dean lacks the insight, as does Adah initially, to comprehend the logic behind Pau Lin's jealousy. Ultimately, she recognizes the contradictions of her own position: "Is it not what we teach these Chinese boys—to become Americans? And yet, they are Chinese, and must, in a sense, remain so" (71). Mrs. Dean, despite her endeavors to the contrary, arrives at the conventional belief that Asians are unassimilable.

Sui Sin Far, then, raises an important question that is integral to this story's cultural work: what is forfeited in coercing Chinese immigrants into becoming Americanized? The result of coercive tactics in "The Wisdom of the New" is that Pau Lin kills her Yen to prevent his attending an American school. On the contact zone, then, Paul Lin teaches Adah the boundaries of her woman's-rights activism. Adah proffers the moral of the story when she asserts to Wou Sankwei: "[I]t is a mistake to try and make a Chinese man into an American—if he has a wife who is to remain as she always has been" (78). "Mrs. Spring Fragrance" depicts as successful and desirable the Americanization of partners equally complicit in the process. Conversely, Wou Sankwei's Americanization isolated him from his wife, and emotionally destroyed her. Although Sui Sin Far never finally rejects the need for the Chinese to accommodate to American ways, she intimates, in the face of the persistent belief that the Chinese were unassimilable, that assimilation is not the best alternative for everyone.[47]

There are multiple thematic and structural echoes between "The Americanizing of Pau Tsu" and "The Wisdom of the New." In "The Americanizing of Pau Tsu," Wan Lin Fo, like Wou Sankwei, is an Americanized Chinese man befriended by a white New Woman, Adah Raymond. Inspired by his friendship with Adah Raymond, Wan Lin Fo announces his plan to marry Pau Tsu, to whom his parents have betrothed him in accordance with Chinese arranged-marriage customs. However, Wan Lin Fo admits he wants Pau Tsu, an immigrant born in China, to be just like Adah Raymond, although Pau Tsu does not want to become Americanized. Like Pau Lin, who is jealous of Adah Charlton, Pau Tsu is troubled by her husband's relationship with Adah Raymond. Unlike Wou Sankwei, Wan Lin Fo coerces Pau Tsu into becoming acculturated by buying American clothes for her and forcing his modest wife to endure the humiliation of a physical examination by Adah's male doctor after Pau Tsu, "a daughter of Southern China," takes ill during the rainy season (153).

Whereas Pau Lin externalizes her anxiety and kills her son, Pau Tsu internalizes her grief and grows ill. But in both "The Americanizing of Pau Tsu" and "The Wisdom of the New," the Adah character is slow to comprehend the wife's jealousy. However, "Pau Tsu" ends less tragically: Wan Lin Fo seeks reconciliation with his wife who had run away, believing her husband had preferred to marry Adah, and Adah finally realizes her own shortsightedness in not seeing Pau Tsu's pain and frustration brought on by Wan Lin Fo's wanting her quickly to adopt American customs and values.

Realistically examining the frontier between cultures, both stories jolt their white audience, for rather than tracing the process by which these Chinese wives acclimate themselves to U.S. culture, they delineate the development of a cultural awareness in white female activists and articulate the limits of patriarchal authority for Wou Sankwei and Wan Lin Fo. The stories not only depict Chinese husbands between worlds, but they also assert that these husbands cannot expect to enjoy the best of both worlds. It is not possible for them to have a Chinese wife who is both traditionally obedient and also perfectly comfortable with U.S. culture and her husband's Americanization.

Interestingly, in both stories Chinese men are aided by white women and enjoy intimate friendships with them. The stories, while ruling out the possibility of interracial romance, entertain the notion of friendship between white women and Chinese men. The women worshiped by the Chinese men are therefore romantically inaccessible to them. Further, certain clues in each story contravene the possibility of interracial love. Adah Charlton, for example, never suspects Pau Lin's jealousy of her because she is "secure in the difference of race." "Adah Raymond started" when Wan Lin Fo told her "you have inspired in me a love," and she is relieved when he specifies that that love is for his intended, Pau Tsu. However, in "The Americanizing of Pau Tsu," Sui Sin Far flirts with the miscegenation phobia by displacing Wan Lin Fo's latent attraction to Adah onto Pau Tsu, whom he wishes to be like Adah. That attraction is defused in the end when Adah chastises him for his treatment of Pau Tsu and he wonders "how he could ever have wished his gentle Pau Tsu to be like this angry woman" (159). Sui Sin Far creates friendships between Chinese men and white women in her fiction, but she realistically displays the intrinsic miscegenation phobia deeply buried in the psyches of these generally well-intentioned social activists.

Adah Charlton's and Adah Raymond's apprehensions about miscegenation are understated compared with those that pervaded U.S. society at the turn of the century. As noted above, marriages between Asians and whites were obstructed by the establishment of antimiscegenation laws. In 1906, California legislators banned marriages between "Mongolians" and whites; soon thereafter, Arizona, Georgia, Idaho, Louisiana, Mississippi, Missouri, Nebraska, Nevada, South Dakota, Utah, Virginia, and Wyoming followed suit.[48] Not only were Chinese men not allowed to wed Chinese women because of the exclusion laws, but Asians of both sexes were prohibited from marrying white Americans. Through antimiscegenation laws, Anglos sought to control the frontiers by interfering in private relationships and regulating interactions between men and women of different cultures.

Although miscegenation was not legally prohibited until 1906, it was socially forbidden much sooner by intense anti-Asian public opinion. In 1885, Senator Aaron A. Sargent, the California senator known for his antagonism toward the Chinese, wrote:

> Yet no fact is better known than that mixed races are the most corrupt and worthless on earth, especially where one of the compounds is Asiatic. A learned German has said of mixed races: "To define their characteristics correctly would be impossible, for their minds partake of the mixture of their blood. As a rule, it may be fairly said that they unite in themselves all the

faults, without any of the virtues, of their progenitors. As men, they are generally inferior to the pure races, and as members of society they are the worst
class of citizens."[49]

Later in this article, Sargent continues: "There is little danger of mixture of
blood, for they remain, after years of residence, Chinese, exclusive in all their
ways and thoughts, and their children born here continue like their fathers."[50]
Unconscious that he proves his own worst apprehensions unfounded, Sargent
employs a common myth about the Chinese—that they are unassimilable—
to assuage his paranoia about miscegenation.

Antimiscegenation rhetoric was exploited by other anti-immigration interests. The Asiatic Exclusion League, formed to suppress Japanese immigration, voiced six principles defending exclusion, among them: "It should be
against public policy to permit our women to intermarry with Asiatics."[51]
Samuel Gompers and Herman Guttstadt, of the American Federation of Labor, an organization bent on reducing job competition between white and
Asian laborers, professed in 1908: "The offspring of miscegenation between
Americans and Asiatics are invariably degenerate."[52] Undoubtedly, this view
of the degeneracy of biracial people espoused by Sargent and the American
Federation of Labor anticipated a central irony of antimiscegenation laws:
their impact was on marriage and the creation of "legitimate" children, and so
they had little affect on the production of mixed children outside of marriage.[53] On the frontier between cultures, antimiscegenation laws and attitudes sought to obliterate culture contact.

Miscegenation phobia was evident in *Overland Monthly* stories, many of
which dramatized marriage, potential or realized, between white men and
Asian women, an example being "The Canton Shawl," by Hazel D. Havermale.[54] Havermale's story, which reads like a cautionary tale to seamen, calls
miscegenation "racial 'contamination.'"[55] John Sargent, "an aesthete" who "worshiped beauty," undertakes a liaison with one of the wives of a Chinese merchant when his ship is docked in Canton (269). The affair satisfies more his
aesthetic than his sexual desires: as the narrator explains, Sargent "simply rev-
eled in her beauty" (271). He suffers for this interracial tryst when he retains
the shawl his Chinese lover drops during their farewell meeting. Later, he
gives that shawl, slightly smudged with lipstick, to his fiancée, a white woman
in San Francisco, and she contracts the smallpox with which it is infected. The

doctor announces, "She won't never be beautiful again!" (272). Sargent's affair with a Chinese woman poisons his potential marriage to the American, and his admiration of Asian exotic beauty occasions his fiancée's disfigurement.[56]

There are more stories about white men and Asian women than there are about Asian men and white women: Americans could accept (if not sanction) the pursuit of an "exotic" Asian lover by a white man, but given the paranoia concerning the rape of white women by men of color, and the conventional view of women as "pure," nonsexual beings, rarely did stories depict, let alone condone, interracial relationships involving white women. Dennis M. Ogawa explains that Anglo society shuddered at the thought of white women, child-bearers of the "pure white race," being tainted by "inferior racial strains."[57] The *Overland Monthly* stories stereotype Chinese lovers of white women as vulgar in their sexuality and associate miscegenation with disease, maiming, suicide, and even homicide. Whereas white men are described in interracial stories as aggressively pursuing acquiescent Asian women, in "Poor Ah Toy," by Mary T. Mott, and "Ah Choo," by Esther Barbara Bock, white women are unwilling participants, the recipients of passionate advances made by Chinese men.[58] In Mott's tale, Ah Toy, a Chinese man, is sent to serve as a domestic for Fanny Siddons, who needs help in caring for her brother's home and three motherless children. The friend who sends Ah Toy warns Fanny he has a "flaw": though an excellent servant, "he is unduly sensitive and has been some-what spoiled. He will need all the praise you can reasonably bestow, and will deserve it; so I hope you will be ready to conciliate his morbid approbativeness" (372). The story suggests that whites desire Chinese laborers who collaborate in their own objectification. Ah Toy is "flawed" because, as an agent, he demands credit and praise. Yet when Fanny follows her friend's advice and commends Ah Toy's talents, when she melds her approbation with her objectification of him, she ironically makes herself romantically vulnerable to him.

Mott is careful to describe Fanny's interactions with Ah Toy as nonsexual, even patronizing. Her "affection" for him is the same as "that [which] caused her to desire the happiness of the dog and cat, and even the big brown toad that lived under the doorstep" (373). Ah Toy becomes ill and Fanny waits on him "with the womanly tenderness her mother had shown to a favorite slave" (375). This analogy is hardly coincidental since the racial qualities attributed to blacks became associated with the Chinese at the turn of the century: Chinese men, like black men, were stereotyped as sensuous creatures who lusted after white women.[59] Ah Toy, unlike the slave who knows his "place," misunderstands the condescension of his "kind" mistress.

Because of what he perceives as her kind attention to him, Ah Toy falls in love with Fanny and, in a flood of emotion, kisses her hand. Through Fanny's reactions, Mott exploits the rape paranoia of the white woman toward the man of color: "mingled fright, anger, and disgust" agonize Fanny (378)—that is to say, miscegenation is encoded in this story as physical/sexual assault. Fanny dismisses Ah Toy from his job and grows distant from her white fiancé. Out of grief and unrequited love, Ah Toy hangs himself by his queue, which serves as symbol of the ethnicity that made him repulsive to Fanny. At his request, Ah Toy is buried at the Siddons home, but Fanny can visit his grave only after she is safely married to her white lover. A story to bolster Chinese exclusion, "Poor Ah Toy" sanctions the miscegenation taboo: Chinese men like Ah Toy, who are unaware of the taboo and consider themselves equal to whites, are shown to be a sexual threat to white women.

Ah Toy's response to unrequited love from a white woman is suicide. In Bock's "Ah Choo," the vehicle through which the Chinese antagonist demonstrates his love for a white woman is, initially, homicide. Unlike Ah Toy, who is a domestic in an upper-class household, Ah Choo is a laborer in a San Joaquin packinghouse, where he endures "gibes, ridiculous questions, and mimicry of his own language" (50). Ah Choo's white supervisor Mabel Marten (like Fanny in "Ah Toy") treats the Chinese male with approbation; at one point, she nurses an injury he receives. In the first part of the story, Ah Choo is portrayed as a sympathetic character, unfairly abused by his white fellow workers. Ultimately, however, the story authorizes the racism of the white abusers.

Like Ah Toy, Ah Choo responds with loving adoration to Mabel. In a depraved show of his love, he kills Frank, a foreman who harasses both him and Mabel. Ah Choo then professes his love for Mabel, who—unlike the ultragenteel Fanny—projects no revulsion but simply rejects him because she is already engaged. Ah Choo commits suicide, but whereas Ah Toy takes such action because he is disappointed in love, Ah Choo's suicide is done in the spirit of revenge: he kills himself because "he foresaw the evils that his spirit would wreak upon Mabel Marten and the man to be her husband" (91). Ah Toy and Ah Choo represent bipolar extremes of the Chinese "other": Ah Toy is childlike and fawning, Ah Choo deranged and criminal.[60]

Interestingly, Bock initially portrays a sympathetic Ah Choo bullied by his fellow workers, but she halts before reaching the conclusion that such racism could contribute to his criminality; rather, the story switches focus to the evils of miscegenation. Both tales caution women against advocating for Chinese men by suggesting such behavior leaves women romantically and sexually vulnerable to the men they have tried to help. Sui Sin Far, on the other hand, in stories like "The Wisdom of the New" and "The Americanizing of Pau Tsu," portrays white women activists in Chinatown who openly befriend and assist Chinese men.

Consistent with the reflexive dialogue in *Mrs. Spring Fragrance*, Sui Sin Far explores interracial marriage between a white woman and a Chinese man in two radical stories, "The Story of One White Woman Who Married a Chinese" and "Her Chinese Husband: Sequel to the Story of the White Woman Who Married a Chinese."[61] Mary V. Dearborn asserts that there are two different significations of intermarriage in ethnic women's fiction. Intermarriage represents "anxieties about taboo, incest, and inheritance," or "it suggests an assertion of melting-pot idealism . . . of love 'regardless of race, creed, or color.'"[62] The latter implies that intermarriage often symbolizes "a solemnization or consummation of American ethnic identity."[63] In "Poor Ah Toy" and "Ah Choo," miscegenation is rendered the brutal violation of taboo. Yet for Sui Sin Far's white heroine Minnie, marriage to Liu Kanghi rescues her from the brink of suicide after her white husband abuses and then spurns her. Ideally, the tales suggest the possibility of melting-pot union; realistically, the tragic ending of the sequel denounces society's destructive meddling in the private lives of individuals. Intermarriage, rather than consummating Liu Kanghi's American identity, enables Minnie to escape life in "man's sphere" and return to a more traditional feminine lifestyle.[64]

The battle between conventional femininity and progressive women's-rights activism is played out between Minnie and her white husband James Carson. Minnie regards as "one of his particular hobbies" her husband's interest in women's rights, but Carson manipulates this interest to perpetuate patriarchal authority (112). Using his "feminism" to abuse his wife, Carson derides her: "You weren't built for anything but taking care of kids" (113). Minnie, who holds a conventional view of gender relations, believes that men and women "keeping step together . . . would . . . make a very unbeautiful and disorderly spectacle" (112). Choosing not to value progressivism for women, Minnie declares: "All I care for is for my husband to love me and be kind to me, for life to be pleasant and easy, and to be able to help a wee bit the poor and sick around me" (114–15).

Carson's dogmatic public and political belief in women's rights robs Minnie of her lifestyle choices, and ironically, rather than empowering her, seeks to make her a better servant to him. Carson's disgust with Minnie's aspirations to be a wife and mother arises because he wishes she would work while he stays home and writes his book, which ironically is on social reform. Obediently, she goes to work to support him despite wanting to care for her baby at home. She eventually leaves Carson when she catches him trying to seduce his female writing partner, a "broad-shouldered, masculine-featured, and, as it seemed to me, heartless" woman (116). Hence, Sui Sin Far shows how the women's-rights agenda can be exploited by men to authorize their maleness, cater to their desires, and sanction their narcissism.

As an alternative to Carson's brand of disempowering progressivism, Minnie finds racial intermarriage to be her means of living a conventionally feminine existence. In other words, Chinese culture, rather than being alien, is a refreshing alternative to American progressivism for Minnie. She is attracted to Liu Kanghi, who saves her from attempted suicide, because he "has never sought to take away from me the privilege of being but a woman. I can lean upon and trust in him" (131). Yet while Minnie embraces her ideal role as a woman through mixed marriage, their racial difference disrupts that role. Liu Kanghi is aware that although Minnie "belong[s] to him as his wife," she is "of the dominant race, which claimed, even while it professed to despise me" (139). The claims of gender and race conflict with each other as they compete to undermine the hierarchical relationship of husband to wife. Throughout *Mrs. Spring Fragrance*, Sui Sin Far represents the conflicts between social action on behalf of the Chinese and the U.S. women's-rights agenda.

Minnie's two-part narrative responds to the cultural disparagement of the Chinese in such antimiscegenation tales as "Poor Ah Toy" and "Ah Choo." In "Poor Ah Toy," Ah Toy is portrayed variously as a toy, a petulant child, and a household pet. Worse yet, Ah Choo is a homicidal criminal and murders the man who harasses his love interest, Mabel. Sui Sin Far disputes these negative images as well as the stereotype of the effeminate Chinese man.[65] Minnie boasts, Liu Kanghi "is always a man" (131). At first he is a good Samaritan who saves Minnie and her child from her suicidal impulses and affords her shelter with his family. Later, he is also an ideal husband who protects her, takes an interest in their domestic life together, and listens to her. Fanny is shamed and revolted by Ah Toy's love, and Mabel mocks Ah Choo's devotion, but Minnie declares: "Loving Liu Kanghi, I became his wife, and though it is true that there are many Americans who look down upon me for so becoming, I have never regretted it" (131). Rather than a disease that destroys, as in "The Canton Shawl," miscegenation saves and then enhances Minnie's life.

In countenancing the intermarriage of Liu Kanghi and Minnie, Sui Sin Far uses unconventional strategies. The narrative is from the white woman's point of view, rather than an omniscient narrator's; consequently, Minnie herself announces her love for Liu Kanghi. The *New York Times* review of *Mrs. Spring Fragrance* calls special attention to Minnie's narratives: "Particularly interesting are two stories in which an American woman is made to contrast her experiences as the wife of an American and afterward of a Chinese."[66] What is "particularly interesting" is that Minnie compares Carson with Liu Kanghi and finds Carson lacking. When Carson confronts her during her courtship with Liu Kanghi, Minnie admonishes him:

> And what are you that dare sneer at one like him. For all your six feet of grossness, your small soul cannot measure up to his great one. You were unwilling to protect and care for the woman who was your wife or the little child you caused to come into this world; but he succored and saved the stranger woman, treated her as a woman, with reverence and respect; gave her child a home, and made them both independent, not only of others but of himself. (130–31)

Minnie's protest undermines the myth that the wives of Chinese men are treated as slaves.[67] Sanctioning intermarriage, Sui Sin Far portrays Liu Kanghi as being, from Minnie's perspective, superior to James Carson.

As Ammons observes, Sui Sin Far counters the numerous negative stereotypes of Chinese men by overidealizing and creating generally unrealistic images of the Chinese men she portrays.[68] Frank Chin describes the tendency among some Chinese writers to imbibe "white supremacy" and portray their Chinese subjects as loyal, obedient, passive, and good.[69] For instance, in "The Wisdom of the New," Wou Sankwei forgives Pau Lin for killing their son and returns with her to China. Sui Sin Far's politics of race and gender place her in a double bind. A Eurasian woman writing within a sinophobic Western culture, Sui Sin Far cannot locate a position for critique: if she were to discuss Chinese men as in any way flawed in their interactions with Chinese women, she would be contributing to Western racism against them.[70] She often resists capitulating to Western racism by romanticizing the character of Chinese men. Nevertheless, though the description of Liu Kanghi borders on the ideal, Sui Sin Far attempts to create a realistic portrait of him. At one point, Minnie admits, "My Chinese husband has his faults" (131). Among them, she explains, is his tendency to think "he knew better about what was good for my health and other things . . . than I did myself" (137).

Sui Sin Far also portrays the social reality of the marriage; society does not support, or even accept, the marriage of Minnie and Liu Kanghi. Carson implies as much when he views her as a bartered bride and accuses her of being Liu Kanghi's slave and of selling her body to him for room and board. In addition, Minnie describes her ordeal with white men who assume "that a white woman does not love her Chinese husband" and who harass her with "sneers and offensive remarks" (139). When Liu Kanghi is murdered, Minnie explains: "There are some Chinese, just as there are some Americans, who are opposed to all progress, and who hate with a bitter hatred all who would enlighten or be enlightened" (143). As opposed to the deaths of Ah Toy and Ah Choo, Liu Kanghi's murder does not suggest the evils of miscegenation. Instead, through Liu Kanghi's death, Sui Sin Far indicts Chinese and American societies for racial intolerance.[71] Minnie finds in her husband's pockets, after his corpse is brought home, the two red balls he promised to bring the children.[72] Liu Kanghi is symbolically castrated by people reacting to their miscegenation phobia as castration speaks to the threat men of color pose to white women. Castration is an appropriate metaphor also because it underscores how custom, legislation, and social pressures create obstacles to the formation of Chinese marriages and families in the United States.

In the end, through Minnie, Sui Sin Far pleads for the cessation of racism and the inauguration of a new social acceptance. In a passage that echoes the conclusion to "Leaves from the Mental Portfolio of an Eurasian," Minnie laments:

> Only when the son of Liu Kanghi lays his little head upon my bosom do I question whether I have done wisely. For my boy, the son of the Chinese

man, is possessed of a childish wisdom which brings the tears to my eyes; and as he stands between his father and myself, like yet unlike us both, so will he stand in after years between his father's and his mother's people. And if there is no kindliness nor understanding between them, what will my boy's fate be? (132)

Echoing Sui Sin Far's personal autobiographical confessions, Minnie pleads on behalf of her biracial child for concord between Anglo and Chinese Americans and toleration of intermarriage. Sui Sin Far does not posit intermarriage as the solution to all of society's ills, but she does suggest that in a democratic United States that professes to be a "melting pot," intermarriage should be a recognized freedom.

The United States' democratic ideals were overcome by an even greater fear of the Yellow Peril that arose in the hearts of Anglos and caused them to close the frontier and end culture contact by excluding the Chinese from living full lives in America. Sui Sin Far writes to open the frontier as she critiques unjust U.S. policies against the Chinese and disputes the myths associated with the Chinese immigrant experience by adopting and then responding to conventional Chinese stereotypes in *Mrs. Spring Fragrance*. Having lived her adult life in West Coast Chinatowns, she offers an inside view of immigrant responses to arranged marriage, intermarriage, and Chinese American family life in her stories. Creating a dialogue that links the stories in her collection, her nuanced responses to frontier conflict are embodied in humanized Chinese and Anglo characters: the happily Americanized Mrs. Spring Fragrance and the resistant Pau Lin and Pau Tsu; enlightened, elitist, and ethnocentric women's-rights activists; partners happy with arranged marriage and those desiring a love match; and, finally, Adah Raymond and Adah Charlton, who evade the possibility of interracial romance and Minnie who is saved by it. Sui Sin Far, then, opens the frontier by writing to Chinese and Anglo audiences, and posing several possible models of Chinese American contact-zone interactions.

Sui Sin Far's sister Onoto Watanna, who passes as Japanese, bears a far more ambiguous relationship to the frontier contact zone. As Amy Ling explains, Onoto Watanna chose to pass as Japanese and write Japanese American romances because the Chinese were "vilified" and the Japanese "admired" in the United States at the turn of the century.[73] Sui Sin Far's "Leaves from the Mental Portfolio of an Eurasian" depicts Chinese immigrants who pass as

Japanese because they aspire to achieve success in U.S. society. Ling argues that in choosing to be the more "admired oriental," Onoto Watanna acts the literary trickster and accommodates to her social situation in order to survive.[74] An analysis of Onoto Watanna's Japanese American romances shows that she encountered the contact zone in her writings, developing strategies to create novels centered on interracial romance at a time when anti-Japanese sentiment was growing in America.

4 Arranged Betrothals and Mixed Marriages

The Japanese American Romances of Onoto Watanna

At first glance, Onoto Watanna (Winnifred Eaton), especially in comparison with her sister Sui Sin Far, seems to be trying to evade the Chinese American contact zone, choosing to pass as Japanese. Sui Sin Far indicates a reason for her sister's ethnic masquerade in "Leaves from the Mental Portfolio of an Eurasian": "The Americans, having for many years manifested a much higher regard for the Japanese than for the Chinese, several half Chinese young men and women, thinking to advance themselves, both in a social and business sense, pass as Japanese. They continue to be known as Eurasians; but a Japanese Eurasian does not appear in the same light as a Chinese Eurasian."[1] It is difficult not to read this as Sui Sin Far's admonishment and understanding of her sister for being what Werner Sollors calls a "transethnic." A photograph of Onoto Watanna, in her novel *The Wooing of Wistaria* (1902), shows her wearing a Japanese kimono, her hair piled on her head in the authentic Japanese style. In another photograph, she poses wearing a kimono and sitting with her legs tucked under her in Japanese posture.[2] When Onoto Watanna began her writing career in 1899 with the publication of her first novel *Miss Numè of Japan*, there were far fewer Japanese than Chinese immigrants in America, and so the Japanese were more admired than the Chinese. Some fault Onoto Watanna for so desiring commercial success as a writer that she chose to pass as Japanese rather than Chinese. Amy Ling asserts, "Winnifred Eaton made a fiction of her life in order to make a success of her work."[3] Yet if Onoto Watanna was seeking refuge from Anglo sinophobia in an effort to achieve popular acclaim as a novelist, why did she not avoid the contact zone altogether? Why did she not simply pass as white?

Onoto Watanna's position on the frontier is complicated by the fact that she is biracial—Anglo and Chinese. But she passes as Japanese. Without question, Onoto Watanna chose a political escape route and exploited American interest in Japanese exoticism in order to secure her fame and fortune as a writer. To win a large commercial audience, she penned sentimental and exotic Japanese American romances. While Sui Sin Far sought to open the frontier by realistically depicting Chinese marriage and immigrant culture in the face of exclusion legislation and growing Chinese "bachelor societies," Onoto Watanna accommodated herself to frontier stereotypes of Japanese people. Yet Onoto Watanna betrays an ambivalent double consciousness in which she seeks to build her reputation as a popular writer even as she laments in an autobiographical work: "Oh, I had sold my birthright for a mess of potage!"[4] She reduplicates stereotypes but simultaneously challenges dehumanized and distorted images of Japanese characters; consequently, she undermines mainstream prejudices more than do writers whose main goal is to achieve success.

While the emblem of Onoto Watanna's double consciousness is her transethnicity, the politics of her transethnicity mirror the frontier dynamics of writers "west of the border"; as Sollors explains, situated between cultures, transethnics undermine "the image of a presumably stable relationship between in-group and out-group."[5] The initiand in a frontier rite of passage also has an unstable relationship to the group from which she separates and the dominant group that seeks to assimilate, exclude, or exterminate her. In the "pure potentiality" of the limen, initiands grapple with their Americanization; Onoto Watanna does so when she dismantles the opposition between Japanese and American, synthesizing both identities in her being. Such synthesis becomes the major strategy for her novels: she does not replace one ethnic identity with another but blends several ethnic identities as she negotiates the Japanese/American contact zone and shapes its fate through cross-cultural dialogue.

Confronting mainstream Anglos and their increasing fears of Japanese people, Onoto Watanna must navigate, for the success of her writing, fast-shifting historical ground. Hence, Onoto Watanna makes the notion of "cultural work" problematic by raising the issue of how social context *at a time of change* influences a writer's generic choices. During Onoto Watanna's literary career, which spanned the years from 1899 to 1932, Americans went from viewing Japanese as interesting exotics to perceiving them as a social threat. Capitalizing on the stereotypes of Japanese people as exotic, Onoto Watanna's novels are replete with "oriental" stereotypes of Japan and Japanese people. Edward Said labels "Orientalism" the viewpoint that defines the social and moral inferiority of Asians:

> Along with all other peoples variously designated as backward, degenerate, uncivilized, and retarded, the Orientals were viewed in a framework constructed out of biological determinism and moral-political admonishment. The Oriental was linked thus to elements in Western society (delinquents, the insane, women, the poor) having in common an identity best described as lamentably alien. Orientals were rarely seen or looked at; they were seen through, analyzed not as citizens, or even people; but as problems to be solved or confined.[6]

Far from drawing on the image of "orientals" as "lamentably alien," Onoto Watanna idealizes Japan and envisions Japanese people as docile, delicate, and obedient. At the center of her "Japanese-American romances," she confines the "other" to his or her exoticism.

As anti-Japanese sentiment evolved, the romance form became a "problem to be solved" for Onoto Watanna. Confronting American antipathy for the Japanese, she eventually had to deal with some of the same problems as Sui Sin Far: how to make interracial marriage and Asian marriage customs, the basis of her romance plots, attractive to an American audience at a time when the Japanese were becoming the new targets of Yellow Peril paranoia. Coincidentally and perhaps ironically, her popular romances not only idealize Japanese life, but embody in their prettily illustrated pages and romantic patter social observations that echo those of Sui Sin Far. *Miss Numè of Japan*[7] demystifies arranged betrothals by comparing them to American betrothals of choice; she makes interracial marriage a legitimate option by portraying it as romantic. *A Japanese Blossom* (1906) depicts intermarriage between a Japanese man and a white American woman and explores the fluid national identities of the Anglo wife and stepchildren. Both Sui Sin Far and Onoto Watanna privatize the frontier in issues of family and marriage relations. Unlike Sui Sin Far, who advocates for Chinese Americans, Onoto Watanna reproduces oriental stereotypes, acts as an apologist for the Japanese, and deflates Yellow Peril paranoia to appeal to the interests of her commercial reading public.

For her nom de plume, Onoto Watanna chose a pseudo-Japanese name.[8] She did not stop at donning Japanese dress; she even claimed to have been born to a Japanese noblewoman in Nagasaki.[9] She enjoyed the popularity and success of a mainstream "best-seller," writing more than two dozen popular Japanese American romance novels, most of them published by Harper's; one of her most popular novels, *A Japanese Nightingale* (1901), achieved such success that it was made into a Broadway play. Between 1924 and 1931, she was chief scenarist for Universal Studios in Hollywood. In her life's work, Onoto Watanna gained greater national attention and fame than her sister Sui Sin Far.[10]

That attention and fame came with a psychological price, and Onoto Watanna renounced her success. In *Me: A Book of Remembrance* (1915), an autobiographical work in which she is evasive about her racial background, she decries her entire vocation as a writer. Espousing regret that embraces her whole career, she proclaims: "What then I ardently believed to be the divine sparks of genius, I now perceived to be nothing but a mediocre talent that could never carry me far. My success was founded upon a cheap and popular device, and that jumble of sentimental moonshine that they called my play seemed to me the pathetic stamp of my inefficiency" (153–54). She continues her complaint: "It seemed a great pity that I was not, after all, to be the savior of the family, and that my dreams of the fame and fortune that not alone should lift me up, but all my people, were built upon a substance as shifting as sand and as shadowy as mist" (194). Wrestling with her double consciousness, Onoto Watanna expresses profound self-reproach over being a "hack" writer; achieving fame at the expense of admitting her true ethnicity; and failing to uplift herself, her family, and her people.

In betraying her Chinese heritage and passing as Japanese, Onoto Watanna attempted to sidestep one set of American prejudices and capitalize on another. Ironically, though, despite the Americans' initial admiration of the Japanese, the Japanese soon became linked with the Chinese as harbingers of the Yellow Peril. As early as 1892, there were anti-Japanese rumblings. In that year, the anti-Chinese agitator Denis Kearney came out of retirement to deliver a harangue against Japanese immigration.[11] Americans feared the economic threat posed by Japanese workers, who, they maintained, contributed to the exploitation of white laborers by working for as little money as the Chinese.[12] In an article in the *San Francisco Call* dated May 4, 1892, one writer details the arrival of the "picturesque" and "pleasant" Japanese, describing them as "polite, courteous, smiling." But, the writer asserts, they "are taking work away from our boys and girls and away from our men and women."[13] Besides anticipating the economic disaster concomitant with Japanese immigration, Americans dreaded the "mongrelization" of society that would result from the intermixing of Anglos and Asians.[14]

By the early twentieth century, anti-Japanese sentiment had risen to the forefront in U.S. society. For one thing, the Japanese population had increased. There were only 148 Japanese in America in 1880, and they were educated individuals who were absorbed into the population.[15] In 1898–99, little more than two thousand Japanese immigrants were arriving in the United States each year. By 1904, however, there were 78,577 Japanese in the United States.[16] With the increase of Japanese immigrants came an increase in Yellow Peril fear. For instance, when Hawaii was annexed to the United States in 1900, a case of bubonic plague was incorrectly linked to the sudden influx of Asian laborers from Hawaii to the mainland.[17] The San Francisco Building Trades Council, concerned about the fate of white laborers, exploited the atmosphere produced by the plague scare and lobbied for the continuation of the Chinese Exclusion Act of 1882, which was to expire a year later, and to include in its restrictions the Japanese. Although Japanese laborers organized a protest against the act, they remained silent on the issue of Chinese exclusion. Rather than uniting with the Chinese, the Japanese fought independently against exclusion. The Japanese escaped being incorporated into the Exclusion Act of 1902, but white laborers continued to petition against their immigration.[18]

Around 1905, anti-Japanese agitation became a permanent fixture in the United States. The conservative but widely circulated and influential *San Francisco Chronicle* published a series of anti-Japanese articles with headlines like "Crime and Poverty Go Hand in Hand with Asiatic Labor," "How Japanese Immigration Companies Override Laws," "Japanese a Menace to American Women," "The Yellow Peril—How Japanese Crowd Out the White Race," and "Brown Artisans Steal Brains of Whites."[19] With Yellow Peril paranoia burgeoning, the legislature of California petitioned the U.S. Congress to "limit and diminish the further immigration of Japanese." Simultaneously, the Asiatic Exclusion League was formed, in May 1905, and did not disband until after World War II.[20] Fearing a diplomatic crisis, in 1907 President Theodore Roosevelt signed a "Gentleman's Agreement" with Japan; it was not an exclusion act, but under the pact both nations prohibited the immigration of Japanese laborers to America. However, Japanese wives were allowed to immigrate, so that Japanese men could establish families.[21] More Japanese than Chinese women thus became U.S. immigrants.

The U.S. government eventually made efforts to impede Japanese women's entry into the United States. After the 1909 Gentleman's Agreement, Japanese women had begun to outnumber men. Based on the custom of arranged marriage, a Japanese man could obtain a picture bride by affixing his seal to a document that was then presented to a registrar in Japan. The groom need not actually meet his bride to marry her, and so among Japanese men in America ensued the tradition of marrying brides they had seen in pictures. When exclusionists grew uneasy about the influx of picture brides, a Ladies' Agreement with Japan was signed (1921), banning the immigration of picture brides.[22] For the exclusionists, preventing the internal proliferation of Asians by limiting the possibilities for marriage combated the threat of the Yellow Peril. Finally, in 1924, the Second Exclusion Act, also known as the Anti-Immigration Act, banned Asian immigration altogether.[23]

As these events unfolded, Onoto Watanna was developing her literary oeuvre. The influx of Japanese immigrants and growing American rancor against them, U.S. culture's mystification and preemption of Asian marriages, and the social attitudes and laws against miscegenation at the turn of the century —all influenced Onoto Watanna as she shaped her Japanese American romances. As anti-Japanese sentiment proliferated, not only did the concept of romance between Americans and Japanese become incongruous, but Onoto Watanna's "romantic" interracial couples began to push against the line of social acceptability. In order to make her interracial love stories romantic and to legitimate her choice of genre, she caters to Western representations of the Japanese other. She draws on the American image of the exotic Orient, creating birdlike geishas crooning mysterious songs, exotic settings replete with bamboo trees and cherry blossoms, and noble heroines who are sheltered, innocent, and delicate.

By making idealistic Japanese stereotypes answer destructive Yellow Peril ideology, Onoto Watanna fashions characters and plots that charm and captivate her American audience. Whereas Americans depict the Japanese as, in Dennis Ogawa's words, "unassimilable, inferior, a threat to white women, and part of a Japanese conspiracy," Onoto Watanna's Japanese characters are assimilable, noble, attractive to white women, and model U.S. citizens.[24] But, one group of scholars observes, idealized portrayals of Asian cultures only reinforce white dominance by depicting Asian Americans as "miracle synthetic white people."[25] Double consciousness, in Onoto Watanna's case, is ambivalent: her stereotyped representations bolster Anglo supremacy, appealing to the prejudices of her audience, and challenge the image of the Japanese as "backward, degenerate, and uncivilized." Confronting a culture that tentatively embraces Japanese people, Onoto Watanna makes her romances more palatable by evoking idealized stereotypes and being an apologist for the Japanese.

Although Onoto Watanna's representations of Japan and Japanese people are idealized, her depiction of Japanese marriage is not entirely inauthentic: as Ling states, Onoto Watanna seems to "have done her homework" when it comes to Japanese customs.[26] The tradition in Japan prior to its opening to the West in 1868 was for marriages in the middle and upper classes to be arranged by families. In *Miss Numè of Japan*, Numè's and Takie's marriage is arranged by their widowed fathers, who function like the traditional go-between in an arranged marriage. Also, like Gozo's betrothed Summer in *A Japanese Blossom*, women chosen for the eldest son were expected to serve the husband's parents.[27] Overall, Onoto Watanna captures in her novels the change from arranged to love matches under way in Japan at the time. With the onset of industrialization, parental control was weakened, family life became modernized, and Western family values were instilled in Japanese culture. The concept of love matches was imparted to the culture and finally made a right of Japanese citizens in the U.S.-imposed Family Code of 1948.[28] The tension between accepting an arranged marriage and choosing a love match is central to the plot of *Miss Numè of Japan*. As Ling finds, Onoto Watanna's novels were considered by some Japanese readers a reflection of the sentiments of a visitor to Japan; nevertheless, those readers credit her with introducing Japanese manners and customs to the West.[29]

Not only does Onoto Watanna replicate Japanese manners and customs, but her efforts to make the Japanese into attractive protagonists ironically result in her responding to Americans' greatest Yellow Peril prejudices. For example, like Sui Sin Far, she illustrates the integrity of arranged marriage and presents a case for the acceptability of intermarriage. At the time of her writing (1899–1932), Americans looked askance at miscegenation, outlawing it in 1906. Yet Onoto Watanna populates her novels with interracial couples, making them the central characters in *A Japanese Nightingale, A Japanese Blossom,* and *Miss Numè of Japan,* among others. Seeking to authorize her own use of the romance form, she deems interracial marriage romantic in both *Miss Numè of Japan* and *A Japanese Blossom.*

According to H. Bruce Franklin, after Japan's "shocking defeat" of Russia in 1905, Japan figured as the archenemy in Yellow Peril fiction.[30] Sidney L. Gulick, author of *The American Japanese Problem* (1914), articulates the American fear: "Japan's amazing victory over Russia has raised doubts among white nations. . . . In the not distant future Asia, armed, drilled, and united, will surpass in power . . . any single white people, and it is accordingly a peril to the rest of the world."[31] Onoto Watanna, facing American apprehensions about Japanese military might, flouts Yellow Peril anxiety in *A Japanese Blossom* (1906), a novel that celebrates, from the perspective of a newly formed Japanese American family, the martial prowess of Japan in that war.

The frontier is reversed in *Miss Numè of Japan,* A Japanese-American Romance, which recounts the exploits of Americans living in Japan. The plot revolves around two young and attractive betrothed couples, one Japanese, the other American—Takashima Orito (Takie) and Numè, whose marriage has been arranged by their fathers; and Cleo Ballard and Arthur Sinclair, who have fallen in love and become engaged in the United States before business relocates Sinclair to Japan. As the plot unfolds, the two couples switch partners. Cleo is traveling to Japan by ship to join Sinclair, who is already in Japan. Takie, a recent graduate of Harvard, is on board the same ship as Cleo. During his long journey home, Takie falls in love with the coquettish Cleo. In Japan, Sinclair meets Numè at a party hosted by his American friend Mrs. Davis. The two new couples court clandestinely, but each partner remains pledged to the original betrothed. Cleo then rejects Takie's marriage proposal, and he, having disappointed his father and suffered shame, commits ritual suicide. Sinclair now breaks his engagement with Cleo, being in love with the beautiful Numè. Cleo matures, acknowledges her role in Takie's suicide, belatedly admits her love for him, and eventually marries a cousin, her confidant Tom.

Setting the story outside the United States, Onoto Watanna sidesteps her audience's association of miscegenation with Yellow Peril. American neighbors living in Japan have described to Takie's family "their home in America, which they said was the greatest country in the world"; consequently, the two Japanese fathers decide to send Takie to Harvard.[32] It is not Japanese desire for conquest and colonization but the boasts of American sojourners in Japan that incite emigration to America.

Having created a safe distance between her U.S. audience and Japanese characters, Onoto Watanna sells Japanese customs to her audience, revising the stereotype of arranged marriage as the commodification of women. Numè is the quintessential delicate and exotic Japanese lady; Takie is the stereotypical inscrutable and emotionless Asian man. The two are motherless children, raised together by indulgent fathers who are also best friends. On the one hand, the betrothal of Numè and Takie smacks of barter. Numè's father, Omi, who has high hopes for Takie, promises him before he leaves to be educated in America: "When you return from this America I will give you Numè as a bride" (7). But the couple rejoices in this arrangement: "They loved each other very dearly; Orito loved Numè because she was one day to be his little wife, and because she was very bright and pretty; whilst Numè loved big Orito with a pride that was pathetic in its confidence" (8). The "sale" of Numè is qualified by the fact that she and Takie know and already love each other. Hence, in dramatizing their betrothal, Onoto Watanna creates a union that is a compromise between the *miai kekkon,* or arranged marriage in which two families unite through the wedding of their children, and the *ren'ai kekkon,* or love marriage in which lovers choose to wed each other.

Onoto Watanna further demystifies the custom of arranged marriage by paralleling it to American betrothal. By having two couples, she critiques both American and Japanese cultures. Both couples—Numè and Takie, Cleo and Sinclair—are found to be not really in love with each other. Numè and Takie's love is more akin to sibling affection; Cleo and Sinclair became engaged in a moment of passion and it has since faded. All four come to have in common that they are betrothed to one person but in love with another. Numè and Takie's sibling love dissolves; Cleo marries her surrogate brother, cousin Tom. Onoto Watanna blurs any strict line of demarcation between Japanese and American marital relations, and in doing so, she critiques efforts to limit the Anglo/Japanese contact zone on the frontier.

The novel also reflects familial and psychological dynamics of the Japanese and American love relationship. Implicit in American discomfort with arranged marriage is the democratic belief that individuals, not their parents, should choose their marriage partners. Numè's and Takie's fathers, Omi and Sachi, arrange their children's marriage and express bitter disappointment when Takie later admits he loves another; similarly, Cleo's mother prevents her daughter from professing her love for Takie. Prior to docking in Japan, the peevish, ailing mother complains: "I am not strong enough to withstand anything like—like the breaking of your engagement now. My heart is quite set on Sinclair, dear—you must not disappoint me" (45). In both the Japanese and American families, the parents seek to control the children's marriage choice.

Moreover, for Americans, the myth about arranged marriage is that because choice is eliminated for the husband and wife, the marriages are necessarily loveless. Onoto Watanna responds to this myth by evoking the Japanese belief that love matches start out hot and grow cold.[33] Both couples illustrate this belief: Numè and Takie declare love for each other *prior* to their arrangement; Sinclair expresses his love for Cleo "with a wild passion . . . that was so unexpected and violent in its coming" (39). As the narrator explains, "The Japanese are not, as a rule, a demonstrative people. It is said to be a weakness to love before marriage, though a great many do so, especially those who are thrown into contact with the opposite sex to any extent" (131). Onoto Watanna realistically challenges the belief that while arranged marriages are loveless, marriages of choice are passionate and fulfilling. Upon his first meeting with Numè, Sinclair, alluding to his engagement with Cleo, muses: "Happiness is a priceless treasure; we throw away our chances of it sometimes recklessly, for a joy of a moment only" (91). When marriage partners are chosen too hastily, Sinclair suggests, those marriages can be stagnant and loveless. In fact, Sinclair informs Numè that in America "one does not always love where one marries" (145). Thus, through the voice of an American character, the novel questions whether it is worse to be in an arranged marriage where one must learn to love after marriage, or in a Western marriage where after marriage one unlearns love. Onoto Watanna foreshortens the frontier between East and West, challenging Western society's presumptions about the virtue of love matches over arranged marriage.

Onoto Watanna also creates a world in which Japanese and Americans are romantically attracted to each other and intermarry. Her work calls attention to the fact that white women have less choice to intermarry than white men have. Turn-of-the-century Anglos held that marriage between a white woman and an Asian man was unthinkable, but because Japanese women were stereotyped as "graceful," "delicate," and "cultured," intermarriage between a white man and Japanese woman was "rather accepted."[34] Accordingly, Takie commits suicide because Cleo cannot admit her love for him, whereas Sinclair and Numè do consummate their interracial romance in marriage.

Sinclair's and Numè's union is a metaphor for melting-pot idealism, but only for an idealism that disrupts neither the gender nor racial ideologies of Americans. Numè's appeal to Sinclair, and to the reader, lies in her innocent naïveté and physical fragility. In fact, she often speaks in a childlike broken English: "Americazan lady is *vaery* pretty. Sometimes she has *great big heart—then* she change, and she is liddle, liddle heart—*vaery* mean woman" (88). This linguistic portrayal diminishes Numè, and, as Ling points out, reveals Onoto Watanna's unfamiliarity with the Japanese accent because the Japanese would pronounce their *l*s as *r*s.[35] Numè's broken English appeals to a white audience's expectations of her oriental innocence and purity as an upper-class Asian girl who has been sheltered from the world for her whole life.

"Orientals" being (to use Said's words again) "problems to be solved or confined," Onoto Watanna contains the relationship between Numè and Sinclair by infantilizing and Americanizing Numè. Contrary to the ideology of the Yellow Peril, Numè's and Sinclair's intermarriage is not at the expense of Sinclair's American nationalism, in part because of Numè's background. Paradoxically, Numè is kept close to home her entire life yet becomes Americanized: Omi and Sachi encouraged her to mingle with the American visitors in order to make her a more appealing wife for Takie after his sojourn in America. Numè enjoys her American friends and even demands that they speak English to her so she can practice the language. In addition, Sinclair's marriage is nonthreatening to his "American" physical identity since Numè's beauty is not ethnic. Sinclair is captivated by her appearance upon meeting her: "her nationality puzzled him" (85). Pondering whether Numè looks more American or Japanese, Mrs. Davis tells her: "No, not an American girl—you are too pretty even for that—you are individual—just yourself, Numè" (69). Mrs. Davis imposes on Numè an essential self, one not defined by culture or ethnicity. In doing so, she echoes Sui Sin Far, who in her autobiographical essay "Leaves from the Mental Portfolio of an Eurasian" declares: "After all I have no nationality and am not anxious to claim any. Individuality is more than nationality."[36] By downplaying the ethnic identity of Numè, Onoto Watanna packages Numè and Sinclair's romance to mollify a U.S. audience.

Even though Cleo never marries Takie, their romance, testing the limits of social acceptability, is more culturally provocative than Numè and Sinclair's. Like Minnie in Sui Sin Far's "The Story of One White Woman Who Married a Chinese," Cleo openly courts Takie and eventually admits her love for him. This thread of the narrative mimics the eighteenth-century tradition of the sentimental novel in which the heroine, sometimes a coquette, puzzles over which is the best suitor to marry: Cleo vacillates between Takie, the Japanese suitor whom she loves, and Sinclair, her emotionally alienating white suitor who is the socially acceptable choice for a mate. This sentimental coquette narrative, interwoven with a miscegenation tale, displaces onto the male, ethnic lover the tragedy that conventionally befalls the heroine.

A typical coquette, Cleo initially pursues a flirtation with Takie to appease her vanity. His ethnicity intrigues her and catalyzes her play: she wishes to see what the inscrutable Japanese is like in love. But Cleo is mindful that "Takashima could never really be anything to her" (22). Curiosity and vanity mingled with prejudice, then, initially impel Cleo toward Takie as she plays into the stereotype of the Asian man as an exotic but unworthy lover. Unlike the typical coquette, however, rather than being seduced and violated, Cleo falls in love. What begins as a blithe flirtation with Takie on the boat becomes an intimate relationship. She admits to Sinclair in the end: "I—I loved *him*—Orito!" (212).

Cathy Davidson explains that the social function of eighteenth-century sentimental novels was to afford women practice in making "shrewd judgments" about potential marriage partners; for instance, Davidson asserts that in Hannah W. Foster's *The Coquette,* the heroine Eliza deliberates over two equally unsuitable choices: a stultifying existence as a minister's wife or an unstable union as the wife of a philandering rake.[37] Eliza's alternatives are bleak; but for Cleo, the tragedy is her belated realization that her personal choice was obvious all along. In the end, she admits to Jenny Davis that Takie was "so much tenderer and truer" than Sinclair (209). In Cleo's case, parental pressure and social factors like race pose obstacles to her accepting Takie's proposal. Hence, society's miscegenation phobia directly effects Cleo's downfall when, like the conventional sentimental heroine, she suffers a moral breakdown. However, the fate of the traditional fallen woman—death—is displaced onto

Takie, underscoring his nobility and honor as well as his bold transgression of interracial boundaries.

Takie's suicide is not evidence of a degenerate personality or of bold contumacy in even daring to love a white woman; rather, Takie's suicide is the result of the conflict between his social duty *(giri)* to Omi and Sachi and his natural feelings *(ninjo)* for Cleo. In fact, this plot conflict, in which a lover's sense of social duty clashes with his forbidden love affair, pervades traditional Japanese literature. According to Japanese custom, *giri* involves reciprocating the kind acts and favors of others; in so doing, a person proves his moral worth. That Takie's feelings for Cleo have violated his social duty to his father is evident when Takie informs his father of his plan to commit ritual suicide: "I have no further desire to live, my father. Should I live I would go on loving—her—who is so unworthy. That would be a dishonor to the woman I would marry for your sakes, perhaps. Therefore, 'tis better to die an honorable death than to live a dishonorable life; for it is even so in this country, that my death would atone for all the suffering I have caused you" (192–93). Takie's suicide serves multiple purposes; first, through suicide Takie honors his father by "aton[ing] for the suffering" he has caused him. In addition—ritual suicide and shame being interconnected in Japanese culture—Takie eradicates his shame even as he shames Cleo and causes her to "lose face" when he kills himself.

To an American audience, Takie's suicide demonstrates that honor is important in Japanese culture. American readers find that Cleo is shamed, for she acts like the "rake" in this story. But she is a reformed rake who is cured of her coquetry in the end. As Davidson asserts, the eighteenth-century sentimental novel with its focus on the dilemma of courtship has as its most important function "the reappropriating of choice."[38] As women read these novels, they actually practiced selecting the right husband. By adopting the form of the eighteenth-century sentimental novel, Onoto Watanna forces her readers to view intermarriage as an appealing option. Readers who favor Cleo's marriage to Sinclair rather than Takie must reappropriate their choice when they realize Cleo's mistake in not selecting the honorable and devoted Takie as her husband. Like Sui Sin Far's "The Story of One White Woman Who Married A Chinese," *Miss Numè of Japan* makes more rational and logical the choice of the ethnic over the white lover for the white woman.

The consequence to Cleo is that she marries her cousin Tom Ballard—a marriage that, given their relationship throughout the novel, borders on incest. Her marriage to her brotherly confidant mirrors the sibling love at the heart of Numè and Takie's arranged betrothal and so authorizes such betrothals. Yet their marriage also poses their incestuous liaison as an alternative to miscegenation. Onoto Watanna contributes to the frontier conversation about East-West culture contact when she caters to her audience's anxieties about miscegenation and quells their fears by having Sinclair marry the Americanized Numè and by allowing Cleo to admit her love for Takie only after his death. At the same time, she portrays her Japanese characters as deeply passionate lovers, draws similarities between Eastern and Western courtships, demonstrates the importance of honor to the Japanese, and suggests the possibility of interracial marriage. Shaping a bona fide romance for a U.S. audience with serious fears of Asian conquest and genetic intermixing, Onoto Watanna capitalizes on the exotic even as she downplays the alien in Japanese culture.

Another of Onoto Watanna's novels actually portrays an interracial marriage between a Japanese man and a white woman. *A Japanese Blossom*, a war romance, was written in 1906. Onoto Watanna chose to author and then publish this novel during the year in which a law banning miscegenation was passed in California, and the year after Japan proved its military might, winning its war against Russia. This novel not only depicts a marriage between a Japanese man and a white woman, but also explores the ways in which a newly formed stepfamily negotiates cultural conflicts. Frederick Jackson Turner's "frontier melting pot thesis" is dramatized as the American children learn to adapt to, and even embrace, Japanese culture, and the bicultural family discovers a new familial identity that is both American and Japanese. Through the vehicle of intermarriage, Onoto Watanna explores cultural flexibility and melting-pot idealism.

In *A Japanese Blossom,* a Japanese man, Kiyo Kurukawa, is a widower with children from his first marriage. The tale begins with the newly married Kiyo, his American wife Ellen, his stepchildren Marion and Billy, and the couple's baby traveling from America to Japan for him to reunite with his Japanese children and form a new family. The novel climaxes when Kiyo leaves to fight in the Russo-Japanese War. When the family is told that he has been killed in the line of duty, Ellen refuses to believe he is dead. Her hopes are fulfilled when Kiyo's estranged son Gozo, a soldier, returns home with the news that his father is alive. Subsequently, Kiyo is restored to his family and they plan to return to the United States after Gozo finishes college.

As we have seen, *Miss Numè of Japan* inverts the U.S. experience by focusing on another frontier—that created by Americans in Japan. *A Japanese Blossom* jostles the conventional American point of view by giving voice to the prejudices of the Kurukawa children. As they anticipate the arrival of their father and his new family, each suffers anger or anxiety arising from fear of the unknown. The eldest son, Gozo, enlists in the army after learning his "father has put a barbarian in my mother's place."[39] Gozo's future wife, Summer, "set up a great wail, declaring between her sobs that never, never, never could she be induced to wash the feet or be the slave of a barbarian woman" (5–6). Plum Blossom, Gozo's sister, while saying it is wrong to speak badly of their new mother, nevertheless blurts out: "I, for one, am going to—to—love the foreign devil!" (10). When they meet their new family, the fear is intensified. They are "frightened" by the odd looks of the group, especially by the boy and girl with eyes "like those of a goblin" (30). Onoto Watanna displaces the conventional viewpoint of Americans onto the Japanese family and in so doing makes that prejudice seem laughable.

In the fashion of sentimental romances, the children overcome their qualms almost immediately by connecting with the familiar in their counterparts. Plum Blossom learns to love her new brother when she hears her attempt at English—"Come agin—come agin—come agin"—echoed in his rhyme, "Come agin, on agin, gone agin, Finnegan!" (33): Billy is a "kindred spirit"—his linguistic cadences appeal to Plum Blossom. When Billy bests Taro, Plum Blossom's little brother, in a scuffle, Taro endows Billy with the respected name of his big brother Gozo. The Japanese children learn racial acceptance; the American children learn to embrace a new culture.

Onoto Watanna symbolizes the need for cultural boundaries to be kept fluid by introducing a story-within-a-story. Kiyo tells the tale, "The Widow of Sanyo," to his family on a picnic, and it serves as a structural and thematic centerpiece for the novel. The widow of Sanyo, Kiyo narrates, is a beautiful woman with "the soul of a man" who desires above all things to serve her country when the Chinese-Japanese war erupts. She goes to a matchmaker and requests that he find her a husband too cowardly to perform military duty. Exploiting her irresistible beauty, she enjoins her husband to prove his love for her by enlisting in the army. Seven times she marries and creates soldiers who are killed in the line of duty for Japan. Then she relinquishes her mission, fearing that the eighth might survive the war. Narrating the Japanese folktale in

English, Kiyo remarks of his storytelling: "I began in the most approved Japanese style, but as I went on I fell under your American influence" (103). Like the family, the story itself is a unified, bicultural collaboration.

Thematically, the story foreshadows Kiyo's decision, as a member of the samurai class, to enlist in the Russo-Japanese war. Onoto Watanna's use of the Russo-Japanese war in the plot evokes the Yellow Peril since Japan's success in this war directly contributed to America's growing anti-Japanese sentiment and Yellow Peril fears of invasion. The proven military might of the Japanese threatened the United States, which feared that Japan would expand into the Philippines.[40] Also, many Americans worried that after the war Japan would be an exhausted nation whose people would be induced to emigrate to America.[41] Addressing American anxieties, the novel celebrates the strong Japanese nationalism of Kiyo and Ellen as well as the identification with Japanese empire that Marion and Billy display.

Ellen's profession of Japanese nationalism occurs when she plays the role of the widow of Sanyo and supports her husband's war efforts. Later—in a reminder of that role—she literally becomes a widow, or at least is viewed as one when she is told that her husband has died in the war. As for Kiyo, like the widow, who has fluid gender boundaries and solid national ones, he learns that he, too, has solid national boundaries despite his flexible cultural self. He defines his ethnic identity upon choosing to go to war. He reveals to Ellen that in America he "seemed to be a living example of the evolution of an Oriental mind long swayed by Occidental environment." He confesses:

> I called myself American many times, as you know. We came back here. The war, with all it meant to Japan, and the old patriotic feeling aroused, began a struggle with my acquired Occidental sense. Now I know that I never can be other than what I am by every inherent instinct—a true Japanese! (111–12)

The claims of a culturally molded and an essential self compete; for Kiyo Kurukawa, that essential self is Japanese. But for Ellen, national allegiance is negotiable. She defines her primary fidelity as being to her husband.

Onoto Watanna tempers the interracial romance, in the case of Numè and Sinclair, when she Americanizes Numè. The converse happens with Ellen, who responds to Kiyo's confession: "I did not require that *you* should become like my people. *I*, as your wife, was willing to become one of you, if you would let me" (112–13). Onoto Watanna has Ellen romantically declare her Japanese nationalism despite there being, for her readership, fears of the Yellow Peril— fears that Japanese expansionism would occur through the formation of Japanese American families. Ellen, a character in a romance novel, thus, unlike some of Sui Sin Far's heroines, leaves patriarchy unchallenged. Although her cultural identity is fluid, it is prescribed by patriarchy: Ellen Kurukawa identifies with her husband's Japanese nationalism much as Numè becomes Americanized for Sinclair.

Intermarriage produces not only the expatriation of Ellen but also of her children. Perhaps the greatest defiance of anti-Japanese sentiment is in the character of Billy, the American boy who wishes to be Japanese. When Billy wrestles his new stepbrother Taro upon their first encounter, he blithely chants: "Yankee Doodle came to town, / Riding on a pony— / Took a little Jappy Jap / Who was a bit too funny!" (37). By the end, Billy, who wishes to be Japanese, no longer defines himself as Yankee Doodle. Instead, he identifies with his stepfather and fantasizes about joining the Japanese army and becoming a great soldier. Playing war with Taro, Billy is "purple" with insult when Taro reasons that he, not Billy, should be Admiral Togo because Billy looks Russian. Billy declares, "Father says when I wear your old kimono I look Japanese. *I'll* be Togo. I'm the oldest" (137). The cultural fluidity of the American is thus emphasized: Billy can change from American, to Russian, to Japanese. Such fluidity is the heart of the American identity, making ridiculous any claims to ethnic/cultural separatism and accounting for Billy's ability to expatriate. The very essence of American identity enables Billy's displacement of national allegiance, though it does not necessitate it.

Ironically, at the story's end, the Japanese and expatriated Anglo American family plans to travel to America after Gozo graduates college. Onoto Watanna celebrates Japanese pride through her American characters and offers to readers the possibility of a renewed frontier of Asian immigrants who are sympathetic people, attractive marriage partners, and beneficial contributors to the cultural mix that is America. In other words, she rejects the negative stereotypes of Yellow Peril fiction and replaces them with idealized ones. As both Dennis M. Ogawa and Frank Chin explain, idealistic stereotypes that imagine people of color as nonthreatening function to bolster Anglo American power by keeping minorities in their place.[42] Though the Japanese characters are idealized, the American characters renounce their national allegiance. *A Japanese*

Blossom leaves readers with a poignant question: as emblems of frontier cultural melting, will the Kurukawas reinforce or dispute Anglo supremacy once they arrive in the United States?

Like Sui Sin Far's short stories, Onoto Watanna's novels respond to the specific anxiety that Asians would conquer America simply by immigrating, forming families, and populating the continent. However, Onoto Watanna's novels embody the conflicts of the burgeoning contact zone between Japanese and Anglos. Encountering the frontier, she had to fashion her Japanese American romances for an audience whose perceptions of the Japanese grew increasingly unromantic. To ensure her continued literary success and the marketability of her writing, Onoto Watanna constructs idealistic stereotypes of the Japanese and critiques negative ones. She responds to Asian-Anglo frontier dynamics characterized by Yellow Peril paranoia when she placates her American audience's fears and anxieties about Japanese invasion. In one sense, Onoto Watanna's novels close the frontier by bolstering dominant Western beliefs about the East; in another sense, they open the frontier by making Japan and Japanese people seem less strange, alien, and foreign to her commercial reading public.

For Onoto Watanna, double consciousness arises from her position between cultures on the frontier—a position symbolized by her posing as Japanese and donning ethnic garb. The author discussed in the next chapter—Mary Austin, the prolific southwestern writer of the Anglo–Mexican–Native American border—also played the transethnic. Austin adopted Native American and Spanish clothes and identified with the Native American tradition in order to lend authority to her life's aesthetic and literary historical projects.

5 Conservation, Anthropology, and the Closed Frontier

The Southwestern Writings of Mary Austin

Mary Austin's relationship to the Native American cultures she esteemed was often ambiguous. In her essay "The Folly of the Officials," she declares:

> Another factor that the Indian Bureau has utterly failed to reckon with, is the rapidly growing appreciation of such Indian culture as remains to us, as a National Asset, having something the same valuation as the big trees of California and the geysers and buffaloes of Yellowstone. The war, which set hundreds of thousands of Americans to touring their native land, went far toward teaching them that in Indian life we have a precious heritage of enjoyment, and of access to forms of culture rapidly disappearing from the earth, superior to anything the rest of the world has to offer.[1]

By equating "Indian culture" with California's "big trees" and Yellowstone's "geysers and buffaloes," she seems to reinforce the primitivist association of Native Americans with nature. Referring to Native America as a "National Asset," Austin also raises questions about the appropriation of tribal cultures by interested Anglo Americans. At the same time, she asserts that Native American "forms of culture" are "superior to . . . the rest of the world." She calls attention not only to the "growing appreciation" of these genuine American natural and cultural assets but also to the need for their equal protection.

"The Folly of the Officials" was written in 1924, thirty-four years after the country had been traversed and the U.S. Census Bureau rather prematurely announced that the frontier was officially "closed." In his landmark essay "The Significance of the Frontier in American History," Frederick Jackson Turner asserts: "The most significant thing about the American frontier is, that it lies at the hither edge of free land."[2] With the promise of inexhaustible land, economic growth, and spiritual renaissance, the frontier enticed floods of pioneering immigrants.[3] The American consciousness easily deferred concerns about the eradication of the original inhabitants and the devastation of natural resources while the frontier remained open. The 1890 "closing of the frontier" signified that the invasion of Native America had come to an end, as had white settlers' enjoyment of seemingly illimitable land. A participant in this historical drama, Austin reflects in her writings the issues raised by the closing frontier: that resources are limited and so conservation is necessary, and that after centuries of violence with, and political mishandling by, the United States, the Native Americans, their culture, and art are vanishing. Consistently throughout her works, Austin dismantles the opposition between nature and culture to assert that the identification of humans with the land results in the production of culture. Austin's goal in her art and political activism is to keep open the frontier through ecological conservation and the revival of Native American culture.

Mary Hunter Austin (1868–1934), one of the most prolific and eclectic writers of the American West, during her career identified herself as a feminist, mystic, "naturist," and ethnologist.[4] She wrote both fiction and nonfiction— essays, short stories, drama, poetry, and novels. A Midwesterner by birth, Austin attended Blackburn College, Illinois, where she studied science. After graduation, she, her mother, and her brother George traveled to California to rejoin brother James and together homestead in the Tejon district. While living in the desert, Austin met many local and native people. They taught her about the land and introduced her to the region's folklore, igniting her interest in the Southwestern landscape and culture.

In 1891, Mary married Stafford Wallace Austin and a year later gave birth to a mentally retarded daughter, Ruth. Unwilling to sacrifice her writing career, in 1904 Mary placed Ruth in an institution, where Ruth died in 1914, the year Wallace and Mary divorced. In the early 1900s, as she pursued her literary career, Austin settled in Carmel, California, where she belonged to a writers' colony that included, among others, Jack London, George Sterling, Ambrose Bierce, and Lincoln Steffens. During the final portion of her life, Austin lived in Santa Fe, New Mexico, among fellow writers and artists of the Southwest.

Between 1915 and 1934, Austin wrote scores of periodical essays about western Native American culture, folklore, and aesthetics. She also published several aboriginal-inspired books: *The American Rhythm* (1923), *The Land of Journeys' Ending* (1924), and *One-Smoke Stories* (1934). Dudley Wynn has commented about Austin's oeuvre: "Mary Austin can never be made simple. There are back-trackings and reversions, and inconsistency holds all along the chronological line."[5] Austin's contradictions and ambivalence are apparent: her three books were in production simultaneously and, not surprisingly, they manifest thematic and theoretical similarities. Austin produced *The American Rhythm, The Land of Journeys' Ending,* and *One-Smoke Stories* from her study of the Southwest landscape as well as from interaction with the inhabitants of the land—Spanish-speaking peoples and Native Americans. *The American Rhythm* is Austin's fullest statement of her Amerind aesthetic; *The Land of Journeys' Ending* is a collection of naturist and anthropological essays; and *One-Smoke Stories* is an anthology of Southwestern, multiregional/multicultural folklore.

Austin alternated between writing *The American Rhythm* and *The Land of Journeys' Ending* while suffering from an illness.[6] In preparation for writing *The Land of Journeys' Ending*, in the spring of 1923 she took an automobile trip through the desert, accompanied by the painter Gerald Cassidy, the writer Ina Sizer Cassidy, and Dr. Daniel T. MacDougal, "naturalist and director of field laboratories sponsored by the Carnegie Institution at Carmel and on Tumamoc Hill in Tucson."[7] At night, around the campfire, Austin would tell the tales she would later publish as *One-Smoke Stories.*[8]

Throughout these writings, Austin entwines the themes of conserving natural and protecting cultural resources. In *The Land of Journeys' Ending,* Austin juxtaposes essays describing cacti and sacred mountains with articles delineating a Mexican Christmas ritual and Lenten ascetic ceremony; and her *One-Smoke Stories* tend either to be folkloric artifacts of the multicultural Southwest or cautionary tales concerning humankind's responsibility to nature. In like manner, in the early twentieth century the sciences of conservation and anthropology, with which Austin was conversant, were interconnected.[9] Conservationists held that the land should be used responsibly by humans, and anthropological preservationists sought to salvage dying Native American cultures in ethnographic records and museums. Interestingly, Austin's conservationist, anthropological, and artistic goals similarly converge in her Southwestern writings.

Seeking to keep open the frontiers, Austin incorporates, extends, and modifies the language and concepts of conservation and anthropology as she shapes her aesthetic theory, literary historical project, and political agenda. Drawing on conservationist notions, Austin fashions an aesthetic theory of "geographic determinism," which holds that because humans are intimately connected to the land, the land determines cultural expression and personal identity. To conserve cultural assets, Austin implies, humans must protect the land. Therefore, she counters aggressive frontier mastery with a feminine, aboriginal, and ultimately spiritualized ethic of mastery.

Through the language and concepts of anthropology, Austin explores the significance to America of aboriginal culture and aesthetics, and she develops a political ideology. Situated between Anglo and Native American cultures, she presumes cultural authority regarding the lives of native people and claims that her own writing is inspired by the Native American tradition. Her writings raise complex issues about the appropriation of Native American culture by Anglo Americans. Should Native American oral and written expression be treated as literature or as cultural artifacts? Does a distinctly American literary tradition necessitate the appropriation of aboriginal elements? Can Native American literature be approached without creating hierarchies or attempting to define a culture's "essence"? To what extent can Native American art be a national resource? What should be done to protect the cultural and social lives of Native Americans? Answering these concerns, Austin ranges between the theories of evolutionary ethnology and Boasian cultural anthropology.

Conservation and anthropology are the two intellectual systems that shape Austin's aesthetic premise: nature must be conserved because it produces culture, and native cultures must be preserved because they are the origin of a distinctly national literary tradition rooted in the North American continent. By pleading for the conservation of nature and the preservation of native cultures, Austin works to keep open the frontiers.

In her aesthetic theory and American literary genealogy, Austin dismantles the opposition between nature and culture. For Austin, the land is both an active and passive participant in shaping American art. As she states in "Regionalism in American Fiction," "The region must enter constructively into the story, as another character, as the instigator of plot."[10] The land in Austin's regionalist philosophy is a character with agency who moves throughout a story and motivates plot. Austin asserts that fiction must "come up through the land, shaped by the author's own adjustments to it."[11] Living on the land, people adopt its rhythms and symbols, and so cultural self-expression is always geographically determined. Since American literature literally emerges from the American soil and environment, she directs her white audience to embrace the aboriginal roots of the American tradition, to cease looking to Europe for forbears, and "to handle our American material in generic American metrics."[12] By asserting that the land is the formative influence on American art, Austin creates a causal link between nature and culture, and divorces the U.S. tradition from its European roots.

Because the land, much more than race, is the determining factor in the lives of people, the American literary tradition that Austin constructs is primarily multigeographic and secondarily multicultural. For Austin, American literature is the literature of many regions; however, since region shapes culture, American literature is implicitly multicultural. In *The Land of Journeys' Ending,* Austin states that at frontier points of contact, "racial strains . . . run together" and create a new race which the land determines in "design."[13] Hence, as groups merge or melt, racial factors are less significant than environmental ones. Similarly, she construes race in terms of the land: race is "a pattern of response common to a group of people who have lived together under a given environment long enough to take a recognizable pattern."[14] She never totally discounts the effects of race on culture and identity, but she does delimit its influence.

Within Austin's multigeographic U.S. tradition, locally unified groups collectively constitute national diversity. Answering Emerson's challenge to define a national literature rooted in America, many have proffered a monolithic American tradition replete with a canon of shared ideals. Austin opposes an American monolith, promoting instead a "genuine regionalism": "We need to be prompt about it, before somebody discovers that our resistance so far has been largely owed to intellectual laziness which flinches from the task of competently knowing, not one vast, pale figure of America, but several Americas, in many subtle and significant characterizations."[15] Austin envisions a multigeographic America in which unity exists among persons within a common region and diversity reigns across the multiregional continent.

While Austin stresses the need to recognize "several Americas," she locates the cultural center of America in the Southwest. Hence, she resembles Mabel Dodge Luhan, D. H. Lawrence, Robinson Jeffers, Witter Bynner, and other modernists of the writers and artists colony in and near Taos, New Mexico, who viewed New Mexico as a "city on a hill," a newfound Eden where the rebirth of humanity would take place. Austin maintains in *The American Rhythm* that from Mexico "the answers to unsolved problems of literary origins will come in completeness."[16] *The Land of Journeys' Ending* expands the terrain of the cultural center:

> Here in the Southwest, and up along the western coast, where our bloodstream reaches its New-World journey's ending, it finds itself possessed with no effort, along with beauty and food- and power-producing natural resources, of a competent alphabet of cultural expression. This it gains so enormously over all other sections, where such notation is still to be produced, that one confidently predicts the rise there, within appreciable time, of the *next* great and fructifying world culture. (441–42)

The aesthetic contours and life-sustaining aspects of the land produce a cultural alphabet so pronounced in the Southwest as to give birth to a new world culture.

Given the prominence of the land in Austin's aesthetic, it is no wonder that, like the conservationists, she desired to protect the environment.[17] A naturist and conservationist in many of her writings, Austin also pursued her ecological interests in the political arena.[18] T. M. Pearce states that Austin "was a vocal conservationist, a champion of finding ways to advance both human and natural resources."[19] Her husband Wallace, too, had an "abiding interest in conservation."[20] In 1892, the Austins moved to Inyo, California, where Wallace worked as an irrigation engineer for the Owens Valley Project. When the Inyo desert farmers discovered that Los Angeles businessmen had bought the land along the Owens River and planned to divert water from Inyo to Los Angeles, Wallace, as registrar of the Land Office, protested the monopolization of the water to the Bureau of Reclamation.[21] "Mary did what she could" and wrote a letter of protest to President Theodore Roosevelt.[22] Roosevelt responded by limiting the water withdrawal to Los Angeles, but Gifford Pinchot, chief of the Division of Forestry, sided with commercial interests.[23] Consequently, Mary "knew that the land of Inyo would be desolated."[24]

Many years later, Mary Austin was again in a battle over shared water rights. She fought against California on behalf of Arizona as a delegate to the 1927 Seven States Conference on Water Resources and the Colorado River. As in the Owens River controversy, California sought to monopolize and divert from Arizona the Colorado River's Upper Basin for its own industry and population. Austin argued against the exploitation of Arizona. Since to Austin the land and its culture were interconnected, she feared that diverting the water to California would affect the artistic self-expression of Arizonans.[25] Austin's ecological quest was like that of conservationist John Wesley Powell, who fought against people, other than those living along a river, having rights to a river and monopolizing a water source to the deprivation of others.[26]

Conservationism responded to the problems posed by the potential of a closed frontier—of the United States being a settled and exhaustible country. The major conservationists formulated a democratic and activist Social Darwinism opposed to Spencerian Darwinism. The latter believed in harsh, competitive evolution, subscribed to the ideal of noninterference in business, and bolstered the creation of monopolies.[27] Conservationists, on the other hand, echoing Darwin, believed that although humans evolved to control nature, sometimes the government must intervene to protect the harmony in nature when it is unduly disturbed.[28] Lester Frank Ward held that while natural selection operates according to mechanical and arbitrary processes, society does not, and so he advocated "social telesis" or "conscious creative planning" for society.[29] Ward insisted on government interference to guard against a possible consequence of the closed frontier: the monopoly and exploitation of natural resources.[30]

With the recognition that the land was neither vast nor illimitable, conservationists had to reinterpret mastery of the environment. Although they accepted that humans were masters of the environment, conservationists did not define mastery as the domination and abuse of natural resources. Samuel P. Hays has argued that early-twentieth-century conservationists believed the earth's resources should be used for commercial development.[31] John R. Ross succinctly summarizes their collective position: "As conservationists, they were concerned with the most efficient and lasting use of resources; as preservationists they wanted to save a remnant of the primeval for economic, aesthetic and scientific purposes."[32] The twin goals of conservationists were the effective use and continued salvaging of natural resources. In other words, they held that while humans freed themselves from bondage to nature by controlling their environment, they should do so responsibly.

However, responsible mastery was not the legacy of the nineteenth-century frontiersman. According to Annette Kolodny, the "literary imagination" of the frontiersman "found itself forced to choose between a landscape that at once promised total gratifications in return for passive and even filial responses and yet, also, apparently tempted, even invited, the more active responses of impregnation, alteration, and possession." In other words, Kolodny argues that the frontiersmen imagined the land as both a nurturing and gratifying mother and as a maiden who desired to be conquered by her lover.[33]

Given the urgent ecological ramifications of the closed frontier, the conservationists rejected the concept of the master as recipient of maternal favors and as sexual conqueror. One such conservationist with Social Darwinist leanings was W. J. McGee, a geologist and hydrologist who in the late nineteenth century became assistant to the first director of the Bureau of Ethnology, John Wesley Powell. For instance, Whitney R. Cross asserts of McGee's notion of conquest: "McGee thought the end of the conquest could easily be foreseen: that man would transform minerals from the bowels of the earth, totally enslave bacteria, and obtain full management of the soil, to become his own master, fitted to civilized life."[34] McGee's positive, activist Darwinism seeks the elimination of disease and the management of the earth's minerals and soil to sustain and improve life. In "The Earth the Home of Man," McGee describes the ideal relationship between people and the earth:

> Mankind, offspring of mother earth, cradled and nursed through helpless infancy by things earthly, has been brought well toward maturity, and like the individual man, he is repaying the debt unconsciously assumed at the birth of his kind by transforming the face of nature, by making all things bet-

ter than they were before, by aiding the good and destroying the bad among animals and plants, and by protecting the aged earth from the ravages of time and failing strength, even as the child protects his fleshly mother. Such are the relations of earth and man.[35]

In this wonderfully poetic passage (does he borrow from Darwin the flair for figurative language?), the mother-child bond symbolizes the best relationship between humans and the earth. McGee emends the metaphor of the gratifying mother to feature the earth as an aging matron requiring protection from a grateful child. If frontier mastery traditionally denotes the control of natural resources, for McGee control means "making ... better," "aiding the good," and "protecting."

Frontier mastery was also traditionally the goal of the individualist frontiersman—a character critiqued by Austin in such stories as "Lone Tree," "Pan and the Pot Hunter," and "The Last Antelope." But, as Richard Slotkin observes, "In America the growth of the settled area and the decline of available land in the open wilderness reinforced the contrast between a world in which man was free to seek God and the good life in solitude and one in which his behavior was compelled by social necessities."[36] Spencer would define the master as the laissez-faire individualist and the victor of natural selection; the Darwinian conservationists, concerned about "the decline of available land," located the master within a cooperative alliance in which he was "compelled by social necessities." Powell, for instance, denounced the individual struggle for survival, battled against monopolies, and advocated sharing water rights to arid lands.[37] In "The Relation of Institutions to Environment," McGee also focuses on the cooperation of desert inhabitants: "The plants, animals, and men are forced into cooperation so intimate that few live unto themselves alone, most live for the general good."[38] This communalism, he continues, breeds intelligence that strives for and creates organizations promoting the common good. The organizations then mature into institutions binding "humans directly" and "subhumans indirectly" and uniting both in a "grander unity."[39] In some cases, both writers suggest, mastery is contingent upon the communal effort. While Powell insists on cooperation, McGee deems it a consequence of desert life; hence, implicit in McGee's scenario is the concept of geographic determinism, that life in the desert results in the formation of beneficent institutions.

From conservation, Austin appropriates the concept of geographic determinism: that region determines the human condition and social organization of a people.[40] Observing the primacy of the land in Austin's writings, James Ruppert asserts that for Austin the land "always shaped the culture more than the culture shaped it."[41] Echoing McGee, Austin describes the *acequia madre*, or mother ditch, in *The Land of Journeys' Ending:* "Rain falls on radical and conservative alike, but the mother ditch makes communists of them all" (89). According to Austin and McGee, communalism arises from the demands foisted upon people by desert life.

Yet Austin's geographic determinism extends beyond modes of social organization: it extends to humans themselves. She sees humans as shaped by the characteristics of a particular environment. In *The Land of Journeys' Ending* Austin muses that man, in fact, is the land:

> Man is not himself only, not solely a variation of his racial type in the pattern of his immediate experience. He is all that he sees; all that flows to him from a thousand sources, half noted, or noted not at all except by some sense that lies too deep for naming. He is the land, the lift of its mountain lines, the reach of its valleys; his is the rhythm of its seasonal processions, the involution and variation of its vegetal patterns. (437)

But if man is the land, the land is consistently gendered female by Austin. Many of the images in *The Land of Journeys' Ending* represent natural processes symbolized by the seduction, rape, or neglect of a female by a male force. For instance, the "thousand-flowered maguey" who is the "wife of Sekala Ka'amja," was stolen away by the Hot Wind (54). The "plants that give character to the arid region" are "raped of their virgin bloom by the seducing wind" (54–55). Austin describes a mountain "which could both glow and pale, pale after the burning, like a lovely neglected woman who burned to no purpose, a dark mountain, whose bareness was like a pain" (386). Nature is, at once, woman caught in the torrent of multiple, sexual conflicts, and man as sexual aggressor. Unlike McGee, who responds to the closed frontier by imagining nature as a mother needing protection, Austin depicts nature in sexual and often disruptive postures, the female principle invaded by the male.

However, Austin herself critiques the conventional frontier symbol of the feminized, raped land in "Lone Tree," a tale from *One-Smoke Stories*.[42] Although Austin essentializes and polarizes gender traits in her allegory of beneficence to nature, she imagines a more symbiotic relationship between men and women on the frontier by presenting the female ethic of nurturance as necessary for survival. Nature, symbolized by the Lone Tree, is a battered woman whose abuser sabotages his own life in threatening hers. Like the conservationists, Austin indicts frontiersmen for their violent exploitation and destruction of the environment. Anticipating the consequences of the closed frontier, she urges cooperation, not only between men and women but between humans and nature in negotiating the frontier.

The relationship between the Lone Tree and Austin's frontiersman, Hogan, is likened to domestic violence. Although Hogan has a hunch about a gold prospect, he must first finish the job in Tucson he is working on—a land-assessment project—in order to fund his mining adventure in Carrizal. Consequently, he is filled with rage at the land that detains him, and his anger and hatred for the Lone Tree is depicted as spousal strife: "Hogan hated the Lone Tree in the same way and for much the same reasons that men occasionally hate their wives" (25). In Austin's imaginative universe, men hate women for replacing their itinerant and adventuring lives with quiet domesticity and dull stability. By gendering the Lone Tree as female, Austin conflates the pioneering frontiersman's disdain for a staid wife with his violence toward the land. To Hogan, the Lone Tree offered "its old-maidish, insufficient shade. It had a very woman's trick of spreading its roots about the ledge from under which the water seeped, as though its frail fibers were all that held Dripping Rock in place, and a woman's air of dispensing the spring, which was the only water in a half-day's journey, with hospitality" (26). Hogan despises the very presumption of strength and sustenance on the part of the Lone Tree, which he perceives to be insufficient and frail. Consequently, he responds with hostility; he "could have slapped the little tree" (26).

Although the feminine tree tenders nourishment and hospitality, Hogan seeks to master and conquer it. Having completed his job, he "served [the Lone Tree] as men occasionally do serve a woman whom they have used merely because she is convenient, and not because they have appreciated her" (27). With his pick he drags the tree up by its roots, leaving it "like a woman fainting" (27). The rape of woman and the rape of the land are entwined in this violent allusion; both the land and woman are exploited as their nurturance and hospitality are rejected by the frontiersman.

The ironic ending of the story insists on the need for respect and cooperation, not exploitation and conquest, between humans and nature, men and women. Upon his return to Tucson from Carrizal, Hogan sets out to return to the Lone Tree area with a pocketful of ore. Realizing that he has veered from his course and is suffering from intense thirst, the fickle and self-centered Hogan begins "to think affectionately" of the Lone Tree, but with no "recollection of what he had done to it" (28). When he finally reaches the tree, eager to quench his thirst, he cannot because the rock that was held in place by the tree's roots has dropped and blocked the water source, drying it up. Ironically, he learns—too late to save his life—that the "frail fibers were all that held Dripping Rock in place" (26). The conservationist moral of Austin's story is that those who treat nature kindly will survive, and those who destroy it will languish and die. In the context of the closed frontier, the blind destruction of the environment by the frontiersman eventually costs him his own life. And contrary to the myth of the rugged pioneer, the frontier is not the domain solely of raw masculinity, for only a synthesis of masculine and feminine culture will enable life in the West.

As "Lone Tree" illustrates, Austin views humans as interconnected with nature and needing its gifts for survival. Like the conservationists, she subscribes to the notion of beneficent, protective, and responsible mastery of the environment by humans. "Pan and the Pot-Hunter," like "Lone Tree," renounces the subjugation and dominance of nature by frontiersmen. The pot-hunter's identity is not determined simply by the environment but by how he chooses to live in it. Another story, "The Last Antelope," tackles the issue of extinction to show that an ethic of cooperative mastery cannot coexist with one of violent mastery.

In "Pan and the Pot-Hunter," the forest, endowed with the agency of Pan, seeks vengeance on the pot-hunter, who uses forest resources wastefully and wantonly. The pot-hunter is improvident and capitalistic toward nature, a "business man" who is "out for what he can get" (250–51). When he hunted, he disregarded game laws; "fouled the waters where he camped with kitchen refuse"; and "left man traces in the trails and neglected to put out his fires" (251). "Pan and the Pot-Hunter" places faith in "a nostalgic vision of the American Indian's relationship to the land."[43] The Native Americans "never shot swimming deer"; they "prayed permission of the Wild" before hunting and "left offal" for the animals in the woods (251). Willfully exploitative in his behavior, the pot-hunter leaves a trail of waste and destruction behind him, ironically deeming Native Americans "improvident."

Whereas Austin uses the theme of pot-hunting to connote the exploitation of nature in this story, pot-hunting comes up again in relation to Austin's anthropological agenda. When artifacts began to disappear from Native American sites, Austin rebuked careless and selfish pot-hunters. Nevertheless, she acted the pot-hunter herself, purchasing Native American artifacts and housing them in museums that worked to preserve the cultures and to revivify their art forms. She believed that as the woodsman could enjoy and benefit from nature without obliterating it, people could interact with native cultures without destroying them.

Like Hogan, the pot-hunter suffers the consequences of mistreating the forest. When the pot-hunter decides to settle down, build a house, and court a woman, Pan sends a seven-point buck to eat the pot-hunter's grapes and torment him by eluding shots from his rifle. As the pot-hunter grows obsessed with killing the deer, his house falls to disrepair and the woman he now neglects finds another beau. At the mercy of the land he abused, he "turns from being hunter to become the hunted" (260). Austin contends that the land inscribes itself upon the people who dwell on it; having lived in the forest carelessly and inconsiderately, the pot-hunter grows disheveled as "the markings of the pot came out on him very strongly" (261). People, then, are not only determined by the land, but by how they live on it; hence, invasive and wanton mastery of nature only precipitates self-destruction.

"The Last Antelope," like "Lone Tree" and "Pan and the Pot-Hunter," compares beneficent mastery of nature to frontier mastery by conquest. A responsible master, Little Pete is a shepherd whose control of nature is symbolized by his management of his flock. He is respectful toward the land: in contrast to a character like Hogan, he refrains from cutting down a lone tree for firewood because he "thought better of it" (270). As a shepherd, he enjoys an affectionate fellowship with his charges: "He loved his dogs as brothers; he was near akin to the wild things. He knew his sheep by name, and had respect for signs and seasons" (271). Befriending the Last Antelope, Little Pete tames it and makes it reliant on his protection. His reason for mastering things is to understand and bond with nature.

In contrast, the homesteader in the story regards the objects of nature as trophies to enhance his ego and as commodities for his use. He kills the Last

Antelope, reasoning that it is better that it fall to him than to the coyotes—apparently oblivious to the irony that, though the antelope would be food for the coyotes, to him it is merely a prize. The homesteader also "coveted the howlers' [coyotes'] ears" for their monetary value (279). Like the pot-hunter, he is a poacher, and he is unable to grasp Little Pete's spiritual and emotional bond with the antelope. When he discovers that Little Pete has observed him killing the animal, his only concern is that the shepherd will "denounce him to the law" (283). In the end, the homesteader chops down the lone tree for firewood, exemplifying frontier dominance and subjugation of natural resources.

The story illustrates that as the frontier—that "keen edge of slaughter"—advances, it obliterates man's cooperative union with nature—symbolized by the friendship between the Last Antelope and Little Pete (273). Although Little Pete regarded the antelope as "the noblest thing he had ever loved," that love contributes to the antelope's demise (281). Tamed by Little Pete, the Last Antelope grew to rely on "the flock and the protection of man-presence" (280). Having unlearned his instinctive fear of man, the Last Antelope is vulnerable to the homesteader. Austin sanctions Little Pete's attitude of sympathetic mastery, but she deems it no longer practical or viable given the violent mastery of the Anglo frontiersman. In all three stories discussed here, Austin looks askance on the frontiersman's ethic of conquest and domination and enjoins its modification via a benevolent moral stance she variously labels female, aboriginal, and native.

Similarly, in *The Land of Journeys' Ending* Austin defines mastery as conservative and responsible. On the one hand, in a bit of wish-fulfillment, Austin's feminized, sexualized landscape is married to the sojourners on it: "There was nothing that betrayed its [the land's] crop capacity to the untutored sense of the Amerind savage and the unlettered American pioneer. Both of these married the land because they loved it, and afterward made it bear" (5). Unlike the male explorers who, Kolodny finds, wish to conquer and impregnate, the Native Americans and American pioneers, Austin argues, love and then marry the land before making it bear (although eventually the U.S. frontiersman abuses his mate). Further, mastery for Austin involves learning agriculture. Rejecting the myth that the whites were the first to farm America, she refers to "the long journey corn and the red man came together in order to secure to us the quick mastery of the American continent, for which we pridefully plume only ourselves" (282–83). Mastery denotes responsibility toward nature as well as the ability to garner nurturance and sustenance from it.

Ultimately, Austin envisages spiritual, rather than physical, mastery of nature. She describes "that sense of mastery over the environment which is the first awakening of man to the presence of God within himself" (377). Also, there is "the lift of mastery which comes of knowing the world you live in" (383). Characteristically, Austin postulates that knowledge of the world, and the mystical link between humans and God, are the definitive qualities of the master. In so doing, she constructs a spiritual basis for conservation.

Austin also delineates how conservation effects the preservation of cultures because the land determines the shape of the culture, its ceremonies, and its self-expression. Employing a Native American aesthetic, in *The Land of Journeys' Ending* she shows how nature shapes cultural expression. Her chapter "Wind's Trail I Am Seeking" explains that Native Americans "read the plant world as a book" until "the plant world begins to stand to man not for itself but for ideas" (46). Her use of Native American idioms in this essay exemplifies this observation. A rainstorm is described as "Rain walking," and then "the People of the Lightning send their spirit-darting arrows" (33–34). Another essay maintains that true connection with a country is evident when one has "adopted or made up myths about its familiar objects" (302). Native Americans invent culture by reading the significations of natural phenomena.

Austin's conservationism, then, is not ever about saving only the earth but the entire ecosystem in which people, nature, and culture are inextricably connected. She often breaks free from the detached, observer perspective to counsel her readers about their potential effects on the natural and cultural environment. For instance, having explained the importance of the sahuaro, or giant cactus festival, in Papagueria, she declares: "It is counted a crime to destroy a sahuaro" (125). Such an act is a "crime" because the sahuaro's destruction threatens the Papago culture that depends upon the cactus. The Papaguerian uses the ribs of the desiccated sahuaro "to roof his house or his family tomb" (122). Also, the tribe celebrates yearly a "sahuaro harvest, and the ceremonial making of sahuaro wine" (123). Consequently, wanton and selfish disregard for the sahuaro would sabotage the architecture and cultural ceremonies of the Papago people.

Conservation in the United States developed at the same time as anthropology, and so the two sciences converged.[44] Many people who enjoyed careers in geology and the natural sciences also pursued studies in anthropology. From conservation, Powell and McGee ventured into anthropology; Powell served as head of the Bureau of Ethnology until he appointed McGee his successor.[45] Conservation and ethnology—the earliest form of anthropology—overlapped in that both sciences used the evolutionary theories of Darwin. In addition, both responded to the consequences of the closed frontier: the devastation of the land and its aboriginal inhabitants. During the nineteenth and early twentieth centuries, the United States built a staunch assimilation policy that compromised the integrity of Native American culture. According to Brian Dippie, conservation and anthropology coincided with the recognition that Native American culture needed as much protection as the big trees of California and the buffaloes of Yellowstone.[46] Both ethnology and the cultural anthropology of Franz Boas reveal the discipline's continued attempt to prevent the cultural and physical extermination of Native Americans and the consequent closing of the frontier.

As a political activist, Austin strove to protect not only the land but also the aboriginal people on it. In *Earth Horizon*, she reveals: "I took to the defense of Indians because they were the most conspicuously defeated and offended against group at hand. I should have done as much even without what I afterward discovered among them of illumination and reformation of my own way of thought."[47] With writer Mabel Dodge Luhan and activist John Collier, Austin fought for Pueblo land rights against the 1922 Bursum Bill, which secured land ownership for non–Native American settlers who had unlawfully encroached on Pueblo lands but had enjoyed peaceable possession since 1900.[48] (John Collier, a Progressive reform agitator for Native Americans, was appointed commissioner of Indian Affairs in 1933. His Indian Reorganization Act coincided with Austin's views: it abolished allotment, instituted Native American self-government, and sought to preserve Native American arts and traditions.)[49] Austin, for example, battled Indian Bureau attempts to interdict ceremonial dancing.[50] She also advocated an educational curriculum for the Spanish speaking in New Mexico that stressed the manual arts and bilingual education.[51] She and Collier, protesting the boarding schools that isolated Native Americans from their homes and villages, argued for the implementation of bilingual day schools on reservations.[52] Finally, in an effort to preserve and propagate native arts, she founded the Indian Arts Fund and the Spanish Colonial Arts Society in the Southwest. The goal of both of these organizations was the "rebuilding of . . . shattered culture."[53]

The earliest form of ethnology, unlike later schools, did not aim at cultural preservation: its theory of polygenesis bolstered such imperial practices as slavery and genocide. Polygeneticists believed in "multiple creations" that resulted in the inherent inequality of humans.[54] Because polygeneticists held that there were biologically separate human species, they subscribed to the hierarchical segregation of the races. It was only later that both environmental ethnology and the cultural anthropology of Franz Boas attempted to prevent the cultural and physical extermination of Native Americans—the closing of the cultural frontier.

Before Boas, however, evolutionary ethnologists opposed the racism of polygenesis by positing an environmentalist, rather than biological, explanation of human difference. They adopted Spencerian Darwinism, which offered them "a sequential theory of social advancement."[55] Evolutionary ethnologists argued that man rose in intelligence and evolved unilinearly in ascending steps.[56] Hubert Howe Bancroft, for instance, charted the gradual development of humans from a lower type. Lewis Henry Morgan distinguished three evolutionary stages ranging from savagery to barbarism to civilization, and within these three stages he posited seven ethnical periods through which all existing cultures progressed.[57] Basing his reasoning on his evolutionary paradigm, Morgan maintained that factory work would be the next logical and gradual step for Native Americans. On the one hand, Morgan's theory of unilinear evolution was used to justify such institutions and policies as assimilation and the reservation system.[58] On the other hand, he worried about the extermination of Native Americans as a result of westward expansion and the establishment of the railroad. An advocate for Native American rights, Morgan declared that the solutions to the "Indian Problem" were education, Christianity, agriculture, and citizenship.[59] His environmental evolutionism served as a theoretical basis for the salvation of the "vanishing Indian."

Morgan's successor, Franz Boas, was concerned about the racist and imperialist implications of environmental evolutionism and challenged its hierarchism in the interest of his preservationist agenda. Incited by the urgent need for Native American cultural preservation, Boas developed the ethnographic method, which aimed to salvage raw cultural data. Although Boas held to the facts of evolution in his physical anthropology, he rejected the claim that humans evolved gradually through a sequence of stages in which whites occupied the pinnacle of civilization while aboriginal people resided in the gutter of primitivism. Responding to the absolutism of evolutionary para-digms, Boas asserted that culture is relative.[60] In other words, he professed that each society possessed its own integrity and rationality, and it was against this that its customs and beliefs should be interpreted.

Although Austin did not personally know Boas, her writings inhabit the margin between evolutionary ethnology and cultural anthropology. Like Boas, Austin studied and wrote about Native American cultures. But her strong identification with those cultures raises issues about her authority as a writer speaking and advocating for the vanishing tribes. Austin both compli-cates and responds to that problem by placing herself between cultures. Occu-pying the border between Native American and Anglo cultures, she identifies herself as both a native and an anthropologist.

Presuming an aboriginal connection, Austin often posed as a transeth-nic.[61] As noted in my introduction, Victor Turner states that, on the limen, ini-tiands experience loss of status; this is often symbolized by the wearing of "strange disguises."[62] Correspondingly, Frederick Jackson Turner implies that transethnicity and cultural transformation are the residual effects of frontier life on Anglo settlers:

> The wilderness masters the colonist. It finds him a European in dress, indus-
> tries, tools, modes of travel, and thought. It takes him from the railroad car
> and puts him in the birch canoe. It strips off the garments of civilization and
> arrays him in the hunting shirt and the moccasin. It puts him in the log cabin
> of the Cherokee and Iroquois and runs an Indian palisade around him. Be-
> fore long he has gone to planting Indian corn and plowing with a sharp stick;
> he shouts the war cry and takes the scalp in orthodox Indian fashion.[63]

According to the historian Turner, as the frontiersman "regresses" into the wilderness, he is stripped of his European dress and customs and literally re-places Native Americans, adopting their identity. He claims that as the Euro-pean settler "transforms the wilderness . . . the outcome is not the old Europe, not simply the development of Germanic germs"; instead, the "new product . . . is American."[64] The frontiersman's transethnicity marks a borderline be-tween Old World and New World cultures. Like Austin, historian Turner suggests that the land shapes the identities of sojourners on it; but unlike Aus-tin, he views this as a developmental stage prior to the frontiersman's mastering the land. This stage is surmounted because it involves a loss of status, but Frederick Jackson Turner is unclear about whether the experience of Native American life leaves any lasting trace on the settler.

Austin, however, never regarded her transethnicity as regressive; rather, she willingly appropriated the culture and aesthetics of Native Americans to foster her own creative goals. Literally an "ethnic transvestite" at times, she wore Spanish and Native American dress in public. In an essay memorializing her death, Mabel Dodge Luhan—who at times had a tempestuous relationship with Austin—derisively describes one such masquerade by Austin:

> She had never cut her hair and it fell to her knees. She braided it and built it up around her head in a coronet. At parties she felt like a Spanish duchess with a high tortoise shell comb stuck behind her coils and a black lace mantilla thrown over the whole, so sitting down, she was as impressive as she felt herself to be, but as soon as she stood up, there she was, ridiculous.[65]

Besides adopting the costume of a Spanish duchess, Austin also liked to wear Native American clothing. When she lived in Carmel, she would don "the leather gown of an Indian princess" and write in a "Paiute wickiup (sacred shelter) perched in a tree."[66] In *The American Rhythm*, she states: "when I say that I am not, have never been, nor offered myself, as an authority on things Amerindian, I do not wish to have it understood that I may not, at times, have succeeded in being an Indian" (41). Not only did Austin mimic the clothing of Southwestern native cultures, but she actually claims—albeit tentatively, given her negative declaration—to have become a Native American.

Another way to understand her self-fashioning is to view it in light of the anthropologist-native relationship. Austin, who often deemed herself an "ethnologist" (a term she used rather broadly to describe those who study people and culture), corresponded with the well-known ethnomusicologist Frances Densmore and obtained informal, methodological training from Frederick Webb Hodge, the expert in Native American culture.[67] As Austin states, Hodge taught her "the way of collecting and recording Indian affairs," advising her to be attentive to "the thing that is always done, the way of the tribe; the way of the average; the way and the why of it."[68] Throughout her autobiography, she describes her folklore collecting excursions in Tejon and other places in the Southwest.[69]

Austin was also very immersed and well-read in anthropology. She studied Bureau of Ethnology reports and constructed a personal "library covering the general subject of Anthropology," which she bequeathed to the library of the Laboratory of Anthropology in New Mexico.[70] She acknowledges in *The American Rhythm* the influence of ethnologists on the development of her Amerindian aesthetic:

> I would unfairly conclude this record of my work if I omitted to return acknowledgments for the help I have had from the ethnological studies of such scholars as Fletcher and Densmore, Goddard and Boaz and Kroeber, Mathews [*sic*] and Cushing and Harrington. In admitting the contribution of their scholarship, I should fall short if I did not also acknowledge the generosity of their personal assistance in elucidating the creative process as it exhibits itself in the aboriginal mind. Though they do not always take me so seriously as I take them, it would be unfair not to admit that they always take me good-humoredly. (64–65)[71]

Austin admits that these anthropologists did not view her work seriously, and there is no apparent evidence that her writings influenced theirs. Lacking formal training in anthropology, Austin, along with a number of other Southwestern women writers of popular anthropology, was considered an outsider by the discipline. Shelby J. Tisdale explains that popular anthropology, the majority of which was written by women, was the "most undervalued and underrewarded" anthropological writing. She continues: "Generally considered atheoretical, descriptive, and unscientific, attempts to educate the public by demystifying, dejargonizing, humanizing, and in many instances romanticizing anthropology are often viewed with mistrust by the profession."[72] As a result, such writers are "stigmatized and peripheralized" to the extent that they are "neither written into the histories of anthropology nor given credit for the contributions they have made to the development of the discipline."[73]

Austin, it seems, never sought membership in the academy; instead, she identified herself as an artist and wrote her own brand of anthropology. Tisdale claims that Austin's "action anthropology" would have marginalized her in the academy even if she had received formal training.[74] Austin herself admits that her approach to ethnographic writing was unscientific. She rather poetically muses: "I felt myself caught up in the collective mind [of the tribe], carried with it toward states of super-consciousness that escape the exactitudes of the ethnologist as the life of the flower escapes between the presses of the herbalist" (*American Rhythm*, 41). Loosely situated within the anthropological tradition, Austin attempts to transcend scientific objectivity and achieve a spiritual, mystical understanding of her subjects. Nevertheless, between her correspondence with anthropologists and her library of sources, Austin was steeped in the discipline of anthropology and adopted the role of the anthropologist to fashion her self-presentation as an artist.

In her desire to "go native," to don the trappings of Native American and Spanish colonial cultures, Austin may have been influenced by the ethnologist Frank Hamilton Cushing, to whom she pays tribute in the passage above from *The American Rhythm*.[75] Though Austin purports a very strong identification with Native Americans in claiming to "have succeeded in being an Indian," the much mythologized Cushing was the first recognized anthropologist to "go native." Sent by the Bureau of Ethnology to study the Zuni, in a novel move he resided with them, "a privileged insider," for five years. He even earned high office in the Society of the Bow, one of the Zuni secret societies.[76] Austin, similarly, in *The Land of Journeys' Ending* describes how in Spanish colonial New Mexico she, a white woman, was allowed to witness the secret ritual *Los Hermanos Penitentes,* and later gained entry to the private chapel of the Third Order of Saint Francis.

Besides imitating Cushing by acting the participant-observer, Austin also adopted his approach to understanding cultural artifacts. Another early-twentieth-century anthropologist, Alice Fletcher, who similarly lived with the Missouri Valley Native Americans she studied, characterized Cushing's archaeological method as one of "unconscious sympathy" that arose from his "power of thinking his way along the lines of aboriginal thought."[77] By immersing himself in the material conditions of aboriginal culture, Cushing tried to duplicate the ways in which the Native Americans created their material artifacts and discovered their technology.

Although the aboriginal artifact is literary for Austin, she seems to commandeer Cushing's archaeological method in translating Native American literature. The ability to form an empathic bond with native cultures is central to Austin's translation method, which she terms "re-expression." Studying aboriginal tribes, Cushing seeks to "surround [him]self with their material conditions," and Austin attempts to "saturate [her]self . . . in . . . the environment that cradled that life." Cushing's goal is to "restore their act and their arts"; Austin's is to produce "a genetic resemblance to the Amerind song that was my point of contact."[78] Cushing and Austin share Boas's assumption that "the most important task in ethnography is to present the culture of a people from their own point of view, as perceived by the people themselves."[79] They flirt with the boundaries of anthropological authority in striving to transcend their own Anglo cultural positions.

But Austin often pushes the limits of the "ethnologist" role to become the transethnic. Historically, in Austin's time the notion of participant-observation developed for fieldworkers in anthropology. While the participant-observer recognized that his personal experience and subjective authorship were central to ethnographic inquiry, he strove for objective distance from his subject.[80] Clifford Geertz sums up the role of the participant-observer when he states: "We are not, or at least I am not, seeking either to become natives (a compromised word in any case) or to mimic them. . . . We are seeking, in the widened sense of the term in which it encompasses very much more than talk, to converse with them."[81] Austin is a transethnic precisely at the moments when she mimics and seeks to become a native.

Related to this point about Austin's transethnicity, Elizabeth Ammons raises a significant question: "What are the ethics of advantaged white women adapting other people's cultural perspectives to their own personal ends?" Ammons maintains: "In the history of modernism the appropriation by white artists of the cultural perspectives of people of color has almost always been racist and exploitative."[82] Austin and countless other writers and artists of Santa Fe and Taos, New Mexico, celebrated primitivism and adopted the perspectives of people of color. Primitivists found in the Southwest exotic women of color; a lack of distinction between material and spiritual worlds; and natural political and social forms that were preferable to highly developed "civilizations." Though appropriating the perspectives of people of color is problematic, is it always racist, exploitive, and socially irresponsible? Austin certainly appropriates Native America in her writings. Yet at a time when the pleas of Native Americans in their struggle for human rights went unheeded, Austin claimed access to their culture and communicated its beauty, spirituality, and humanity to whites.

Some Anglo writers, like Willa Cather, were inspired by the community and human values in the Southwest but refused to become involved in the struggle for Native American rights. Intrigued by New Mexico's rich history and the priests, settlers, and Native American traders she interviewed, Cather penned *Death Comes for the Archbishop*. However, she rejected Mabel Dodge Luhan's request that she join the fight for Pueblo religious freedom.[83] A great many other Southwestern artists fought for Native American rights. For example, Luhan established a coalition of artists, writers, and reformers who struggled to change federal policies regarding Native Americans. Many formed watchdog and lobbying groups like the New Mexico Association of Indian Affairs and the American Indian Defense Association.[84] Members of the American Indian Defense Association—Austin, Luhan, and Collier—implemented a national publicity campaign, "Protest of Artists and Writers Against the Bursum Bill." Among those who signed this protest were Witter Bynner, Zane Grey, D. H. Lawrence, Harriet Monroe, Carl Sandburg, Elsie Clews Parson, William Allen White, Vachel Lindsay, and Edgar Lee Masters. Lawrence even published an article against the Bursum Bill in the *New York Times*. Political activism on behalf of the Native Americans was part of the primitivist movement in New Mexico.

Politically and artistically, Austin was absorbed in the primitivist beliefs of the Taos circle (although she eventually settled down with artists and writers in nearby Santa Fe). On the one hand, Austin's appropriation of the natives at times threatened their free agency. Arguing for the development of a more sensible and humane Native American policy by the Indian Bureau, she concludes: "And we want this policy in the hands of a group of properly qualified people who will remember that the Indians do not belong to them, but to us, and will hold themselves reasonably sensitive to public opinion on the subject."[85] This *us,* presumably, refers to the public sympathetic to the Native American cause; nevertheless, she objectifies the tribes as national assets, possessions of philanthropic and humanitarian groups.

On the other hand, Austin did not swallow wholesale the potential racist implications of primitivism. She refers to the Native Americans as "primitives," but asserts that primitive does not mean "a savage or a degenerate or even a mental dwarf."[86] Lois Rudnick states that D. H. Lawrence viewed his quest as messianic; he adopted a Native American mythos to effect the rebirth of modern humanity. Yet overall he was ambivalent toward Native Americans, exhibiting a "latent racist paranoia" toward people of color in general.[87]

Austin, however, was unlike many white, modernist artists who appropriated the perspectives of people of color in an era in which Freud made primitivism attractive by professing that civilized people repressed primitive desires to their detriment.[88] Austin did not come by the Native Americans via Freud, primitivism, or dime novels. She apprenticed with them before she embraced their perspectives and their art. In *Earth Horizon,* referring to herself in the third person, she asserts:

> There was a part for her in the Indian life. She had begun the study of Indian verse, strange and meaningful; of Indian wisdom, of Indian art. The Paiutes were basket-makers; the finest of their sort. What Mary drew from them was their naked craft, the subtle sympathies of twig and root and bark; she consorted with them; she laid herself open to the influences of the wild, the thing done, the thing accomplished. She entered into their lives, the life of the campody, the strange secret life of the tribe, the struggle of Whiteness with Darkness, the struggle of the individual soul with the Friend-of-the-Soul-of-Man. She learned what it meant; how to prevail; how to measure her strength against it. Learning that, she learned to write.[89]

As opposed to the modernist writers whom Luhan took on "guided tours" of the land and its people, Austin "consorted" with Native Americans and attempted to learn their culture from the inside.[90] Like the anthropologist, she "entered into their lives"; she did not merely borrow from them—"she learned to write." She states in *The American Rhythm* that the Native American influence "has given to my literary style its best thing" (39). By appropriating the point of view of Native Americans, Austin believed she invigorated and refined her art, her personal self-expression.

Having adopted the role of the anthropologist, Austin strives politically and aesthetically to keep open the frontier to Native Americans by reviving their art and fighting for their cultural rights. However, she puzzles over whether to do this through a unilinear hierarchical system of evaluative literary criticism or via a theory of cultural relativism. For example, she dissociates America from Europe and posits a continuous and successive evolution between unrelated American cultures. In her introduction to *The Path on the Rainbow,* George Cronyn's anthology of Native American songs, Austin asserts: "Probably never before has it occurred that the intimate thought of a whole people should be made known through its most personal medium to another people whose unavoidable destiny it is to carry that thought to fulfillment and make of that medium a characteristic literary vehicle."[91] She provides the immigrant Americans with a tradition rooted in the continent but mysteriously borrowed from Native Americans who become American literary forefathers. Austin also describes evolution as occurring within individual, native cultures; in their art, the Zuni and the Hopi have "surpassed ... every other tribe of the same stage of civil development."[92] Her essay on Native American literature for *The Cambridge History of American Literature* states: "Tribal ceremonies in all stages of ... logical development can be found among the American tribes, well on their way to becoming epic and drama." And the Navajo chant with its "songs, dances, and interpolated comedy ... is akin to that most American and popular variety of entertainment, the musical comedy."[93]

Perhaps Austin falls prey to this evolutionary, hierarchizing tendency given her view that "ethnologists" and literary scholars must work together to reconstruct the roots of American literary history. She praises ethnologists in some of her writings because they, "rather than literary specialists," were responsible for collecting and preserving aboriginal literature. Herself a translator, she recognizes "the debt of American literature to Washington Mathews [*sic*] and Frank Cushing." Further, she claims that one cannot understand the relation of Edgar Lee Masters, Carl Sandburg, and Sherwood Anderson to the American experience "without some understanding of the work of Alice Fletcher."[94] Yet Austin declares the need for collaboration between ethnologists "who occupy themselves with the collection and preservation of our aboriginal art" and literary scholars "whose work is about art in all its manifestations."[95] She displaces the Native American author with anthropologist/translators like Fletcher, Matthews, and Cushing. She never broaches the issue of the cultural authenticity of Native American literature translated by Anglos.

Like Austin, late-nineteenth-century anthropologists were interested in discovering principles of development and origins as well as a unified natural history and cultural past for humankind.[96] Hence, influenced by Darwin, they structured their findings according to unilinear schemes. For many anthropologists, this study was impelled by the fervor of nationalism, the need to provide "romantic ethnic roots for emerging nations."[97] Additionally, if Austin wished to recover Native American works as *literature,* she could not escape making hierarchical judgments. In the 1930s and 1940s, philosophers debated about evaluative literary criticism, some arguing that "value judgments" were "vacuous pseudostatements" that relegated the literary critic to "the intellectually insubstantial activity of a dilettante," and others "invok[ing] the humanistic mission of literary studies." The humanistic-mission people believed that "literary studies had moral responsibilities," and so they ranked novels, poems, poets, genres, verse forms, and even centuries as good or bad.[98] Austin expresses disappointment in Stith Thompson's *Tales of the North American Indians* because the Kato and the Zuni myths are included with no explanation that the Zuni is the superior group, and the Kato and the Zuni myths are "as far apart as Beowulf and 'Paradise Lost.'" Austin's ranking of the Zuni as superior to the Kato implies the "good Indian/bad Indian" dichotomy that privileges "civilized" and heroic over "savage" and "debased" tribes. She criticizes the folklorist Thompson for lacking a "creative literary intelligence" that would perceive "comparative literary form" and "give the key to the cultural backgrounds" of these stories.[99] Austin exploits the hierarchical methods of early-twentieth-century literary studies to recuperate aboriginal literature into the discipline.

In *The American Rhythm,* Austin arrives at a theory of cultural relativism that enables her to avoid the hierarchizing tendencies of the unilinear paradigm and construct a unified American cultural history. Eventually she incorporates her position of cultural relativism into some of her more politically and socially potent *One-Smoke Stories. The American Rhythm* contains a developed statement of Austin's "Amerind" aesthetic as well as several of her translations of Amerind poetry. Austin states in her theory that poetry arises from people's interaction with the land. Europeans, "the becoming race of Americans," are bombarded by "streams of rhythmic sights and sounds" that inform their poetry (14). For example, she contends that a passage from Abraham Lincoln's "Gettysburg Address" mimics the rhythm of a man walking a woodland path with an ax, heaving the ax aloft, and then bringing it down as he chops a piece of wood (16). Austin insists that by listening to aboriginal verse on a phonograph, she can distinguish the rhythms of woodland, plains, and desert tribes. With this revelation, she "awoke to the relationships that must necessarily exist between aboriginal and later American forms" (19). She emphasizes later American forms because earlier American poetry—like Longfellow's, which employed Finnish measures—imitated the European tradition. Austin's effort to bridge the gap between the aboriginal and European American is the most controversial aspect of her theory. She states, "I, at any rate, became convinced as early as the first years of the present century, that American poetry must inevitably take, at some period of its history, the mold of Amerind verse, which is the mold of the American experience shaped by the American environment" (42). Amerind and "later" Anglo American poetry evince similar forms because both groups utilize the rhythms of a common land.

Austin's theory specifically compares Amerind to imagist verse. What she terms the "landscape line" in Amerind verse is the "cadenced verse" or free verse of the imagists. Also, "Imagism" is equivalent to Native American "glyphic" or "the placing of this [landscape] line, and the additional items by which it is connoted and decorated" (56). James Ruppert asserts that Austin's "glyphic" embodies the first two principles of imagism—treat the object directly and use no word that does not contribute to the presentation. "Landscape line" refers to the third tenet—"compos[e] in the sequence of the musical phrase."[100] According to Austin, aboriginal glyphic anticipates imagism. Collections of Native American verse translated by anthropologists as well as Austin's own aboriginal-inspired play *The Arrow Maker* had been published by 1914, "about which time the free versifiers burst upon the world with loud cries of self-discovery" (65).

Given that Austin's theory was radical, her style ambiguous and suggestive, and her claims unsupported, *The American Rhythm* was challenged by many of her friends and contemporaries. Her friends, the modernist, western poets Witter Bynner and Arthur Davison Ficke, took Austin to task in personal correspondence for designating an essential, cross-cultural American rhythm. Regarding her translations, Bynner argues: "You could never convince me that your rhythms in the translations have anything to do with the American soil in the sense that the original Indian rhythms belong to it."[101] Bynner doubts whether Austin can escape her European heritage and create translations that are authentically Native American. Ficke debates her statement of "the *existence* of a general 'American rhythm'": if poets produce rhythms from the environment, will they not "produce similar poetic rhythms all over the world quite irrespective of mere nationality"?[102] Hence, he prods Austin to pinpoint what exactly is American in her poetic rhythms. While Bynner mistrusts Austin's ability to capture the American essence in her translations, Ficke is skeptical about whether the essence of a land can be assigned a nationality.

Austin's comparison of European and Native American poetic practices was disputed by both Bynner and the imagist poet Amy Lowell. Lowell declares in a letter to Austin prior to the publication of *The American Rhythm:* "I am quite sure there is nothing at all like it [Lowell's polyphonic prose] in Amerind verse. It is not a type of technique which a primitive people would think of."[103] Undoubtedly, Austin alludes to this exchange in *The American Rhythm* when she conjectures about an "unpatterned Ute melody" recorded by Frances Densmore: "Is it perhaps the 'polyphonic prose' which Miss Lowell found lurking in a dim, ancestral corner of her mind, and brought forward as a new discovery?" (79). Emphatically reiterating that imagism is neither novel nor unique, Austin recoils from the evolutionary assumption of sophistication on the part of Lowell and the consequent "general snootiness of the classic tradition [to] primitivism."[104]

Bynner repudiates the notion that the American rhythm is influenced by Native Americans. He sardonically quips: "I should say that there is more influence from Queen Elizabeth down through Gershwin on Hopi Indian songs than on so-called American rhythm from any Amerindian whatever."[105] Bynner's argument helps account for the final assertion in this confession from *Earth Horizon*: "I should say that there was a general withdrawal of interest in the subject of Indian poetry, an unwillingness to give it attention. There was an indisposition to admit it to discussion, especially on the basis on which I had introduced it. Most of the reviewers took it for granted that I had said that American poetry was derived from Indian, and scoffed at the idea."[106] Given Austin's statements elsewhere that the Anglo immigrant will bring Native American poetry to fruition, this misunderstanding of reviewers is not so surprising. Yet *The American Rhythm* does not suggest a unilinear model of evolution in which Anglo Americans inherit and develop the Amerind aesthetic or find themselves in parallel stages of development to Native Americans. Nor does Austin imply, as Bynner alleges, that Native Americans actually create the American rhythm that is eventually diffused to white, modern American poets. Instead, she replaces hierarchically arranged categories with geographic determinism: the land creates the American rhythm. Austin discovers in the land the consolidating agent from which to construct a unified history of America. She keeps open the frontier by uniting in the land Anglos and Amerinds, two cultures supposedly removed from each other on the evolutionary scale.

Austin performs the "archaeological" work of excavating an American literary tradition, which she traces to its roots in the land. Because art forms reflect peoples' interaction with the land, Austin espouses cultural relativism, which becomes relevant to her political activism. Like the ethnographers who adhered to the tenets of cultural relativism, Austin followed Boas's ideological shift away from natural history and to salvage ethnography. But salvage ethnographers accepted the passing of cultures as inevitable and worked to retain a written account of them. Austin desired both to preserve and to revivify the vanishing American cultures.

James Clifford discusses the politics of salvage ethnography in his essay "On Ethnographic Allegory." The purpose of salvage ethnography is to represent the native person or "disappearing object" who is a "rhetorical construct," asserts Clifford. He critiques the assumptions of salvage ethnography: that a culture's "essence" is lost with change and that purportedly weak cultures need to be represented by an outsider, the anthropologist, who then becomes "custodian of an essence." Finally, he speculates about how ethnography might change if the focus was placed on the future of these societies and not their vanishing past.[107] Clifford's points illuminate Austin's writings in interesting ways, although it must be remembered that the vanishing native was much more than a "rhetorical construct" to Austin, who witnessed the active cultural and even physical extermination of Native Americans on the frontier. Nevertheless, does Austin see herself as custodian of an essence? Is she future-oriented or past-oriented regarding aboriginal cultures? To what extent does she reinforce the belief in the Vanishing American? In other words, what are the politics of her salvage operation as she reclaims the native for the American tradition?

While Austin admits that Native Americans are vanishing in most parts of the United States, she seeks to reverse the closing frontier by arguing their artistic worth. Yet the rhetoric of vanishing pervades many of her writings. For instance, she rather dismissively states:

> It is not, however, the significance of Amerind literature to the social life of the people which interests us. That life is rapidly passing away and must presently be known to us only by tradition and history. The permanent worth of song and epic, folk-tale and drama, aside from its intrinsic literary

quality, is its revelation of the power of the American landscape to influence form, and the expressiveness of democratic living in native measures.[108]

Given the gradual demise of Native Americans, Austin suggests, their artistic culture is less significant to their own society, which is "rapidly passing away," than to the conquering society, which it serves as a model of genuine American literature.

Elsewhere, Austin is less willing to concede the native's disappearance. She summons her audience to remove the barriers from the "evolutionary progression" of Native American dance drama so that it can develop into a "legitimate theatrical expression":

> What he [the average American] does not realize is that, with his and the government's connivance, a steady propaganda has been going on for the past thirty years in Indian schools to overcome both the religious and the art values of Amerind drama. . . . What is required for this, as for any other cultural salvage, is the co-operative activity of an enlightened group. And it may as well be stated here as anywhere that any Indian dance drama which the miscellaneous public is permitted to attend has already lost most of its religious implication. If the schools and the missionaries will let him alone, the Indian is perfectly able to maintain his own spiritual integrity.[109]

Austin redefines "cultural salvage" in a broader, sociopolitical context, making it more than the preservation of raw data in a paper record. She urges the schools and missionaries to eschew interference in Native American life and allow the Native Americans to salvage their own spirituality and thereby redeem and invigorate their dramatic practice.

In the desert Southwest, where ancient artistic survivals remain, Austin discovered the natives who are not vanishing and who are the hope for the future of American culture. *The Land of Journeys' Ending* prophesies that the Southwest will be the seat of the next great world culture. According to Dippie, the Southwestern tribes, who persisted amid genocide, historically represented the hope for Native American endurance. The Plains tribes were the true vanishing Americans because their hunting and raiding culture died with the demise of the buffalo and the emergence of the reservation system. The Navajos and Pueblos, however, retained their cultural integrity largely because the Southwest desert held little attraction for Anglo settlers.[110] The desert Southwest is the land of journeys' ending where New Mexican and Native American art flourishes. It is a place to witness "Art Becoming," where "art renews itself" (445, 444).

In an act akin to the "social telesis" of conservationists, Austin intervened to prevent the extinction of Native American art. She inaugurated one of her major salvage projects by cofounding the Spanish Colonial Arts Society with Frank Applegate. The society's purpose was to revive in the Southwest the Spanish colonial arts, syncretic art forms made "in the likeness of the things of old Spain, modified by what they [the Spanish colonists] found here among the Indians." Applegate collected the material artifacts and Austin the folklore. Effecting the revival of the arts, they established a Spanish market "and an exhibition with prizes."[111] The Spanish Colonial Arts Society dedicated itself to preserving and rebuilding New Mexican culture. Similarly, Austin established the Indian Arts Fund, which sought to preserve the essence of native Southwest cultures and also to perpetuate dying cultures. Because she feared that artifacts were disappearing as the country was being "combed by a new type of 'pot-hunters' who often destroy as much as they take away," she created a museum for the artifacts.[112] Applying a conservationist metaphor to an archaeological problem, Austin indicates the equivalent urgency of conserving the environment and preserving vanishing cultures.

Austin wished to help New Mexican and aboriginal cultures survive life in the postcontact milieu; hence, she established museum collections for the Indian Arts Fund and the Spanish Colonial Arts Society and critiqued the government's assimilation policies. True, as Vernon Young observes about Austin's work: "Museums of anthropology and Indian ceremonial do not constitute the tools of new culture; they memorialize a vanishing culture."[113] Yet unlike other museums, Austin's were intended for the native peoples, to inspire them to replicate ancient art forms. She opposed the Indian Bureau that defaced Native American culture "in a dull smear of ugly and ineffectual imitation of white life."[114] She tried to salvage native cultures and to reanimate their art while remaining attuned to the pressures placed upon Native Americans on the frontier.[115]

As opposed to the salvage ethnographers whose goal is only to preserve the past, Austin's museums anticipated the future of Native Americans. Rudnick argues that Austin's patronage of the arts, though well-intentioned, is just another form of colonization as Austin appropriates symbols from

Native America for her own tradition.[116] Austin imagined the ultimate purpose of the Indian Arts Fund museum to be its contributions "to the evolving
American aesthetic." But keeping in mind her political agenda, she also states:
"Always it must be borne in mind that the primary object of the collection is
not merely to anticipate their complete demise but to keep the arts alive."[117]
Austin stimulated the Native American economy by keeping their arts alive
and encouraging them to make crafts.[118]

Austin's quest to nurture the American aesthetic resulted in her role as
custodian of an aboriginal aesthetic essence. Stineman claims that by encouraging the people to reproduce traditional crafts, Austin imprisoned them in a
nonindustrial past.[119] However, Austin is not a cultural purist who wishes to
return the tribes to their precontact states; she advocates the adoption of certain Anglo cultural practices. At the same time, incorporating Boasian cultural
relativism into her political activism, Austin abjures extremist assimilation
policies that seek to turn Native Americans into whites.

In "Why Americanize the Indian?" Austin takes to task the government
boarding schools for Native American children. She accuses these schools of
kidnaping students to supply white teachers with jobs, providing nutritionally
deficient food and unclean surroundings, forcing students to perform hard labor, and overworking them. She also critiques the philosophy of the "Indian
schools," which presumes that the Native American student is an inferior
white who must be transformed, through education, into an "imitation poor
white."[120] Consequently, the student, who is both unfit for Native American
life and rejected by white society, becomes "a social outcast and an economic
drifter."[121] Given this cogent analysis, Austin questions whether Americanization is the answer to the "Indian Problem," adopting a stance of cultural relativism in her writings.

She depicts the absurdity of white education for Native Americans in
"White Wisdom," in *One-Smoke Stories*. Through the character of Dan Kearny,
the gray-eyed Ute, she maintains that regardless of physical appearance and cultural demeanor, the white-educated Native American will always be a pariah in
Anglo American society. The frame of the story portrays a Ute speaker, offering
his tale as a caution to the Navajos—"a tree of protection" as they "pray Washington to build schools for them" (182). The speaker warns them not to be
"twice-bitten" by white wisdom—bitten by their desire to obtain it and then
again when it betrays them.

The protagonist of the story, Dan, the gray-eyed Ute, has been "twice-bitten." The speaker, who gives his readers to understand that Dan is his cousin, explains that Dan has been raised by the speaker's aunt. This Ute woman had helped nurse Dan's white mother on her deathbed, then she later married Dan's white father and raised the gray-eyed son. Although the young Dan is educated in a white school, his Ute relatives, believing Dan to be the Ute woman's biological child, attend to his education in Native American traditions; hence, as a child he is "two-minded." However, when he is older, his Ute "mother" sends him to a white school according to the wishes of his now-deceased father.

The story is set on a reservation, and its political backdrop is institutionalized assimilation. The speaker complains: "Washington will have all Indians to live wholly in the White way" (189). They may choose only from "among the White man's religions" and are debarred from performing their ceremonial dances (189). In all things, they must follow the white way "except for the one thing of living according to their heart's need of living" (189). The "one thing" the speaker refers to is intermarriage. The story examines the absurdity of acculturation without the possibility of cultural mixing through intermarriage. The newly "whitewashed" Dan Kearny serves a purpose for the reservation agents. Believing Dan to be part Ute, the agents seemingly admit him to their society and then use him to control the tribe. Dan Kearny is "as one painted with Whiteness" (187): in physical appearance he is white and is treated with the deference accorded a white man. The traders on the reservation call him Mr. Kearny; he often eats meals with the white missionary agents; and on his rides around the reservation, he is accompanied by their daughter. Kearny speaks to the Utes on behalf of the agents, mocking the tribe's customs and affirming the need for assimilation: "As for dancing, it is nothing to me that you dance buffalo trot or fox trot. . . . But if you dance, saying to the rain or to the corn, obey me, that is the talk of savages" (191). Having become a privileged participant in white life, Kearny renounces the culture of the Utes.

Kearny learns, though, that there are definite limits to this liberal acceptance on the part of whites. After he asks the missionary's daughter to marry him, he discovers his outsider status. She is "sickened" at his proposal and cries to her mother, "Don't let him touch me!" Her mother responds with anger; despite having treated Dan as one of her children, she objects when he dares to propose to her daughter "as though [he] were White" (196). Austin suggests that while white education does not make Native Americans equal to whites, its purpose is to make them less different and more tractable.

Kearny rebels against such control and runs away to join the Ute dance at Big Meadows. When the speaker and the speaker's mother (the sister of Dan's Ute "mother") discover him, he has adopted Ute dress and married a Ute wife. The story momentarily seems to endorse the fixity of race and the fluidity of culture. However, in an ironic twist, the speaker's mother reveals to her son that although Kearny was brought up by his Ute "mother," he is actually the son of his father's first wife, and she was white. The story, then, depicts the arbitrariness of race categories that are not innate but socially determined. Though Kearny looks and acts white, the missionary's daughter is revolted by him because she supposes him to be part Ute. Her reaction to his proposal is based not on his projected cultural identity, but on his assumed Native American heredity. By disclosing that Kearny is white, the speaker satirizes the girl's bigotry and reveals the irrationality of society's racial prejudices. At the story's end, Kearny, who remains deceived about his racial identity, is no longer manipulated by white wisdom but uses it defiantly, as "a shield under which the tribal use flourishes, and a thorn in the side of the Agency which they can in no wise pluck out" (182).

"White Wisdom" discloses Austin's skepticism about the viability of assimilation policies when Anglos continue to endorse the belief that there are essential differences between races. Proffering the perspective of cultural relativism, the story asks: What is the virtue of white wisdom for its own sake? Similarly, Austin questions the assumption that so-called "civilized" white customs are more rational and valid than Native American ones. In "Why Americanize the Indians?" she worries that schools have "saddle[d] upon these simple primitives some of the most ridiculous fetishes of our complex civilization—the fetish of bundling up the human body in cloth, the fetish of steam-heated houses, the fetish of substituting the fox trot and the bunny hug for the buffalo and deer dances, the fetish of high-heeled shoes for women and $9.98 custom-made suits for men." Through these comparisons, Austin makes white customs seem primitive. As whites foist these customs upon the Native Americans, the reasons for them "are completely hidden from the Indian."[122] By repeating the word "fetish," Austin accentuates the fact that undisputed reverence is attributed to white culture, arbitrarily making high-heeled shoes more "civilized" than moccasins.

Somewhat moderate in her views about the coerced Americanization of Native Americans, Austin advocates fluid acculturation or biculturality. "Mixed Blood," for example, is the story of Venustiano, a man who is half Spanish, half Native American and who is educated Presbyterian. Ironically, though he is of "mixed blood," he adopts a Presbyterian identity and renounces his Native American self, even "refusing to let his hair grow." Venustiano had "no occasion for instruction in his own tribal rites" and so "was glad to call himself by their [the Presbyterians'] name." In addition, Venustiano is ethnocentric in his religious belief, proclaiming to his uncle, the cacique, "I get me a God that is the true one and not no old people's story." He disowns his Native American heritage, but with unconscious irony reminds his mother "that he was of mixed blood and no Indian." Despite his disavowal of his Pueblo roots, Venustiano exploits his heritage by marrying Abieta of the Turquoise clan and claiming his "allotment of pueblo land" (286, 288).

Venustiano's ethnocentric Presbyterianism causes the tribe to spurn him. Although he marries a Native American wife and lives on tribal land, to the chagrin of the Pueblo people he refuses to partake in Native American ceremonies or even to wear native dress when working with the tribe. When the people alienate him, he complains to his wife "that they ought to remember that he was after all of mixed blood and proper Indian feelings" (289). Venustiano acknowledges his Pueblo ancestry and avails himself of his "mixed blood" identity when it benefits him. The tribe isolates Venustiano because he is consistently unable to embrace his mixed identity and view ethnicity as flexible. To the tribe, Venustiano is in "bad form" since "nothing in pueblo custom inhibited the utilization of as many rites as a man found served his purpose." The "good Catholics," for example, did not let "making the Roman sign inhibit the salutary pinch of sacred meal on entering a friend's house." (287–88). The Pueblos scorn Venustiano for failing to syncretize his mixed identity yet wishing to live among the people whose culture he repudiates.

In the end, through the "witchcraft" and machinations of his wife and her aunt, Venustiano learns tribal pride and respect for native customs and is eventually readmitted to the "community of labor" (294). The story resists making value judgments about cultural traditions and illustrates that only by viewing culture as fluid can Venustiano capitalize on the potential of his "mixed blood" identity.

Besides depicting the "mixed blood" character who resists fluid biculturalism, Austin portrays the difficulties some Native Americans have with the uncompromising assimilation policies of whites. "Hosteen Hatsanai Recants" faults Christian assimilationists with being inflexible and fetishistic. Hatsanai— a Native American—converts to Christianity when he meets and falls in love with Tuli, a Native American Christian. When Tuli goes blind, Hatsanai seeks a second wife, pending the approval of Tuli, to assist her at home. The missionaries are enraged when the threesome request that they marry Hatsanai and his pregnant second wife according to Christian law.

Austin reconciles Christianity with the polygamy of Hatsanai by radically suggesting that biblical doctrines, rather than being fixed in meaning, are interpreted within cultural contexts and are, therefore, fluid with culture. The missionaries deem Hatsanai a sinner and rebuke him: "You have a wife whom you married in the sight of God, and would you insult her by bringing into her house a —?" (232–33). Further, they call his wife Tuli "a pagan and a backslider" (233). Interpreting Hatsanai's polygamy from their own cultural perspective, the missionaries deem his second wife a "whore," imply that the relationship is purely sexual, and accuse him of insulting Tuli. However, Tuli is not "insulted," for he has married the second wife to honor her, not satisfy his sexual appetite. He complains that he has practiced monogamy "according to their [the missionaries'] convenience" (228). In other words, monogamy is not an absolute moral standard, and within certain cultures it even prevents the family from functioning fully and smoothly. Hatsanai dumbfounds the missionaries when he challenges them to cite any sayings of Jesus that forbid him to marry his second wife, the mother of his child. Although he has honored his wife, Hatsanai is berated by the missionaries and accused of sinning. Because Christian doctrine is not flexible—because it is culture bound— Hatsanai cannot reconcile his Native American lifestyle to Anglo Christianity. Austin does not so much object to introducing Christianity to the Native Americans as she does to the dogmatism of the missionaries, who are unable to see that from Hatsanai's cultural perspective finding a mate to assist his blind wife and then wishing to marry this new bride when she becomes pregnant are, within his own culture, acts of love and kindness.

Fearing that they are doomed to Christian hell, Hatsanai and his wives recant their Christianity. Hatsanai relates that they "threw into the Cleft all our fetishes that we had from the Mission," including "Sunday-school cards, a silver cross . . . a Bible . . . our writing of marriage" (235). Along with these "fetishes," they expel white cultural prescriptions that ascribe unquestioned reverence to Anglo practices. The story endorses cultural relativism by judging the morality of polygamy within its cultural context. Like Dan Kearny, the gray-eyed Ute, Hatsanai and his wives return in the end to the more amenable Native American spirituality. From within his native religion, Hatsanai can somewhat reconcile his spiritual beliefs. Although he renounces Christianity, Hatsanai dreams of Christ: "It is His face I see, and yet as though it were also one of the Diné, and the face is kind" (236). He dreams of Christ, the European God with the face of a Native American. Moreover, he appeases himself with the knowledge "that *there is no Saying*" of Jesus that makes his act of polygamy sinful and defiant (236). Similar to "Mixed Blood," Austin's story "Hosteen Hatsanai Recants" depicts Native American religion as flexible and accepting of other religious beliefs.

For Austin, Americanization benefits native cultures when it is a syncretic process. Austin's own solutions to the "Indian Problem" are syncretic ones, based on a "more rational Americanization." For instance, she asserts that the Native Americans should be given their religious freedom and the liberty to create their own art, rather than having to mimick white forms. Also, Native American family and village life should be restored but with improved sanitation. Upon the reinstitution of family life, village schools should replace government boarding schools and in each village adult-education programs should be coordinated to lessen the alienation between parents and their white-educated children. Children should attend classes until the age of sixteen, when they should be allowed to choose whether or not they would like to continue their education at a white school. Normal schools should be established for students wishing to become teachers and craftsmen among their own people. Instead of paternalistically denying Native Americans access to an industrialized future, Austin declares: "Open all the doors to civilized opportunity . . . but neither nag nor compel them to enter."[123] While Austin endeavors through her salvage project to preserve the essence of aesthetic culture, politically she does not attempt to fix Native Americans in a sentimental past. Rather, she locates their cultural essence in their art and without force or coercion welcomes them to all other aspects of white life.

Austin's intercultural relationship to Native America raises complex questions about the adoption of nonwhite cultures by white artists, writers, and reformers. Can white writers and artists ever respectfully portray nonwhite cultures? (For that matter, can white scholars who study such writers and artists ever adequately depict such cultures?) Austin does not transcend the critical problems arising from her writing other cultures; however, she does make an effort to carve out a respectful position for herself by dismantling the imperialist nature-culture binary, redefining primitivism, and adopting a position of cultural relativism in both her political activism and in her attempts to redefine American literary history.

Austin's conservationism and anthropology directly responded to the problems posed by the closing of the frontier in 1890; her understanding was that the land and its inhabitants needed to be protected. Austin attempted to re-open the frontier by sustaining culture contact. To the white, masculine frontier ethic of conquest and destruction, she opposed a genteel feminine or spiritualized Native American regard for the environment. Yet conservation for her involved more than just saving the earth. Since she maintained that the land was like a text containing various cultural forms, the destruction of the land threatened the existence of cultures. By saving the land, Austin thought she could salvage the aboriginal cultures on it.

Hence, Austin also sought to keep open the frontier by preventing the cultural annihilation of Native America. Culturally, she constructed a national literary tradition rooted in the American soil and originating from Native American culture. Politically, she opted for a position of cultural relativism as she reclaimed the vanishing Americans from oblivion by advocating an Americanization agenda that was syncretic and progressivist. In so doing, she nurtured the roots of the stem upon which the second wave of Americans engrafted itself to form a unified American tradition.

Epilogue

The myth that describes the pioneering Anglo frontiersman does not, for the most part, explain the experiences of people who already resided west of the border of encroaching Anglo pioneers. In the American imagination, the frontiersman was a rugged individual, a self-reliant adventure-seeker. His travels West were fueled by an innate aggression that prompted him to possess and conquer, tame and alter the land that was there for his taking. He thrived on the freedom from societal restraints and limitations the West offered him as he sought economic prosperity in his progress toward becoming a self-made man. For the frontiersman, travel west promised the fulfillment of the American Dream. Pointing out the problems inherent in this view, the frontier historian Henry Nash Smith critiques his own groundbreaking study *Virgin Land* (1950). In a 1986 article, Smith admits that, like Frederick Jackson Turner, he viewed the frontier wilderness as "free land," and in so doing "assume[d] that this area was in effect devoid of human inhabitants."[1] This was not true, and it was the human inhabitants who already lived there who had to encounter the pioneering frontiersman.

People west of the border had to manage the pioneering frontiersman's active fantasies of conquest in order to assure their survival. Such management was necessary after it became painfully clear that the Anglo American worldview and values often clashed with those of people west of the border. Native Americans exhibited a communal rather than an individual ethic: survival depended not on any one individual but on the tribe. Instead of conquering nature, Native Americans nurtured and received nurturance from the land. Alienated from their lands, Native Americans and Mexicans suffered the colonial experience of being dispossessed of their homes. Asians, however, like their Anglo counterparts, chose to immigrate; they hoped to gain wealth and prosperity in America. While there is no evidence that their ultimate goal was to conquer and colonize the nation, they nevertheless became the objects of Yellow Peril paranoia, an Anglo American concept that successfully denied Asian people their individuality.

What westering pioneers and persons west of the border had in common, however, was the experience of the frontier as a contact zone—that is, a place where cultures meet, interact, and grapple for power. And in the contact zone, people underwent a frontier rite of passage. Simply put, a rite of passage is a ceremony that accompanies a person's change of status. Rites of passage, then, mark the end of one stage and the beginning of another for a person or group. While anthropologists view rites of passage as occurring to individuals within a culture (for example, when people undergo rituals of circumcision, baptism, ordination, and so on as they move through one stage of community life to another), people who meet at the border undertake rites of passage as they negotiate the frontiers between cultures on the contact zones. Such people, situated in the liminal position between cultures, confront cultural others and contemplate their impending change of status. The choices frontier authors are faced with include adapting to the dominant group, resisting assimilation, or instituting social changes through their writings.

The rite of passage, then, is an apt metaphor to explain frontier literature from both sides of the border because it emphasizes the concepts of initiation into a new social and cultural order as well as the sense of self-discovery and self-making that is so prominent in American literature. In fact, multicultural frontier literature addresses a central canonical question in American literature, a question first posed by J. Hector St. John de Crevecoeur: What is an American? Crevecoeur answers that North Americans are "a mixture of English, Scotch, Irish, French, Dutch, Germans, and Swedes. From this promiscuous breed, that race now called Americans have arisen [*sic*]."[2] Conversely, writers west of the border expand the boundaries of that definition of American identity to include Mexican, Native, Asian, and African Americans. In broadening the borders of American identity, this model of the frontier contact zone also seeks to open the boundaries of the American canon to include works of western American literature by multicultural writers.

Yet this concept of intercultural frontiers also suggests an alternative model of what it means to be an American. Rather than drawing on the archetypal Anglo American self-made man who achieves the Horatio Alger, capitalist fantasy of moving from "rags to riches," writers west of the border reconceive the concept of self-making. They exhibit fluid selves that are able to change by adapting to diversity. In other words, they do not seek an ideal American image after which they pattern themselves; instead, their works constantly invent and reinvent what it means to be, for example, an Asian or Paiute or African American man or woman.

The issues about American identity raised by this model of the frontier contact zone as a rite of passage persist in contemporary cultural debates, which metaphorically attack the issue of American assimilation or diversity by asking whether society is a "melting pot" or a "salad bowl." Assimilationists concede that America's roots are multiethnic, yet they often define American identity as British-based. Arguing American identity is more cultural than ethnic, John O'Sullivan claims: "it is possible to *become* an American—or in effect, a WASP."[3] Pluralists, however, argue that ethnic and cultural diversity defines America, and that America's plural cultures never completely lose their separate ethnic identities; that is, they never completely become Anglo or WASP. Hence, the debates sparked by nineteenth- and early-twentieth-century multicultural American literature of the contact zones continue to resonate in U.S. society at the turn into the twenty-first century as contact sometimes threatens to close a frontier.

Through the study of frontier literature, *West of the Border* has engaged in this debate, posing the question: What happens when cultures meet in the contact zone where they face initiation into another social order, and they anticipate the inescapable change of status that contact demands? How do these writers exemplify their experiences with the rite of passage? How do they textualize the contact zone? External contact zones become internalized and ultimately reexternalized as writers arbitrate their cultural identities and seek the means of survival in America.

The contact zone is internalized for writers west of the border in their double consciousness or awareness of being between two cultures, an awareness that shapes the writers' self-perceptions. Double consciousness enables Sarah Winnemucca Hopkins to develop sophisticated techniques for persuading an audience; it leaves James Beckwourth vacillating between Crow and Anglo cultures; it allows Sui Sin Far to invent realist techniques as she speaks on behalf of the Chinese to a sinophobic audience; and it complicates Onoto Watanna's identity as a part-Chinese writer of Japanese American romances. Double consciousness is not an essentialist model that describes the experiences of all border groups; rather, it is a mode of perception that lets frontier writers invent a repertoire of literary and rhetorical techniques.

Double consciousness is reexternalized by those writers who adopt a new identity and become "transethnics." Many of the writers in *West of the Border* don the clothing and identities of ethnic groups to which they do not belong. Beckwourth's transethnicity allows him access to economic and political power in Crow culture—power he, as a person of color, would otherwise have been denied in mainstream white culture. While transethnicity empowers him, it is at the expense of the Crows, whom he threatens economically, culturally, and, in the end, physically. Conversely, Mary Austin's transethnicity arises from her desire to use the folklore and art of Southwestern Native Americans to create her own authentically American literature and to revive dying Native American cultures. Transethnicity reveals a conflicted self for Onoto Watanna, who in passing as Japanese attains success as a romance writer by creating idealized representations of Japanese culture and people in order to conciliate an audience growing fearful of Japanese aggression.

Although not all writers west of the border are transethnics, most externalize the contact zone when they act as literary mediators. Hopkins, Mourning Dove, Sui Sin Far, and Austin seek empathy and understanding from persons on the other side of the border in an effort to negotiate the rite of passage. Facing the change in cultural status accompanying frontier contact, these writers must establish boundaries and limitations as they define their place in America and their newly emerging cultural identities. Conversely, for Beckwourth and John Rollin Ridge, mediation ends in the closing of the frontiers and the creation of boundaries that exclude people west of the border. Ultimately, the role of mediation in the rite of passage is to articulate the many different versions of American identity for multicultural frontier writers.

Notes

Introduction

1. Robert Laxalt, "The Melting Pot," in *The Best of the West: An Anthology of Classic Writing from the American West,* ed. Tony Hillerman (New York: HarperCollins, 1991), 147.

2. Frederick Jackson Turner, *The Frontier in American History* (New York: Henry Holt, 1920), 22–23.

3. Laxalt, "Melting Pot," 148.

4. Gloria Anzaldúa, *Borderlands/La Frontera: The New Mestiza* (San Francisco: Aunt Lute, 1987), 86.

5. Ibid., 79.

6. See Charles Stewart and Rosalind Shaw's collection of essays, *Syncretism/Anti-Syncretism: The Politics of Religious Synthesis* (New York: Routledge, 1994).

7. Ibid., Rosalind Shaw and Charles Stewart, introduction, "Problematizing Syncretism," 21.

8. For an extended discussion about the debate over Turner's thesis, see Gerald D. Nash, *Creating the West: Historical Interpretations, 1890–1990* (Albuquerque: University of New Mexico Press, 1991).

9. Turner, *Frontier,* 1.

10. Harold P. Simonson, *Beyond the Frontier: Writers, Western Regionalism, and a Sense of Place* (Fort Worth: Texas Christian University Press, 1989); Richard Slotkin, *Regeneration through Violence: The Mythology of the American Frontier, 1600–1860* (Middletown, Conn.: Wesleyan University Press, 1973).

11. See, for example, John M. Faragher, *Women and Men on the Overland Trail* (New Haven: Yale University Press, 1979); Elizabeth Hampsten, *Read This Only to Yourself: The Private Writings of Midwestern Women, 1880–1910* (Bloomington: Indiana University Press, 1982); Sandra L. Myres, *Westering Women and the Frontier*

Experience, 1800–1915 (Albuquerque: University of New Mexico Press, 1982); Lillian Schlissel, Vicki L. Ruiz, and Janice Monk, eds., *Western Women: Their Land, Their Lives* (Albuquerque: University of New Mexico Press, 1988); and Lillian Schlissel, *Women's Diaries of the Westward Journey* (New York: Schocken, 1982).

12. Henry Nash Smith, *Virgin Land: The American West as Myth and Symbol* (Cambridge: Harvard University Press, 1950).

13. Annette Kolodny, *The Land Before Her: Fantasy and Experience of the American Frontiers, 1630–1860* (Chapel Hill: University of North Carolina Press, 1984); Kolodny, *The Lay of the Land: Metaphor as Experience and History in American Life and Letters* (Chapel Hill: University of North Carolina Press, 1975).

14. James Axtell, "The Ethnohistory of Early America: A Review Essay," *William and Mary Quarterly* 35, no. 1 (1978): 110. See also Axtell, *The Invasion Within: The Contest of Cultures in Colonial North America* (New York: Oxford University Press, 1985).

15. Leonard Thompson and Howard Lamar, "Comparative Frontier History," in *The Frontier in History: North America and Southern Africa Compared,* ed. Howard Lamar and Leonard Thompson (New Haven: Yale University Press, 1981), 7.

16. Mary Louise Pratt, *Imperial Eyes: Travel Writing and Transculturation* (New York: Routledge, 1992), 4.

17. Anzaldúa, *Borderlands,* preface and 78.

18. Slotkin, *Regeneration,* 22.

19. Eric Heyne, "The Lasting Frontier: Reinventing America," in *Desert, Garden, Margin, Range: Literature on the American Frontier,* ed. Eric Heyne (New York: Twayne, 1992), 7.

20. Victor W. Turner, *The Ritual Process: Structure and Anti-Structure* (Ithaca, N.Y.: Cornell University Press, 1969), 94–95. Arnold van Gennep, *The Rites of Passage,* trans. Monika B. Vizedom and Gabrielle L. Caffee (Chicago: University of Chicago Press, 1960), 11. The anthropologist Victor Turner bears no relation to the historian Frederick Jackson Turner.

21. Turner, *Ritual Process,* 95.

22. Annette Kolodny, "Letting Go Our Grand Obsessions: Notes Toward a New Literary History of the American Frontiers," *American Literature* 64, no. 1 (1992): 11.

23. Ronald Takaki, *A Different Mirror: A History of Multicultural America* (Boston: Little, Brown, 1993), 11.

24. Turner, *Ritual Process,* 103.

25. Ibid., 167.

26. Victor Turner, *From Ritual to Theatre: The Human Seriousness of Play* (New York: PAJ, 1982), 47.

27. Ronald L. Grimes, "Victor Turner's Definition, Theory, and Sense of Ritual," in *Victor Turner and the Construction of Cultural Criticism: Between Literature and Anthropology,* ed. Kathleen M. Ashley (Bloomington: Indiana University Press, 1990), 144.

28. Turner, *From Ritual to Theatre,* 28, 44.

29. Turner, *Ritual Process,* 128.

30. Qtd. ibid., 94. In *Rites of Passage,* van Gennep discusses, among others, territorial change, pregnancy, childbirth, childhood, initiation, betrothal, marriage, and funerals as rites of passage.

31. Turner, *Ritual Process,* 112.

32. *International Encyclopedia of the Social Sciences,* s.v. "Myth and Symbol"— encyclopedia article written by Victor Turner.

33. Mikhail Bakhtin, *The Dialogic Imagination: Four Essays,* trans. Caryl Emerson and Michael Holquist (Austin: University of Texas Press, 1981), 360.

34. David Murray, *Forked Tongues: Speech, Writing and Representation in North American Indian Texts* (Bloomington: Indiana University Press, 1991), 65.

35. Turner, *Ritual Process,* 201.

36. Turner, *From Ritual to Theatre,* 44. See also C. Clifford Flanigan, "Liminality, Carnival, and Social Structure: The Case of Late Medieval Biblical Drama," in Ashley, *Victor Turner and Cultural Criticism,* 53. Flanigan notes that Turner's theory is "ill equipped to deal" with rituals whose "implications are so deeply subversive."

37. Turner, *Ritual Process,* 116–17.

38. Victor Turner, "Myth and Symbol," 577.

39. Turner, *From Ritual to Theatre,* 58.

40. Frederick Jackson Turner, *Frontier,* 2–3.

41. Ibid.

42. Anzaldúa, *Borderlands,* preface.

43. Pratt, *Imperial Eyes,* 6.

44. Robert F. Berkhofer Jr., "The North American Frontier as Process and Context," *The Frontier in History: North America and Southern Africa Compared,* 52.

45. Turner, *Frontier,* 4.

46. Gerald D. Nash, "New Approaches to the American West," *Old West–New West: Centennial Essays,* ed. Barbara Howard Meldrum (Moscow: University of Idaho Press, 1993), 19.

47. Ibid.

48. Thompson and Lamar, "Comparative Frontier History," 7; Axtell, "Ethnohistory," 110.

49. Thompson and Lamar, "Comparative Frontier History," 7.

50. Berkhofer, "North American Frontier," 71.

51. Ibid., 70–71; Takaki, *Different Mirror,* chaps. 4 and 9; and Brian W. Dippie, *The Vanishing American: White Attitudes and U.S. Indian Policy* (Middletown, Conn.: Wesleyan University Press, 1982).

52. Takaki, *Different Mirror,* chap. 7.

53. See also Robert Daly, "Liminality and Fiction in Cooper, Hawthorne, Cather, and Fitzgerald," in Ashley, *Victor Turner and Cultural Criticism,* 70–85. Daly argues that on the limen persons stand apart from society and formulate a "potentially unlimited series of alternative social arrangements" (71). Daly connects the liminal to the

frontier in his discussion of Cooper, viewing it as a margin of "freedom and cultural possibility" between the wilderness and civilization (73).

54. Pratt, *Imperial Eyes,* 7. Emphasis in the original deleted.

55. Turner, *Ritual Process,* 177.

56. Chicano writers, who have made great contributions to the canon of borderland writings, have been studied in great detail. See, for example, Jose David Saldivar, *The Dialectics of Our America: Genealogy, Cultural Critique, and Literary History* (Durham: Duke University Press, 1991); Hector Calderon and Jose David Saldivar, eds., *Criticism in the Borderlands: Studies in Chicano Literature, Culture, and Ideology* (Durham: Duke University Press, 1991); and Leticia Garza-Falcon, *Gente Decente: A Borderlands Response to the Rhetoric of Dominance* (Austin: University of Texas Press, 1998).

Chapter 1

1. I will use the standard spelling of Paiute rather than either of Hopkins's variations—Piute or Pah-Ute.

2. Sarah Winnemucca Hopkins, *Life among the Piutes: Their Wrongs and Claims* (Bishop, California: Sierra Media, Inc., 1969), 18–19; punctuation is as in the original. All subsequent references to this work are cited parenthetically in the text.

3. T. D. Bonner, *The Life and Adventures of James P. Beckwourth* (New York: Arno Press, 1969), iv. All subsequent references to this work are cited parenthetically in the text.

4. Arnold Krupat, *For Those Who Come After: A Study of Native American Autobiography* (Berkeley: University of California Press, 1985), 31, 33.

5. W. E. B. Du Bois, *The Souls of Black Folk* (New York: Johnson Reprint Corporation, 1968), 3.

6. Pratt, *Imperial Eyes,* 7.

7. Henry Louis Gates, *The Signifying Monkey: A Theory of African-American Literary Criticism* (New York: Oxford University Press, 1988), 51, 107–10.

8. Karl Kroeber, "American Indian Persistence and Resurgence," *boundary 2* 19, no. 3 (1992): 9.

9. William Loren Katz, *Black Indians: A Hidden Heritage* (New York: Atheneum, 1986), 120–25.

10. Norman B. Plummer, *Crow Indians* (New York: Garland, 1974), 39–43.

11. Delmont R. Oswald, introduction, *The Life and Adventures of James P. Beckwourth* as told to T. D. Bonner (Lincoln: University of Nebraska Press, 1972), ix; Elinor Wilson, *Jim Beckwourth: Black Mountain Man and War Chief of the Crows* (Norman: University of Oklahoma Press, 1972), chaps. 12 and 13.

12. Arnold Krupat, "American Autobiography: The Western Tradition," *Georgia Review* 35, no. 2 (1981): 310.

13. Krupat, *For Those Who Come After,* 43.

14. Murray, *Forked Tongues,* 67.

15. Ibid., 68.

16. See also H. David Brumble III, *American Indian Autobiography* (Berkeley: University of California Press, 1988), 12.

17. Although Bonner, above, refers to himself as author, I regard the author of *The Life and Adventures of James P. Beckwourth* to be Beckwourth/Bonner; for simplicity, however, I will designate Beckwourth as author.

18. Helen Carr, "In Other Words: Native American Women's Autobiography," *Life/Lines: Theorizing Women's Autobiography,* ed. Bella Brodzki and Celeste Schenck (Ithaca: Cornell University Press, 1988), 136.

19. Krupat, *For Those Who Come After,* 33.

20. Mary V. Dearborn, *Pocahontas's Daughters: Gender and Ethnicity in American Culture* (New York: Oxford University Press, 1986), 152.

21. Robert B. Stepto, *From Behind the Veil: A Study of Afro-American Narrative* (Urbana: University of Illinois Press, 1979), 7.

22. Charles Godfrey Leland, preface to the new English edition of *The Life and Adventures of James P. Beckwourth, Mountaineer, Scout, Pioneer, and Chief of the Crow Nation of Indians,* written from his own dictation by T. D. Bonner (London: T. Fisher Unwin, 1892), 9, 12.

23. Oswald, introduction, xi.

24. Katz, *Black Indians,* 116. Katz does not document the identity of this "more modern scholar."

25. Qtd. in Wilson, *Jim Beckwourth,* 6.

26. Christy scathingly notes Beckwourth's biracial roots and remarks that he "was born in that section of the United States where they spell Afro-American with a double g." White, who lived near the Beckwourth family in Saint Louis, observes Beckwourth's "proclivities were low," and he was an arrogant liar. Qtd. in Wilson, *Jim Beckwourth,* 7, 17.

27. Ibid., 18.

28. See Eugene Exman, *The House of Harper: One Hundred and Fifty Years of Publishing* (New York: Harper & Row, 1967).

29. "Story of James P. Beckwourth," *Harper's New Monthly Magazine,* Sept. 1856, 457. All subsequent references to this work will be cited parenthetically in the text.

30. Oswald, introduction, ix.

31. Brumble, *Autobiography,* 23.

32. A. Irving Hallowell, "American Indians, White and Black: The Phenomenon of Transculturalization," *Current Anthropology* 4, no. 5 (1963): 523. Hallowell terms "transculturalization" an individual's "temporarily or permanently" taking on the culture, ideas, and traditions of a group to which he does not originally belong.

33. Elizabeth Ammons, introduction to *Tricksterism in Turn-of-the-Century American Literature,* ed. Elizabeth Ammons and Annette White-Parks (Hanover: University Press of New England, 1994), xi.

34. Katz, *Black Indians,* 115.

35. Plummer, *Crow Indians,* 48.

36. Ibid., 45–60.

37. George Devereux and Edwin M. Loeb, "Antagonistic Acculturation," *American Sociological Review* 8, no. 2 (1943): 140.

38. Roy Harvey Pearce, *Savagism and Civilization: A Study of the Indian and the American Mind* (Berkeley: University of California Press, 1988), 106, 130.

39. Herman Melville, *The Confidence-Man* (1857; New York: Penguin, 1990); James Hall, *Sketches of History, Life, and Manners in the West* (Philadelphia, 1835). My quotes from Hall will be taken from the Penguin edition of *The Confidence-Man*, which includes Hall's sketch of Moredock in an appendix.

40. Hall, qtd. in Melville, 348. Similarly, Melville states "some signal outrage" inspires the Indian-hater (179).

41. Hall, qtd. in Melville, 350. For Melville's Moredock, "to kill Indians had become his passion" (184).

42. Louise K. Barnett, *The Ignoble Savage: American Literary Racism, 1790–1890* (Westport, Conn.: Greenwood, 1975), 130.

43. Ibid., 133.

44. Hall, qtd. in Melville, 347. Melville states that the child "learns that a brother is to be loved, and an Indian to be hated" (175).

45. Barnett, *Ignoble Savage*, 137.

46. Jane Tompkins, *Sensational Designs: The Cultural Work of American Fiction, 1790–1860* (New York: Oxford University Press, 1985), 8.

47. Barnett, *Ignoble Savage*, 17–18. Barnett states that frontier romances were popular between 1790 and 1860.

48. Forrest G. Robinson, "The New Historicism and the Old West," in *Old West–New West: Centennial Essays,* ed. Barbara Howard Meldrum (Moscow: University of Idaho Press, 1993), 84, 90.

49. Exman, *House of Harper,* 71.

50. Don J. Kraemer Jr., "Gender and the Autobiographical Essay: A Critical Extension of the Research," *College Composition and Communication* 43, no. 3 (1992): 335.

51. Barnett, *Ignoble Savage*, 86.

52. Mary Rowlandson, "A Narrative of the Captivity, Suffering, and Removes of Mrs. Mary Rowlandson," in *Puritans among the Indians: Accounts of Captivity and Redemption, 1676–1774,* ed. A. T. Vaughan and E. W. Clark (Cambridge, Mass.: Belknap, 1981), 32–75.

53. Rayna Green, "The Pocahontas Perplex: the Image of Indian Women in American Culture," *Massachusetts Review* 16, no. 4 (1975): 698–714.

54. Ibid., 711.

55. Ibid., 703.

56. Gae Whitney Canfield, *Sarah Winnemucca of the Northern Paiutes* (Norman: University of Oklahoma Press, 1983), 17.

57. Dippie, *Vanishing American,* 16.

58. Ibid., 175.

59. Canfield, *Sarah Winnemucca*, 209, 249.

60. Murray, *Forked Tongues*, 65.

61. Krupat, *Ethnocriticism: Ethnography, History, Literature* (Berkeley: University of California Press, 1992), 219; Kathleen Mullen Sands, "Indian Women's Personal Narrative: Voices Past and Present," in *American Women's Autobiography: Fea(s)ts of Memory*, ed. Margo Culley (Wisconsin: University of Wisconsin Press, 1992), 273.

62. Canfield, *Sarah Winnemucca*, 200.

63. Ibid., 211.

64. Ibid., 201.

65. Qtd. ibid., 203.

66. Ibid., 203, 209.

67. Ibid., 232–40.

68. Ibid., 249.

69. Qtd. ibid., 203.

70. Sands, "Personal Narrative," 271.

71. Canfield, *Sarah Winnemucca*, 204.

72. Dippie, *Vanishing American*, 144–46.

73. Canfield, *Sarah Winnemucca*, 204.

74. Dippie, *Vanishing American*, 262.

75. Edward Byron Reuter, *The Mulatto in the United States* (New York: Haskell House, 1969), 328.

76. F. James Davis, *Who Is Black?* (University Park: Pennsylvania State University Press, 1991), 25.

77. Interestingly, Elizabeth Palmer Peabody was friends with Schurz, who was the product of a German kindergarten and whose wife started a kindergarten in the United States. When Peabody traveled abroad, Schurz's letter of introduction afforded her access to kindergartens. See Louise Hall Tharp, *The Peabody Sisters of Salem* (Boston: Little, Brown, 1950), 322.

78. Far from being permanently perturbed by Schurz's rebuff, Hopkins lectured extensively, not only in San Francisco but also in New York, Connecticut, Rhode Island, Maryland, Massachusetts, and Pennsylvania. For information on Hopkins's career as a lecturer, see Canfield, *Sarah Winnemucca*, chaps. 15 and 19.

79. Qtd. in Canfield, *Sarah Winnemucca*, 204.

80. Stepto, *From Behind the Veil*, 10.

81. Tharp does not document her sketch on Hopkins; many of her claims are contradicted by Canfield in *Sarah Winnemucca*.

82. Tharp, *Peabody Sisters*, 327.

83. Ibid., 328.

84. See Hertha D. Wong, "Pre-literate Native American Autobiography: Forms of Personal Narrative," *MELUS* 14, no. 1 (1987): 17–32.

85. Canfield, *Sarah Winnemucca*, 214. In 1884, Hopkins appeared before a U.S. Senate subcommittee, chaired by Senator Dawes, with her petition. A bill was passed to

give the Paiutes land in severalty in Camp McDermitt. However, General Sheridan countermanded the decision and, instead, Leggins's and Winnemucca's bands received 160 acres for each head of the family at Pyramid Lake. The Paiutes regarded this a loss because they already nominally owned land on Pyramid Lake and many foreigners were settled there on the choice lands. They feared that there was not room enough for five hundred displaced Paiutes on Pyramid Lake.

86. Qtd. in Canfield, *Sarah Winnemucca,* 65.

87. Hopkins was exposed to Anglo culture from a young age. She attended a white convent school until the parents of some of the students complained about their daughters being educated with Native Americans. In *Life among the Piutes,* she claims to have attended the San Jose school for only three weeks. In an 1873 interview, however, she maintained that she attended the Convent of Notre Dame in San Jose for three years. She also related that she lived with a Mrs. Roach, of Stockton, at one time. Further, as described in her narrative, in 1857 she and her sister Elma lived with Major William Ormsby, his wife, and young daughter. At their home, she helped with the chores and learned English and the rudiments of reading and writing. Canfield states that many Paiute children were adopted into settlers' homes at this time. See Canfield, *Sarah Winnemucca,* 31–33.

88. Jarold Ramsey, *Reading the Fire: Essays in the Traditional Indian Literatures of the Far West* (Lincoln: University of Nebraska Press, 1983), 126.

89. Martha C. Knack and Omer C. Stewart, *As Long as the River Shall Run: An Ethnohistory of Pyramid Lake Indian Reservation* (Berkeley: University of California Press, 1984), 60–61.

90. Qtd. in Canfield, *Sarah Winnemucca,* 42.

91. Ibid., 39.

92. Ibid., 37.

93. These descriptions are taken from a review of one of the performances, quoted ibid., 39–41.

94. Of course, the Winnemuccas might signify on conventional images of Native Americans in their tableaux vivants, but there is no record detailing the script of these performances.

95. Knack and Stewart, *As Long as the River Shall Run,* 88.

96. Ibid.

97. Dippie, *Vanishing American,* 50.

98. Knack and Stewart, *As Long as the River Shall Run,* 109.

99. Krupat, *Ethnocriticism,* 229.

100. Patricia Stewart, "Sarah Winnemucca," *Nevada Historical Society Quarterly* 14 (winter 1971): 28. Knack and Stewart, in *As Long as the River Shall Run,* enumerate other reasons cited by historians for the start of the war, ranging from revenge for the theft of a Native American's horse to simply "an unmotivated outbreak of Paiute racial aggression" (71).

101. Krupat, "Western Tradition," 314.

102. Pearce, *Savagism,* 103.

103. Gates, *Signifying Monkey,* 44–88.

104. Karl Kroeber, "Deconstructionist Criticism and American Indian Literature," *boundary 2* 7, no. 3 (1979): 76.

105. See Barbara Babcock-Abrahams, "'A Tolerated Margin of Mess': The Trickster and His Tales Reconsidered," *Journal of the Folklore Institute* 11 (1974): 147–86.

Chapter 2

1. *International Encyclopedia of the Social Sciences,* s.v. "Myth and Symbol"—Turner's article.

2. Babcock-Abrahams, "'A Tolerated Margin,'" 148.

3. Culturally, Trickster is thought to be of undefined gender, appearing in both male and female guises throughout trickster cycles. In this essay, for the sake of brevity, I will refer to Trickster simply as *he.*

4. Mac Linscott Ricketts, "The North American Indian Trickster," *History of Religions* 5, no. 4 (1966): 327–50.

5. Andrew Wiget, "His Life in His Tail: The Native American Trickster and the Literature of Possibility," in *Redefining American Literary History,* ed. A. LaVonne Brown Ruoff and Jerry W. Ward Jr. (New York: MLA, 1990), 87.

6. Ake Hultkrantz, *The Religions of the American Indians,* trans. Monica Setterwall, (Berkeley: University of California Press, 1967), 26.

7. In *The Trickster: A Study in American Indian Mythology* (New York: Philosophical Library, 1956), Paul Radin records two such cycles: "The Winnebago Trickster Cycle" and "The Winnebago Hare Cycle."

8. Hultkrantz, *Religions,* 34.

9. Robert H. Ruby and John A. Brown, *Dreamer-Prophets of the Columbia Plateau: Smohalla and Skolaskin* (Norman: University of Oklahoma Press, 1989), 3–9.

10. Amanda Porterfield, "American Indian Spirituality as a Countercultural Movement," in *Religion in Native North America,* ed. Christopher Vecsey (Moscow: University of Idaho Press, 1990), 157–58.

11. Ibid., 155–58; Ruby and Brown, *Dreamer-Prophets,* 3–9. See also Ake Hultkrantz, *Belief and Worship in Native North America,* ed. Christopher Vecsey (Syracuse, N.Y.: Syracuse University Press, 1981), 270.

12. James Mooney, *The Ghost Dance Religion and the Sioux Outbreak of 1890,* part 2, 1892–1893 (Washington, D.C.: Government Printing Office [U.S. Bureau of American Ethnology], 1896), 795.

13. Mooney, *Ghost Dance,* 795–96.

14. Ibid., 820.

15. Hultkrantz, *Belief and Worship,* 270.

16. Ricketts, "Indian Trickster," 343.

17. Hultkrantz, *Religions,* 33.

18. Ricketts, "Indian Trickster," 340.

19. *Dictionary of Native American Literature,* s.v. "Revitalization Movements and Oral Literature."

20. Porterfield, "Spirituality," 156–57.

21. Ruby and Brown, *Dreamer-Prophets,* 9.

22. Porterfield, "Spirituality," 157.

23. While most primary and secondary sources on trickster tales record and discuss "authentic" precontact versions, anthologies and journals of Native American folklore contain examples of trickster border narratives, a genre that is only beginning to be examined. I have yet to find a collection of postcontact trickster tales in any published source; rather, the tales exist scattered throughout anthologies and journals. Ramsey, in *Reading the Fire,* explains that many hybridized narratives went unrecorded by anthropologists, who exhibited a classical bias and so collected mainly precontact stories and regarded postcontact ones as "impure curiosities" (167). Although Ramsey's book does not discuss the genre of trickster tales, it does include essays on hybridized Indian myths, hero stories, prophecy, and Bible stories (see chaps. 7–10). Ramsey collects some hybridized narratives in *Coyote Was Going There: Indian Literature of the Oregon Country* (Seattle: University of Washington Press, 1977).

24. *Dictionary of Native American Literature,* s.v., "The White Man in Native Oral Tradition."

25. *Dictionary of Native American Literature,* s.v., "The Native American Trickster."

26. Babcock-Abrahams, "'A Tolerated Margin,'" 152.

27. For an analysis of the African American Trickster, see John Roberts, *From Trickster to Badman: The Black Folk Hero in Slavery and Freedom* (Philadelphia: University of Pennsylvania Press, 1989), chap. 2.

28. H. H. St. Clair, coll., "Shoshone and Comanche Tales," *Journal of American Folk-Lore* 22, no. 85 (1909): 276–77.

29. William T. Hagan, *United States–Comanche Relations: The Reservation Years* (New Haven: Yale University Press, 1976), 45–46; Dee Brown, *Bury My Heart at Wounded Knee: An Indian History of the American West* (New York: Holt, 1970), 396.

30. Morris W. Foster, *Being Comanche: A Social History of an American Indian Community* (Tucson: University of Arizona Press, 1991), 38; Hagan, *Relations,* 171.

31. Hagan, *Relations,* 171–72.

32. Foster, *Being Comanche,* 38–52.

33. Galen Buller, "Comanche and Coyote, The Culture Maker," in *Smoothing the Ground: Essays on Native American Oral Literature,* ed. Brian Swann (Berkeley: University of California Press, 1983), 255–57. Buller states that the "newest function" of trickster tales is to comment on white–Native American relations and that in these tales Coyote often tricks white culture-bringers like priests and soldiers.

34. Wiget, "His Life," 90.

35. Buller, "Comanche and Coyote," 257.

36. There is a version of the self-burning kettle story ascribed to the Comanche Coyote and Pedro de Urdemalas. See St. Clair, "Tales," 276–77; "Pedro de Urdemalas," in J. Frank Dobie, ed., *Puro Mexicano* (Dallas: Southern Methodist University Press, 1935), 49–55. The stories of the tree that grows money and of the mule that excretes gold are attributed to both the Apache Coyote and Pedro de Urdemalas. See Richard Erdoes and Alfonso Ortiz, "Coyote Gets Rich Off the White Men," *American Indian Myths and Legends* (New York: Pantheon, 1984), 369–71; "Pedro de Urdemalas," 52; Frances Toor, *A Treasury of Mexican Folkways* (New York: Crown, 1947), 529–31; and "Pedro de Urdemalas and the Gringo," *Folktales of Mexico,* ed. and trans. Americo Paredes (Chicago: University of Chicago Press, 1970), 155–56. The tale of Trickster's blatant theft of a white man's horse and clothes exists in the folklore of Mexican, Apache, and Comanche cultures. See St. Clair, "Tales," 277; Erdoes and Ortiz, "Coyote Gets Rich," 369–71; and Paredes, "Pedro and the Gringo," 156–57.

37. Wiget, "His Life," 94.

38. Erdoes and Ortiz, "Coyote Gets Rich," 369–71.

39. Wiget, "His Life," 88.

40. Paula Gunn Allen, *The Sacred Hoop: Recovering the Feminine in American Indian Traditions* (Boston: Beacon, 1992), 225, 244.

41. Allen, *Sacred Hoop,* 240.

42. Ruby and Brown, *Dreamer-Prophets,* 132.

43. Ibid., 154.

44. Mourning Dove, *Mourning Dove: A Salishan Autobiography,* ed. Jay Miller (Lincoln: University of Nebraska Press, 1990), 29, 24. All subsequent references to this work are cited parenthetically in the text.

45. Qtd. in Alanna Kathleen Brown, "Mourning Dove, Trickster Energy, and Assimilation-Period Native Texts," in Ammons and White-Parks, *Tricksterism,* 133.

46. Mourning Dove's autobiography was not published in her lifetime. It exchanged hands among several editors before it was finally edited by Jay Miller and published in 1990. For a chronicle of the autobiography's history, see Miller, introduction, *Mourning Dove: A Salishan Autobiography,* xxxi–xxxvi.

47. For information on Guie's influence, see Miller, introduction, *Mourning Dove,* xxiii; Miller, introduction, *Coyote Stories* (Lincoln: University of Nebraska Press, 1990), vi; and Dexter Fisher, "The Transformation of Tradition: A Study of Zitkala Sa and Mourning Dove, Two Transitional American Indian Writers," in *Critical Essays on Native American Literature,* ed. Andrew Wiget (Boston: Hall, 1985), 208.

48. Miller, introduction, *Mourning Dove,* xxiv; and Miller, introduction, *Coyote Stories,* x.

49. Miller, introduction, *Mourning Dove,* xxiii.

50. Jay Miller, "Mourning Dove: The Author as Cultural Mediator," in *Being and Becoming Indian: Biographical Studies of North American Frontiers,* ed. James A. Clifton (Chicago: Dorsey, 1989), 167.

51. Miller, "Cultural Mediator," 167.

52. Mourning Dove, *Coyote Stories* (1933; Lincoln: University of Nebraska Press, 1990), 12. All references to this work are cited parenthetically in the text. For information on the beliefs and rituals concerning guardian spirits in Salishan tribes, see Verne F. Ray, *Cultural Relations in the Plateau of Northwestern America* (Los Angeles: Southwest Museum, 1939), 68–77. A dream vision is a sacred religious rite in which prepubescent Native American children are sent to desolate areas where they engage in sleepless vigils, awaiting dream visions from guardian spirits who confer instructions and offer them help in life. By presenting his idea for *Coyote Stories* to Mourning Dove as a dream vision, McWhorter both attempts to persuade Mourning Dove of the project's cultural value and makes the project sacred.

53. Miller, "Cultural Mediator," 175.

54. Ibid., 175.

55. Kristin Herzog, "Mourning Dove," in *The Heath Anthology of American Literature,* 3rd ed., vol. 2, ed. Paul Lauter et al. (Lexington, Mass.: Houghton Mifflin, 1998), 1829.

56. Ramsey, *Coyote,* xxx.

57. James A. Teit et al., colls., "Owl and Ntsaa'.z," *Folk-Tales of Salishan and Sahaptin Tribes* (Lancaster, Penn.: American Folk-Lore Society, 1917), 26.

58. The Comanche story is in St. Clair, "Tales," 275–76.

59. Ramsey, *Reading,* 37. See also Barre Toelken, "The 'Pretty Languages' of Yellowman: Genre, Mode, and Texture in Navaho Coyote Narratives," in *Folklore Genres,* ed. Dan Ben-Amos (Austin: University of Texas Press, 1976), 155.

60. Miller, *Coyote Stories,* 233.

61. Mary V. Dearborn, *Pocahontas's Daughters: Gender and Ethnicity in American Culture* (New York: Oxford University Press, 1986), 29.

62. Miller, introduction, *Mourning Dove,* xxiv.

63. Ray, *Cultural Relations,* 36.

64. "How the People Got Arrowheads" is collected in Erdoes and Ortiz, 356–57. The Shasta tribe, living in northern California, exists in geographical proximity to the Salishan tribes that inhabit northern Oregon, Idaho, Wyoming, and the southern portion of western Canada.

65. Erdoes and Ortiz, "How the People," 356.

66. For a study of northern tribes and the fur trade, see Charles A. Bishop, *The Northern Ojibwa and the Fur Trade: An Historical and Ecological Study* (Toronto: Holt, Rinehart, Winston, 1974), and Ray, *Cultural Relations,* 78–79.

67. Ramsey, *Coyote,* 258.

68. Ramsey notes "the sharp irony implicit in white newcomers asking the Indians 'where they had come from,' and in transferring the name 'Snake' from Indians to whites." Ramsey, *Coyote,* 286.

69. Franklin Walker, *San Francisco's Literary Frontier* (New York: Knopf, 1939), 49; Joseph Henry Jackson, introduction to *The Life and Adventures of Joaquin Murieta* (Norman: University of Oklahoma Press, 1955), xv.

70. Walker, *San Francisco's Literary Frontier,* 47.

71. Grant Foreman, *The Five Civilized Tribes* (Norman: University of Oklahoma Press, 1934), 281–95; Walker, *San Francisco's Literary Frontier,* 47.

72. Qtd. in James W. Parins, *John Rollin Ridge: His Life & Works* (Lincoln: University of Nebraska Press, 1991), 56.

73. See James Mooney, *Myths of the Cherokee* (1900; Michigan: Scholarly Press, 1970), 267–68 and 269. In "How the Rabbit Stole the Otter's Coat" and "Why the Possum's Tail Is Bare," Otter has the most beautiful coat and Possum the bushiest tail of all the animals. In both tales, Trickster upsets a "beauty contest" or boasting ritual when he steals the animals' furs from them.

74. Roberts, *From Trickster to Badman,* 185, 200. Roberts argues that the African American Trickster manipulated the master to attain material and social necessities within the slave system. After slavery, the badman evolved and exhibited trickster-like behaviors but operated outside the law that did not protect blacks' interests.

75. Roberts, *From Trickster to Badman,* 183.

76. Babcock-Abrahams, "'A Tolerated Margin,'" 159.

77. The quoted words are from Anne Doueihi, "Trickster: On Inhabiting the Space between Discourse and Story," *Soundings: An Interdisciplinary Journal* 67 (fall 1984): 308.

78. Louis Owens, *Other Destinies: Understanding the American Indian Novel* (Norman: University of Oklahoma Press, 1992), 39.

79. John Rollin Ridge, *The Life and Adventures of Joaquin Murieta* (1854; Norman: University of Oklahoma Press, 1955), 9, 8. All subsequent references to this work are cited parenthetically in the text.

80. In *Other Destinies,* Owens notes the parallel to the Cherokees' plight as they were also driven from their lands by Anglos (37).

81. Kroeber, "Deconstructionist Criticism," 78.

82. Lydia D. Hazera, "Joaquin Murieta: The Making of a Popular Hero," *Studies in Latin American Popular Literature* 8 (1989): 202; A. LaVonne Brown Ruoff, *American Indian Literatures* (New York: MLA, 1990), 65; Parins, *John Rollin Ridge,* 103; Walker, *San Francisco's Literary Frontier,* 53; and Owens, *Other Destinies,* 38. Owens refers to the novel as "a disguised act of appropriation, an aggressive and subversive masquerade" (33).

83. Hazera, "Joaquin Murieta," 202; Owens, *Other Destinies,* 38; Ruoff, *American Indian Literatures,* 65; and Walker, *San Francisco's Literary Frontier,* 53.

84. Kroeber, "Deconstructionist Criticism," 78.

85. John Rollin Ridge, *Poems* (San Francisco: Payot, 1868), 7.

86. Ridge's reference is to a novel about a romance—*Rinaldo Rinaldini, the Border Captain,* written by August Vulpius in 1797.

87. Ridge, *Poems,* 6.

88. Parins, *John Rollin Ridge,* 55.

89. Qtd. ibid., 57.

90. Owens, *Other Destinies,* 39.
91. Doueihi, "Trickster," 308.
92. Walker, *San Francisco's Literary Frontier,* 50.
93. Annette White-Parks, *Sui Sin Far/Edith Maude Eaton: A Literary Biography* (Urbana: University of Illinois Press, 1995), 168.

Chapter 3

1. Smith, *Virgin Land,* 15–37.
2. William F. Wu, *The Yellow Peril: Chinese Americans in American Fiction, 1850–1940* (Hamden, Conn.: Archon, 1982), 1.
3. Charles Frederick Holder, "Chinese Slavery in America," *North American Review* 165 (September 1897): 288, 290–91. Holder was a Quaker teacher, naturalist, editor, lecturer, historian, archaeologist, and sportsman. He is best known for his writings on the science of zoology and for his religious and political history of the Society of Friends, *The Quakers of Great Britain and America.*
4. William Wu, *Yellow Peril,* 74–76.
5. See, for example, Patricia Buckley Ebrey, *The Inner Quarters: Marriage and the Lives of Chinese Women in the Sung Period* (Berkeley: University of California Press, 1993), 61–65.
6. Sui Sin Far, "Betrothals in Chinatown," *Mrs. Spring Fragrance and Other Writings,* ed. Amy Ling and Annette White-Parks (Urbana: University of Illinois Press, 1995), 201.
7. Limin Chu, *The Images of China and the Chinese in the Overland Monthly 1868–1875, 1883–1935* (San Francisco: R & E Research Associates, 1974), 221. The *Overland Monthly* was published from 1868 to 1875, and from 1883 to 1935. The *Californian* was the interim magazine published between 1880 and 1882. Thus, the time span of these magazines parallels China's entrance into the United States, its evolution as a modern state, and its fated stand against Japan.
8. Limin Chu, *Images of China,* 226.
9. Tompkins, *Sensational Designs,* 200.
10. Pratt, *Imperial Eyes,* 7; White-Parks, *Sui Sin Far/Edith Maude Eaton,* 118.
11. White-Parks, *Sui Sin Far/Edith Maude Eaton,* 5.
12. Sui Sin Far, "Leaves from the Mental Portfolio of an Eurasian" (1909), *The Heath Anthology of American Literature,* 3rd ed., ed. Paul Lauter et al. (Boston: Houghton Mifflin, 1998) 2:836–37. All subsequent references to this work are taken from this edition and cited parenthetically in the text.
13. S. E. Solberg, "Sui Sin Far/Edith Eaton: First Chinese-American Fictionist," *MELUS* 8, no. 1 (1981): 28 and n.5.
14. Amy Ling, *Between Worlds: Women Writers of Chinese Ancestry* (New York: Pergamon, 1990), 26–28; and Solberg, "Sui Sin Far/Edith Eaton," 28.

15. Ling, *Between Worlds,* 21; Solberg, "Sui Sin Far/Edith Eaton," 27.

16. Sui Sin Far, *Mrs. Spring Fragrance* (Chicago: A. C. McClurg, 1912). All subsequent references to this work are cited parenthetically in the text. In the acknowledgments, she thanks the *Independent, Out West, Hampton's, Century, Delineator, Ladies' Home Journal, Designer, New Idea, Short Stories, Traveler, Good Housekeeping, Housekeeper, Gentlewoman, New York Evening Post, Holland's, Little Folks, American Motherhood, New England, Youth's Companion, Montreal Witness, Children's, Overland, Sunset,* and *Westerner.*

17. Xiao-Huang Yin, "Between the East and West: Sui Sin Far—the First Chinese-American Woman Writer," *Arizona Quarterly* 47, no. 4 (1994): 75.

18. See also Elizabeth Ammons, *Conflicting Stories: American Women Writers at the Turn into the Twentieth Century* (New York: Oxford University Press, 1992), 108; Ling, *Between Worlds,* 35.

19. Frank Chin et al., "An Introduction to Chinese- and Japanese-American Literature," in *Aiiieeeee! An Anthology of Asian-American Writers,* ed. Frank Chin et al. (Washington, D.C.: Howard University Press, 1974), xlviii.

20. Cheng-Tsu Wu, *"Chink"* (New York: World, 1972), 2.

21. Limin Chu, *Images of China,* 70; William Wu, *Yellow Peril,* 72.

22. Qtd. in Cheng-Tsu Wu, *"Chink,"* 33–34.

23. Ronald Takaki, *A Different Mirror: A History of Multicultural America* (Boston: Little, Brown, 1993), 210.

24. William Wu, *Yellow Peril,* 72.

25. Robert A. Wilson and Bill Hosokawa, *East to America: A History of the Japanese in the United States* (New York: Morrow, 1980), 137.

26. Jack Chen, *The Chinese of America* (San Francisco: Harper & Row, 1980), 176; Elaine H. Kim, *Asian American Literature: An Introduction to the Writings and Their Social Context* (Philadelphia: Temple University Press, 1982), 96; William Wu, *Yellow Peril,* 77.

27. William Wu, *Yellow Peril,* 77.

28. "In the Land of the Free" was written in 1909. In 1904, according to Chen, *Chinese of America,* Theodore Roosevelt appointed Victor Metcalf "secretary of commerce and labor in charge of immigration." Following his appointment, the exclusion laws were rigidly maintained: all Chinese were excluded from immigrating with the exception of the exempt classes, which were narrowly defined (170).

29. Robert Hewes, "A Little Prayer to Joss," *Overland Monthly and Out West Magazine,* 2nd ser., 81 (August 1923): 10+.

30. Marguerite Stabler, "The Sale of Sooy Yet," *Overland Monthly,* 2nd ser., 35 (May 1900): 414–16.

31. White-Parks, *Sui Sin Far/Edith Maude Eaton,* 121.

32. Xiao-Huang Yin, "Between East and West," 79.

33. White-Parks, *Sui Sin Far/Edith Maude Eaton,* 45.

34. Ibid., 120–21.

35. Ibid., 229.

36. I borrow this apt phrase from Carolyn Karcher.

37. Elizabeth Ammons, "The New Woman as Cultural Symbol and Social Reality," in *1915, the Cultural Moment: The New Politics, the New Woman, the New Psychology, the New Art & the New Theatre in America,* ed. Adele Heller and Lois Rudnick (New Brunswick, N.J.: Rutgers University Press, 1991), 93.

38. White-Parks, *Sui Sin Far/Edith Maude Eaton,* 165.

39. Ammons, *Conflicting Stories,* 110–11.

40. Historically, the United States' imperialistic goals were behind its efforts to "protect" China. In 1899, as France, Britain, Japan, and Russia were gaining control of commerce, America issued an Open Door Policy to secure equal trade and investment opportunities in China. Following the Boxer Rebellion in China, during which the Chinese attacked foreigners, in 1900 the United States issued a Second Open Door Policy. The United States, promising to protect China's territory and political administration, consequently preserved its own commercial interests.

41. For another discussion of this story, see Ling, *Between Worlds,* 42–43.

42. Ammons, "New Woman," 93.

43. White-Parks, *Sui Sin Far/Edith Maude Eaton,* 167.

44. For other discussions of "The Wisdom of the New," see Ling, *Between Worlds,* 44–45; Ammons, "New Woman," 92–93.

45. Henry James first used the term New Woman to "evoke his image of female independence and rebellion." Ammons, *Conflicting Stories,* 7.

46. Ibid., 113.

47. On the persistence of the belief in unassimilability, see Chen, *Chinese of America,* 147.

48. Ibid., 154. In 1948, California repealed its miscegenation laws. In 1967, the U.S. Supreme Court declared all such laws unconstitutional. For a history of the miscegenation laws in the United States by state, see Edward Byron Reuter, "The Legal Status of Racial Intermarriage," in *Race Mixture: Studies in Intermarriage and Miscegenation* (New York: McGraw-Hill, 1931), 75–103.

49. Aaron A. Sargent, "The Wyoming Anti-Chinese Riot," *Overland Monthly,* 2nd ser., 6 (November 1885): 509.

50. Ibid.

51. Roger Daniels, *The Politics of Prejudice: The Anti-Japanese Movement in California and the Struggle for Japanese Exclusion* (New York: Atheneum, 1969), 28.

52. Chen, *Chinese of America,* 154.

53. My thanks to Dan Ross for this insight.

54. Hazel H. Havermale, "The Canton Shawl," *Overland Monthly,* 2nd ser., 64 (September 1914): 269–72.

55. William Wu, *Yellow Peril,* 58.

56. Compare with Frank Norris's "After Strange Gods," *Overland Monthly,* 2nd

ser., 24 (October 1894): 375–79. In this story, Norris depicts a love affair between a French sailor and a half-Chinese woman. When the woman is horribly marred by smallpox, she blinds her lover to prevent him from seeing her disfigurement and abandoning her.

57. Dennis M. Ogawa, *From Japs to Japanese: An Evolution of Japanese-American Stereotypes* (Berkeley: McCutchan, 1971), 57.

58. Mary T. Mott, "Poor Ah Toy," *Californian* 5 (April 1882): 371–81; Esther Barbara Bock, "Ah Choo," *Overland Monthly,* 2nd ser., 76 (September 1920): 49–56, 87–91.

59. Ronald Takaki, *Strangers from a Different Shore: A History of Asian Americans* (Boston: Little, Brown, 1989), 101.

60. Americans held that the Chinese character was excessively criminal: "Statistics were developed which were designed to prove that the Chinese population contributed a disproportionate share to the criminal population in the United States. One table based on the 1890 census showed that although the Chinese and Japanese made up less than one-quarter of 1 percent of the foreign population, they were responsible for more than 1.25 percent of homicides in the United States." See Robert McClellan, *The Heathen Chinee: A Study of American Attitudes Toward China, 1890–1905* (Columbus: Ohio State University Press, 1971), 37.

61. "Her Chinese Husband" being a sequel to "The Story of One White Woman Who Married a Chinese," I will discuss both tales as if they are one.

62. Mary V. Dearborn, *Pocahontas's Daughters: Gender and Ethnicity in American Culture* (New York: Oxford University Press, 1986), 103.

63. Ibid., 101.

64. Ammons states that these stories challenge the "middle- and upper-middle-class white ideal of the New Woman." See "New Woman," 93. She also asserts, "'The Story of One White Woman Who Married a Chinese' develops openly Sui Sin Far's criticism of white middle-class feminism, portraying it as a culturally and class-biased ideology that is arrogant and authoritarian in its ethnocentricity. . . . Its sequel, 'Her Chinese Husband,' also flies in the face of stereotypes" (*Conflicting Stories,* 115).

65. Chin et al., "An Introduction to Chinese- and Japanese-American Literature," xxx.

66. "A New Note in Fiction," *New York Times,* 7 July 1912, 405.

67. Ammons, "New Woman," 94.

68. Ammons, *Conflicting Stories,* 114.

69. Chin et al., preface to *Aiiieeeee!*

70. As Ammons asserts, "At the turn of the century the dominant culture was filled with vicious, racist stereotypes of Chinese men. To admit any flaws in them beyond the most minor foibles was to give the racist script credibility" (*Conflicting Stories,* 114).

71. Xiao-Huang Yin, "Between East and West," 71.

72. Ling, *Between Worlds,* 46. Ling remarks that this is "an image with undeniable sexual implications."

73. Ibid., 25.

74. Amy Ling, "Creating One's Self: The Eaton Sisters," in *Reading the Literatures of Asian America,* ed. Shirley Geok-lin Lim and Amy Ling (Philadelphia: Temple University Press, 1992), 305–18.

Chapter 4

1. Sui Sin Far, "Leaves," 2:841.

2. Yuko Matsukawa, "Cross-Dressing and Cross-Naming: Decoding Onoto Watanna," in Ammons and White-Parks, *Tricksterism,* 106–25. Matsukawa includes and discusses both of these pictures in her essay.

3. Amy Ling, "Edith Eaton: Pioneer Chinamerican Writer and Feminist," *American Literary Realism* 16, no. 2 (1983): 288.

4. Onoto Watanna, *Me: A Book of Remembrance* (New York: Century, 1915), 154. All subsequent references to this work are cited parenthetically in the text.

5. Werner Sollors, *Beyond Ethnicity: Consent and Descent in American Culture* (New York: Oxford University Press, 1986), 252.

6. Edward W. Said, *Orientalism* (New York: Pantheon, 1978), 207.

7. Onoto Watanna, *Miss Numè of Japan: A Japanese-American Romance* (New York: Rand, McNally, 1899).

8. Ling, "Creating One's Self," 310.

9. Ling, *Between Worlds,* 25.

10. S. E. Solberg, "Sui Sin Far/Edith Eaton," n.5.

11. Daniels, *Politics of Prejudice,* 19–21.

12. Kim, *Asian American Literature,* 123.

13. Qtd. in Wilson and Hosokawa, *East to America,* 116.

14. Ibid., 56.

15. Daniels, *Politics of Prejudice,* 3.

16. McClellan, *Heathen Chinee,* 117.

17. Wilson and Hosokawa, *East to America,* 108.

18. Ibid., 120–21.

19. Daniels, *Politics of Prejudice,* 25.

20. Ibid., 25–29.

21. Kim, *Asian American Literature,* 124.

22. Wilson and Hosokawa, *East to America,* 55–56; Takaki, *A Different Mirror,* 247–51.

23. Chen, *The Chinese of America,* 176.

24. Ogawa, *From Japs to Japanese,* 50.

25. Chin et al., preface to *Aiiieeeee!* xv.

26. Ling, *Between Worlds,* 55.

27. Robert O. Blood Jr., *Love Match and Arranged Marriage* (New York: Free Press, 1967), 4–5.

28. Ibid., 7–9.

29. Ling, *Between Worlds,* 54.

30. H. Bruce Franklin, *War Stars: The Superweapon and the American Imagination* (New York: Oxford University Press, 1988), 36.

31. Sidney L. Gulick, *The American-Japanese Problem* (New York: Scribner's, 1914), 225.

32. *Miss Numè of Japan,* 6. All subsequent references to this work are cited parenthetically in the text.

33. Blood, *Love Match,* 6. The full Japanese saying is that arranged marriages start out cold and grow hot, and love matches start out hot and grow cold.

34. Ogawa, *From Japs to Japanese,* 59.

35. Ling, *Between Worlds,* 54.

36. Sui Sin Far, "Leaves," 843.

37. Cathy N. Davidson, *Revolution and the Word: The Rise of the Novel in America* (New York: Oxford University Press, 1986), 113.

38. Ibid., 123.

39. Onoto Watanna, *A Japanese Blossom* (New York: Harper & Brothers, 1906), 3. All subsequent references to this work are quoted parenthetically in the text.

40. Ling holds that the exercise of might and military prowess in winning the war against China in 1895 and the Russo-Japanese war gained Japan more respect from the world. Ling, *Between Worlds,* 24.

41. Wilson and Hosokawa, *East to America,* 122.

42. Ogawa, *From Japs to Japanese,* 50; Chin et al., "An Introduction to Chinese- and Japanese-American Literature," xi.

Chapter 5

1. Mary Austin, "The Folly of the Officials," *Forum* 71, no. 3 (1924): 287.

2. Frederick Jackson Turner, *Frontier,* 3.

3. Charles R. Van Hise, "History of the Conservation Movement," in *Readings in Resource Management and Conservation,* ed. Ian Burton and Robert W. Kates (Chicago: University of Chicago Press, 1960), 179.

4. Austin uses the term *naturist,* not the more common *naturalist:* "This is the way a Naturist is taken with the land, with the spirit trying to be evoked out of it." Mary Austin, *Earth Horizon* (Albuquerque: University of New Mexico Press, 1932), 188.

5. Dudley Wynn, "Mary Austin, Woman Alone," *Virginia Quarterly Review* 13 (April 1937): 255.

6. Austin, *Earth Horizon,* 341.

7. Larry Evers, "Mary Austin and the Spirit of the Land," introduction to *The Land of Journeys' Ending,* by Mary Austin (Tucson: University of Arizona Press, 1983), xiv.

8. Esther Lanigan Stineman, *Mary Austin: Song of a Maverick* (New Haven: Yale University Press, 1989), 181.

9. Dippie, *The Vanishing American,* chap. 14.

10. Mary Austin, "Regionalism in American Fiction," *English Journal* 21 (February 1932): 105.

11. Ibid., 101.

12. Mary Austin, "New York: Dictator of American Criticism," *Nation,* 31 July 1920: 129.

13. Mary Austin, *The Land of Journeys' Ending* (New York: AMS Press, 1969 [1924]), 438. All subsequent references to this work are cited parenthetically in the text.

14. Austin, "Regionalism," 97.

15. Ibid., 98.

16. Mary Austin, *The American Rhythm: Studies and Reexpressions of Amerindian Songs* (New York: Cooper Square, 1970 [1923]), 84. All subsequent references to this work are cited parenthetically in the text.

17. For an excellent discussion of Austin's conservationism, see Vera Norwood, "The Photographer and the Naturalist: Laura Gilpin and Mary Austin in the Southwest," *Journal of American Culture* 5 (summer 1982): 1–28.

18. For discussions of Austin as a conservationist and naturist, see Henry Chester Tracy, *American Naturists* (New York: Dutton, 1930), 244–61, and Peter Wild, *Pioneer Conservationists of Western America* (Missoula: Mountain, 1979), 81–91. Wild places Austin in the company of such well-known conservationists as John Muir, Gifford Pinchot, and John Wesley Powell.

19. T. M. Pearce, introduction to *Literary America, 1903–1934: The Mary Austin Letters,* ed. T. M. Pearce (Westport, Conn.: Greenwood, 1979), xiv.

20. Stineman, *Mary Austin,* 74.

21. T. M. Pearce, *Mary Hunter Austin* (New York: Twayne, 1965), 37.

22. Austin, *Earth Horizon,* 308.

23. Pearce, *Mary Hunter Austin,* 38; Stineman, *Mary Austin,* 48–49.

24. Austin, *Earth Horizon,* 308.

25. Pearce, *Mary Hunter Austin,* 56–57.

26. John R. Ross, "Man over Nature: Origins of the Conservation Movement," *American Studies* 16 (spring 1975): 52–53.

27. Ibid., 52, 58; Whitney R. Cross, "W. J. McGee and the Idea of Conservation," *Historian* 15, no. 2 (1953): 155–56; Paul F. Boller Jr., *American Thought in Transition: The Impact of Evolutionary Naturalism, 1865–1900* (Chicago: Rand McNally, 1969), 49–52. The major scientists and philosophers of conservation—George Perkins Marsh, John Wesley Powell, Lester Frank Ward, and W. J. McGee—knew and influenced each other; some even shared interests in anthropology. Marsh inspired Powell in his work, and Powell was mentor to Ward and McGee. The latter three were all geologists who worked for the U.S. Geological Survey.

28. Ross, "Man over Nature," 50.

29. Boller, *American Thought in Transition,* 67.

30. Ross, "Man over Nature," 55.

31. Samuel P. Hays, "Conservation and the Gospel of Efficiency," in *Readings in Resource Management and Conservation,* ed. Ian Burton and Robert W. Kates (Chicago: University of Chicago Press, 1960), 202–3.

32. Ross, "Man over Nature," 55.

33. Kolodny, *The Lay of the Land,* 71.

34. Cross, "W. J. McGee," 158.

35. Qtd. ibid., 159.

36. Slotkin, *Regeneration,* 471.

37. Ross, "Man over Nature," 55.

38. W. J. McGee, "The Relation of Institutions to Environment," in *Annual Report of the Board of Regents of the Smithsonian Institution, 1895* (Washington, D.C., 1896), 709.

39. Ibid., 709.

40. James Ruppert also applies the phrase "geographic determinism" to Austin. See Ruppert, "Mary Austin's Landscape Line in Native American Literature," *Southwest Review* 68 (autumn 1983): 378. Some anthropologists, like conservationists, held that the environment affects and determines the cultural development of a people. For instance, Frank Hamilton Cushing maintained that the Zuni people betrayed the vestiges of "civilization"—a well-developed government and society—because they lived in the desert and were forced to cooperate in practicing agriculture. Boas, however, objected to the concept of geographic determinism. See Ronald P. Rohner and Evelyn C. Rohner, "Franz Boas and the Development of North American Ethnology and Ethnography," introduction to *The Ethnography of Franz Boas,* ed. Ronald P. Rohner (Chicago: University of Chicago Press, 1969), xix.

41. Ruppert, "Landscape Line," 377. Norwood argues that although there are preservationist and conservationist elements in Austin's writing, she falls outside both movements in making the land primary ("Photographer and Naturalist," 2).

42. Mary Austin, *One-Smoke Stories* (Boston: Houghton Mifflin, 1934). All subsequent references to this work are cited parenthetically in the text.

43. Norwood, "Photographer and Naturalist," 6.

44. Dippie, *Vanishing American,* 223.

45. Cross, "W. J. McGee," 151.

46. Dippie, *Vanishing American,* 228.

47. Austin, *Earth Horizon,* 266.

48. Stineman, *Mary Austin,* 173–74.

49. Takaki, *A Different Mirror,* 239.

50. Stineman, *Mary Austin,* 174.

51. Ibid., 176; Pearce, *Mary Hunter Austin,* 59.

52. Stineman, *Mary Austin,* 177.

53. Austin, *Earth Horizon,* 359.

54. Dippie, *Vanishing American,* 82–84.

55. Ibid., 102.

56. Robert E. L. Faris, "Evolution and American Sociology," in *Evolutionary Thought in America,* ed. Stow Persons (New Haven: Yale University Press, 1950), 164–66.

57. Dippie, *Vanishing American,* 98–106.

58. Ibid., 169–70.

59. Bernard J. Stern, *Lewis Henry Morgan: Social Evolutionist* (Chicago: University of Chicago Press, 1931), 50, 52.

60. Dippie, *Vanishing American,* 282.

61. *Harvard Encyclopedia of American Ethnic Groups,* s.v. "Literature and Ethnicity." The author of the encyclopedia article, Werner Sollors, uses this term to describe the transethnic writers Waldo Frank and John Howard Griffin.

62. *International Encyclopedia of the Social Sciences,* s.v. "Myth and Symbol"—Turner's article.

63. Turner, *Frontier,* 4.

64. Ibid.

65. Mabel Dodge Luhan, "Mary Austin: A Woman," in *Mary Austin: A Memorial* (Santa Fe: Laboratory of Anthropology, 1944), 19–20.

66. Stineman, *Mary Austin,* 95.

67. Ibid., 172.

68. Austin, *Earth Horizon,* 291.

69. For example, see Austin, *Earth Horizon,* 237–38, 246–47, 250–51, and 258.

70. Ibid., 288; "The Indian Arts Fund," in *Mary Austin: A Memorial,* 61.

71. Frances Densmore was an ethnomusicologist who studied and translated the songs of the Teton Sioux, Choctaw, Menominee, and British Columbia tribes. Pliny Earle Goddard was a linguist and the foremost Athnabaskanist of his time. He was also in close intellectual alliance with the influential Franz Boas, the German anthropologist who rebutted the theories of cultural evolutionists. Alfred L. Kroeber was a student of Boas; he made contributions in all four fields of anthropology. Kroeber studied the Zuni, Arapahoe, Mohave, and Yurok tribes. John Peabody Harrington, through Kroeber and Goddard, developed an interest in Native American languages, especially those of the Southwest. He was the first ethnologist to realize the import of Native Americans' knowledge of the world around them. Washington Matthews was a collector and translator of Navajo myths, prayers, and songs. Alice Fletcher, a pioneering fieldworker in anthropology, studied Native American music and Plains Indian religious ceremonies. Her best-known works are *The Hako: A Pawnee Ceremony* and *The Omaha Tribe.* Frank Hamilton Cushing, who studied the Zuni, lived with them for five years.

72. Shelby J. Tisdale, "Women on the Periphery of the Ivory Tower," in *Hidden Scholars: Women Anthropologists and the Native American Southwest,* ed. Nancy J. Parezo (Albuquerque: University of New Mexico Press, 1993), 311.

73. Ibid., 330.

74. Ibid., 325.

75. Austin praised Cushing for obtaining parts of the sacred tribal epic of the Taos Pueblo, which had never before been shared with whites. With Hodge, she prepared a second edition of and wrote an introduction to Cushing's *Zuni Folk Tales* for its reissue in 1931. See "The Indian Arts Fund," 60. Many scholars today find problematic Cushing's sojourn with the Zuni. They charge that he obtained the trust of the Zuni people only to betray them by revealing their sacred ceremonies. See Dippie, *Vanishing American*, 285. Austin applauds Cushing in "The Folk Story in America," *South Atlantic Quarterly* 33 (January 1934): 18.

76. Sylvia Gronewold, "Did Frank Hamilton Cushing Go Native?" in *Crossing Cultural Boundaries: The Anthropological Experience*, ed. Solon T. Kimball and James B. Watson (San Francisco: Chandler, 1972), 44.

77. *American Anthropologist*, "In Memoriam: Frank Hamilton Cushing," n.s., 2 (April–June 1900), 367, 370.

78. Ibid., 368; Austin, *American Rhythm*, 38.

79. Rohner and Rohner, "Franz Boas," xxiii.

80. James Clifford, "Partial Truths," introduction to *Writing Culture: The Poetics and Politics of Ethnography*, ed. James Clifford and George E. Marcus (Berkeley: University of California Press, 1986), 13.

81. Clifford Geertz, *The Interpretation of Cultures* (New York: Basic, 1973), 13.

82. Ammons, *Conflicting Stories*, 101.

83. Lois Palken Rudnick, *Mabel Dodge Luhan: New Woman, New Worlds* (Albuquerque: University of New Mexico Press, 1984), 189.

84. Ibid., 177–78.

85. Austin, "Folly," 288.

86. Mary Austin, "Why Americanize the Indian?" *Forum* 82 (September 1929): 170.

87. Rudnick, *Mabel Dodge Luhan*, 194.

88. Dippie, *Vanishing American*, 290.

89. Austin, *Earth Horizon*, 289.

90. The reference to Luhan's "guided tours" is from Rudnick, *Mabel Dodge Luhan*, 293.

91. Mary Austin, introduction to *The Path on the Rainbow: An Anthology of Songs and Chants from the Indians of North America*, ed. George W. Cronyn (New York: Liveright, 1934), xv.

92. Mary Austin, "Indian Arts for Indians," *Survey* (1 July 1928): 382.

93. Mary Austin, "Non-English Writings II," *The Cambridge History of American Literature*, ed. William Peterfield Trent et al. (New York: Putnam's, 1921), 4:616, 633.

94. Ibid., 4:612; Austin, "New York," 130.

95. Mary Austin, "Aboriginal Fiction," *Saturday Review of Literature*, 28 Dec. 1929, 599.

96. Simon J. Bronner, *American Folklore Studies: An Intellectual History* (Lawrence: University Press of Kansas, 1986), 39.

97. Bronner, *American Folklore Studies,* 29.

98. Barbara Herrnstein Smith, "Contingencies of Value," *Critical Inquiry* 10, no. 1 (1983): 3–4.

99. Austin, "Aboriginal," 598.

100. James Ruppert, "Discovering America: Mary Austin and Imagism," in *Studies in American Indian Literature: Critical Essays and Course Designs,* ed. Paula Gunn Allen (New York: MLA, 1983), 253.

101. Witter Bynner, letter to Mary Austin, 26 May 1930—letter 98 of Pearce, *Literary America,* 232.

102. Arthur Davison Ficke, letter to Mary Austin, 11 March 1930—letter 102 of Pearce, *Literary America,* 241.

103. Amy Lowell, letter to Mary Austin, 28 April 1922—letter 66 of Pearce, *Literary America,* 160.

104. Stineman, *Mary Austin,* 173.

105. Bynner, letter to Mary Austin, 26 May 1930—letter 98 of Pearce, *Literary America,* 232.

106. Austin, *Earth Horizon,* 345.

107. James Clifford, "On Ethnographic Allegory," in *Writing Culture: The Poetics and Politics of Ethnography,* 112–13, 115.

108. Austin, "Non-English," 633.

109. Mary Austin, "American Indian Dance Drama," *Yale Review* 19 (1929–30): 743.

110. Dippie, *Vanishing American,* 286–87.

111. Austin, *Earth Horizon,* 358.

112. Austin, "Indian Arts," 383.

113. Vernon Young, "Mary Austin and the Earth Performance," *Southwest Review* 35 (summer 1950): 161.

114. Austin, "Folly," 287.

115. Pearce, *Mary Hunter Austin,* 55.

116. Lois Rudnick, "Re-Naming the Land: Anglo Expatriate Women in the Southwest," in *The Desert Is No Lady: Southwestern Landscapes in Women's Writing and Art,* ed. Vera Norwood and Janice Monk (New Haven: Yale University Press, 1987), 25.

117. Austin, "Indian Arts," 381, 386.

118. Rudnick, "Re-Naming the Land," 25.

119. Stineman, *Mary Austin,* 178.

120. Austin, "Why Americanize?" 168.

121. Austin, "Folly," 285.

122. Austin, "Why Americanize?" 169.

123. Stineman, *Mary Austin,* 178; and Austin, "Why Americanize?" 170, 171.

Epilogue

1. Henry Nash Smith, "Symbol and Idea in *Virgin Land*," in *Ideology and Classic American Literature,* ed. Sacvan Bercovitch and Myra Jehlen (London: Cambridge University Press, 1986).

2. J. Hector St. John de Crevecouer, *Letters from an American Farmer,* in *The Heath Anthology of American Literature,* 3rd ed., ed. Paul Lauter et al. (Boston: Houghton Mifflin, 1998), 1:855.

3. John O'Sullivan, "Nationhood: An American Activity," *National Review,* 21 February 1994, 43.

Bibliography

Allen, Paula Gunn. *The Sacred Hoop: Recovering the Feminine in American Indian Traditions.* Boston: Beacon, 1992.

American Anthropologist. "In Memoriam: Frank Hamilton Cushing." N.s., 2 (April–June 1900): 354–80.

Ammons, Elizabeth. *Conflicting Stories: American Women Writers at the Turn into the Twentieth Century.* New York: Oxford University Press, 1992.

———. "The New Woman as Cultural Symbol and Social Reality." In *1915, the Cultural Moment: The New Politics, the New Woman, the New Psychology, and the New Theatre in America,* ed. Adele Heller and Lois Rudnick. New Brunswick, N.J.: Rutgers University Press, 1991.

———. Introduction to *Tricksterism in Turn-of-the-Century American Literature,* ed. Elizabeth Ammons and Annette White-Parks. Hanover: University Press of New England, 1994.

Anzaldúa, Gloria. *Borderlands/La Frontera: The New Mestiza.* San Francisco: Aunt Lute, 1987.

Ashley, Kathleen M., ed. *Victor Turner and the Construction of Cultural Criticism: Between Literature and Anthropology.* Bloomington: Indiana University Press, 1990.

Austin, Mary. "Aboriginal Fiction." *Saturday Review of Literature,* 28 December 1929: 597–99.

———. "American Indian Dance Drama." *Yale Review* 19 (1929–30): 732–45.

———. *The American Rhythm: Studies and Reexpressions of Amerindian Songs.* 1923; New York: Cooper Square, 1970.

———. "Art Influence in the West." *Century* 80 (April 1915): 829–33.

———. *Earth Horizon.* Albuquerque: University of New Mexico Press, 1932.

———. "The Folk Story in America." *South Atlantic Quarterly* 33 (January 1934): 10–19.

———. "The Folly of the Officials." *Forum* 71 (March 1924): 281–88.

———. "Indian Arts for Indians." *Survey,* 1 July 1928: 381–88.

————. Introduction to *The Path on the Rainbow: An Anthology of Songs and Chants From the Indians of North America,* ed. George W. Cronyn. New York: Liveright, 1934.

————. *The Land of Journeys' Ending.* 1924. New York: AMS, 1969.

————. "Mrs. Austin Protests." *New Republic,* 5 January 1921, 170.

————. "New York: Dictator of American Criticism." *Nation,* 31 July 1920, 129–30.

————. "Non-English Writings II." In *The Cambridge History of American Literature,* ed. William Peterfield Trent et al., vol. 4. New York: Putnam's, 1921.

————. *One-Smoke Stories.* Boston: Houghton Mifflin, 1934.

————. "Regionalism in American Fiction." *English Journal* 21 (February 1932): 97–107.

————. "Why Americanize the Indian?" *Forum* 82 (September 1929): 167–73.

Axtell, James. "The Ethnohistory of Early America: A Review Essay." *William and Mary Quarterly* 35, no. 1 (1978): 110–44.

————. *The Invasion Within: The Contest of Cultures in Colonial North America.* New York: Oxford University Press, 1985.

Babcock-Abrahams, Barbara. "'A Tolerated Margin of Mess': The Trickster and His Tales Reconsidered." *Journal of the Folklore Institute* 11 (1974): 147–86.

Bakhtin, Mikhail. *The Dialogic Imagination: Four Essays.* Trans. Caryl Emerson and Michael Holquist. Austin: University of Texas Press, 1985.

Barnett, Louise K. *The Ignoble Savage: American Literary Racism, 1790–1890.* Westport, Conn.: Greenwood, 1975.

Beckwourth, James P. *The Life and Adventures of James P. Beckwourth. . . .* written from his own dictation by T. D. Bonner. 1856. New York: Arno, 1969.

Berkhofer, Robert F., Jr. "The North American Frontier as Process and Context." In *The Frontier in History: North America and Southern Africa Compared,* ed. Howard Lamar and Leonard Thompson. New Haven: Yale University Press, 1981.

Bishop, Charles A. *The Northern Ojibwa and the Fur Trade: An Historical and Ecological Study.* Toronto: Holt, Rinehart & Winston, 1974.

Blood, Robert O., Jr. *Love Match and Arranged Marriage.* New York: Free Press, 1967.

Boas, Franz. *Race, Language, and Culture.* Chicago: University of Chicago Press, 1940.

Boatright, Mody C. "The Western Bad Man as Hero." In *Mesquite and Willow,* ed. Mody C. Boatright, Wilson M. Hudson, and Allen Mexwell. Dallas: Southern Methodist University Press, 1957.

Bock, Esther Barbara. "Ah Choo." *Overland Monthly,* 2nd ser., 76 (September 1920): 49–56, 87–91.

Boller, Paul F., Jr. *American Thought in Transition: The Impact of Evolutionary Naturalism, 1865–1900.* Chicago: Rand McNally, 1969.

Bright, William. "The Natural History of Old Man Coyote." In *Recovering the Word: Essays on Native American Literature,* ed. Brian Swann and Arnold Krupat. Berkeley: University of California Press, 1987.

Bronner, Simon J. *American Folklore Studies: An Intellectual History.* Lawrence: University Press of Kansas, 1986.

Brooks, Paul. *Speaking for Nature*. New York: Houghton Mifflin, 1980.

Brown, Alanna. "The Evolution of Mourning Dove's *Coyote Stories*." *American Indian Literatures* 4 (1992): 161–80.

————. "Mourning Dove, Trickster Energy, and Assimilation-Period Native Texts." In *Tricksterism in Turn-of-the-Century American Literature,* ed. Elizabeth Ammons and Annette White-Parks. Hanover: University Press of New England, 1994.

Brown, Dee. *Bury My Heart at Wounded Knee: An Indian History of the American West.* New York: Holt, 1970.

Brumble, H. David, III. *American Indian Autobiography*. Berkeley: University of California Press, 1988.

Buller, Galen. "Comanche and Coyote, The Culture Maker." In *Smoothing the Ground: Essays on Native American Oral Literature,* ed. Brian Swann. Berkeley: University of California Press, 1983.

Burton, Ian, and Robert W. Kates, eds. *Readings in Resource Management and Conservation*. Chicago: University of Chicago Press, 1960.

Bynner, Witter. Letter to Mary Austin, 26 May 1930. In *Literary America, 1903–1934: The Mary Austin Letters*, ed. T. M. Pearce, letter 98. Westport, Conn.: Greenwood, 1979.

Calderon, Hector, and Jose David Saldivar, eds. *Criticism in the Borderlands: Studies in Chicano Literature, Culture, and Ideology.* Durham: Duke University Press, 1991.

Canfield, Gae Whitney. *Sarah Winnemucca of the Northern Paiutes.* Norman: University of Oklahoma Press, 1983.

Carr, Helen. "In Other Words: Native American Women's Autobiography." In *Life/Lines: Theorizing Women's Autobiography,* ed. Bella Brodzki and Celeste Schenck. Ithaca: Cornell University Press, 1988.

Chen, Jack. *The Chinese of America.* San Francisco: Harper & Row, 1980.

Chin, Frank, Jeffery Paul Chan, Lawson Fusao Inada, and Shawn Hsu Wong, eds. *Aiiieeeee! An Anthology of Asian-American Writers.* Washington, D.C.: Howard University Press, 1974.

Chu, Limin. *The Images of China and the Chinese in the Overland Monthly, 1868–1875, 1883–1935.* San Francisco: R & E Research Associates, 1974.

Clifford, James. "On Ethnographic Allegory." In *Writing Culture: The Poetics and Politics of Ethnography,* ed. James Clifford and George E. Marcus, 1–26. Berkeley: University of California Press, 1986.

————. "Partial Truths." Introduction to *Writing Culture: The Poetics and Politics of Ethnography,* ed. James Clifford and George E. Marcus. Berkeley: University of California Press, 1986.

Cross, Whitney R. "W. J. McGee and the Idea of Conservation." *Historian* 15, no. 2 (1953): 148–62.

Daly, Robert. "Liminality and Fiction in Cooper, Hawthorne, Cather, and Fitzgerald." In *Victor Turner and the Construction of Cultural Criticism: Between Literature and Anthropology,* ed. Kathleen M. Ashley. Bloomington: Indiana University Press, 1990.

Daniels, Roger. *The Politics of Prejudice: The Anti-Japanese Movement in California and the Struggle for Japanese Exclusion.* New York: Atheneum, 1969.

Davidson, Cathy N. *Revolution and the Word: The Rise of the Novel in America.* New York: Oxford University Press, 1986.

Davis, F. James. *Who Is Black?* University Park: Pennsylvania State University Press, 1991.

Dearborn, Mary V. *Pocahontas's Daughters: Gender and Ethnicity in American Culture.* New York: Oxford University Press, 1986.

Devereux, George, and Edwin M. Loeb. "Antagonistic Acculturation." *American Sociological Review* 8, no. 2 (1943): 133–47.

Dippie, Brian W. *The Vanishing American: White Attitudes and U.S. Indian Policy.* Middletown, Conn.: Wesleyan University Press, 1982.

Dobie, J. Frank, ed. *Puro Mexicano.* Dallas: Southern Methodist University Press, 1935.

Doueihi, Anne. "Trickster: On Inhabiting the Space Between Discourse and Story." *Soundings* 67 (fall 1984): 283–311.

Drinnon, Richard. *Facing West: The Metaphysics of Indian Hating and Empire Building.* Minneapolis: University of Minnesota Press, 1980.

Du Bois, W. E. B. *The Souls of Black Folk.* New York: Johnson Reprint, 1968.

Ebrey, Patricia Buckley. *The Inner Quarters: Marriage and the Lives of Chinese Women in the Sung Period.* Berkeley: University of California Press, 1993.

Erdoes, Richard, and Alfonso Ortiz. *American Indian Myths and Legends.* New York: Pantheon, 1984.

Evers, Larry. "Mary Austin and the Spirit of the Land." Introduction to *The Land of Journeys' Ending,* by Mary Austin. Ed. Larry Evers. Tucson: University of Arizona Press, 1983.

Exman, Eugene. *The House of Harper: One Hundred and Fifty Years of Publishing.* New York: Harper & Row, 1967.

Faragher, John M. *Women and Men on the Overland Trail.* New Haven: Yale University Press, 1979.

Faris, Robert E. L. "Evolution and American Sociology." In *Evolutionary Thought in America,* ed. Stow Persons. New Haven: Yale University Press, 1950.

Ficke, Arthur Davison. Letter to Mary Austin, 11 March 1930. In *Literary America, 1903–1934: The Mary Austin Letters,* ed. T. M. Pearce, letter 102. Westport, Conn.: Greenwood, 1979.

Fink, Augusta. *I—Mary: A Biography of Mary Austin.* Tucson: University of Arizona Press, 1983.

Fisher, Dexter. "The Transformation of Tradition: A Study of Zitkala Sa and Mourning Dove, Two Transitional American Indian Writers." In *Critical Essays on Native American Literature,* ed. Andrew Wiget. Boston: Hall, 1985.

Flanigan, C. Clifford. "Liminality, Carnival, and Social Structure: The Case of Late Medieval Biblical Drama." In *Victor Turner and the Construction of Cultural Criti-*

cism: Between Literature and Anthropology, ed. Kathleen M. Ashley. Bloomington: Indiana University Press, 1990.

Foreman, Grant. *The Five Civilized Tribes.* Norman: University of Oklahoma Press, 1934.

Foster, Morris W. *Being Comanche: A Social History of an American Indian Community.* Tucson: University of Arizona Press, 1991.

Franklin, H. Bruce. *The Victim as Criminal and Artist.* New York: Oxford University Press, 1978.

—————. *War Stars: The Superweapon and the American Imagination.* New York: Oxford University Press, 1988.

Fukuyama, Francis. "Immigrants and Family Values." *Commentary* (May 1993): 26–32.

Garza-Falcon, Leticia. *Gente Decente: A Borderlands Response to the Rhetoric of Dominance.* Austin: University of Texas Press, 1998.

Gates, Henry Louis. *The Signifying Monkey: A Theory of African-American Literary Criticism.* New York: Oxford University Press, 1988.

Geertz, Clifford. *The Interpretation of Cultures.* New York: Basic, 1973.

Georgi-Findlay, Brigitte. "The Frontiers of Native American Women's Writing: Sarah Winnemucca's *Life among the Piutes.*" In *New Voices in Native American Literary Criticism,* ed. Arnold Krupat. Washington, D.C.: Smithsonian Institution Press, 1993.

Gilbert, Sandra. "Costumes of the Mind: Transvestism as Metaphor in Modern Literature." In *Writing and Sexual Difference,* ed. Elizabeth Abel. Chicago: University of Chicago Press, 1980.

Gleason, Philip. "The Melting Pot: Symbol of Fusion or Confusion?" *American Quarterly* 16 (1964): 20–46.

Goetzmann, William H. "The Mountain Man as Jacksonian Man." *American Quarterly* 15 (1963): 402–15.

Gordon, Milton M. *Assimilation in American Life.* New York: Oxford University Press, 1964.

Green, Rayna. "The Pocahontas Perplex: the Image of Indian Women in American Culture." *Massachusetts Review* 16, no. 4 (1975): 698–714.

Grimes, Ronald L. "Victor Turner's Definition, Theory, and Sense of Ritual." In *Victor Turner and the Construction of Cultural Criticism: Between Literature and Anthropology,* ed. Kathleen M. Ashley. Bloomington: Indiana University Press, 1990.

Gronewold, Sylvia. "Did Frank Hamilton Cushing Go Native?" In *Crossing Cultural Boundaries: The Anthropological Experience,* ed. Solon T. Kimball and James B. Watson, 33–50. San Francisco: Chandler, 1972.

Hagan, William T. *United States–Comanche Relations: The Reservation Years.* New Haven: Yale University Press, 1976.

Hall, James. *Sketches of History, Life, and Manners, in the West.* Philadelphia: 1835.

Hallowell, Irving A. "American Indians, White and Black: The Phenomenon of Transculturalization." *Current Anthropology* 4, no. 5 (1963): 519–29.

Hampsten, Elizabeth. *Read This Only to Yourself: The Private Writings of Midwestern Women, 1880–1910.* Bloomington: Indiana University Press, 1982.

Hanson, James. "The Winning of Josephine Chang." *Overland Monthly* 75 (June 1920): 493–98.

Havermale, Hazel H. "The Canton Shawl." *Overland Monthly,* 2nd ser., 64 (September 1914): 269–72.

Hays, Samuel P. "Conservation and the Gospel of Efficiency." In *Readings in Resource Management and Conservation,* ed. Ian Burton and Robert W. Kates. Chicago: University of Chicago Press, 1965.

Hazera, Lydia D. "Joaquin Murieta: The Making of a Popular Hero." *Studies in Latin American Popular Literature* 8 (1989): 200–213.

Herzog, Kristin. "Mourning Dove." In *The Heath Anthology of American Literature,* ed. Paul Lauter et al. 3rd ed., vol. 2. 1829–30. Lexington, Mass.: Houghton Mifflin, 1998.

Hewes, Robert. "A Little Prayer to Joss." *Overland Monthly and Out West Magazine,* 2nd ser., 81 (August 1923): 10+.

Heyne, Eric. "The Lasting Frontier: Reinventing America." In *Desert, Garden, Margin, Range: Literature on the American Frontier,* ed. Eric Heyne. New York: Twayne, 1992.

Holder, Charles Frederick. "Chinese Slavery in America." *North American Review* 165 (September 1897): 288–94.

Hopkins, Sarah Winnemucca. *Life among the Piutes: Their Wrongs and Claims.* 1883. Bishop, Calif.: Sierra Media, 1969.

Hultkrantz, Ake. *Belief and Worship in Native North America.* Ed. Christopher Vecsey. Syracuse, N.Y.: Syracuse University Press, 1981.

———. *The Religions of the American Indians.* Trans. Monica Setterwall. Berkeley: University of California Press, 1967.

Ichihashi, Yamato. *Japanese in the United States.* New York: Arno, 1969.

"Indian Arts Fund, The." In *Mary Austin: A Memorial.* Santa Fe: Laboratory of Anthropology, 1944.

Inness, Sherrie A., and Diana Royer. *Breaking Boundaries: New Perspectives on Women's Regional Writing.* Iowa City: University of Iowa Press, 1997.

Jackson, Joseph Henry. Introduction to *The Life and Adventures of Joaquin Murieta,* by John Rollin Ridge. Norman: University of Oklahoma Press, 1955.

Katz, William Loren. *Black Indians: A Hidden Heritage.* New York: Atheneum, 1986.

Kellogg, E. Lincoln. "A Partly Celestial Tale." *Overland Monthly* 26 (September 1895): 315–19.

Kim, Elaine H. *Asian American Literature: An Introduction to the Writings and Their Social Context.* Philadelphia: Temple University Press, 1982.

Knack, Martha C., and Omer C. Stewart. *As Long as the River Shall Run: An Ethnohistory of Pyramid Lake Indian Reservation.* Berkeley: University of California Press, 1984.

Knoll, Tricia. *Becoming Americans: Asian Sojourners, Immigrants, and Refugees in the Western United States.* Portland, Ore.: Coast to Coast, 1982.

Kolodny, Annette. "The Integrity of Memory: Creating a New Literary History of the United States." *American Literature* 57 (1985): 291–307.

———. *The Land Before Her: Fantasy and Experience of the American Frontiers, 1630–1860.* Chapel Hill: University of North Carolina Press, 1984.

———. *The Lay of the Land: Metaphor as Experience and History in American Life and Letters.* Chapel Hill: University of North Carolina Press, 1975.

———. "Letting Go Our Grand Obsessions: Notes Toward a New Literary History of the Frontiers." *American Literature* 64, no. 1 (1992): 1–18.

Kraemer, Don J., Jr. "Gender and the Autobiographical Essay: A Critical Extension of the Research." *College Composition and Communication* 43, no. 3 (1992): 323–39.

Kroeber, Karl. "American Indian Persistence and Resurgence." *boundary 2* 19, no. 3 (1992): 1–25.

———. "Deconstructionist Criticism and American Indian Literature." *boundary 2* 7 (spring 1979): 73–89.

Krupat, Arnold. "American Autobiography: The Western Tradition." *Georgia Review* 35, no. 2 (1981): 307–17.

———. *Ethnocriticism: Ethnography, History, Literature.* Berkeley: University of California Press, 1992.

———. *For Those Who Come After: A Study of Native American Autobiography.* Berkeley: University of California Press, 1985.

Lankford, George E. *Native American Legends.* Little Rock, Ark.: August House, 1987.

Laughlin, Ruth. "Mary Austin: An Interview." In *Mary Austin: A Memorial.* Santa Fe: Laboratory of Anthropology, 1944.

Laxalt, Robert. "The Melting Pot." In *The Best of the West: An Anthology of Classic Writing from the American West,* ed. Tony Hillerman. New York: HarperCollins, 1991.

Leland, Charles Godfrey. Preface to the New English edition of *The Life and Adventures of James P. Beckwourth, Mountaineer, Scout, Pioneer, and Chief of the Crow Nation of Indians, Written from his own dictation by T. D. Bonner.* London: T. Fisher Unwin, 1892.

Limon, Jose E. "Oral Tradition and Poetic Influence: Two Poets From Greater Mexico." In *Redefining American Literary History,* ed. A. LaVonne Brown Ruoff and Jerry W. Ward Jr. New York: MLA, 1990.

Ling, Amy. *Between Worlds: Women Writers of Chinese Ancestry.* New York: Pergamon, 1990.

———. "Chinese American Women Writers: The Tradition Behind Maxine Hong Kingston." In *Redefining American Literary History,* ed. A. Lavonne Brown Ruoff and Jerry W. Ward Jr. New York: MLA, 1990.

———. "Creating One's Self: The Eaton Sisters." In *Reading the Literatures of Asian America,* ed. Shirley Geok-lin Lim and Amy Ling. Philadelphia: Temple University Press, 1992.

———. "Edith Eaton: Pioneer Chinamerican Writer and Feminist." *American Literary Realism* 16, no. 2 (autumn 1983): 287–98.

Lowell, Amy. Letter to Mary Austin, 28 April 1922. In *Literary America, 1903–1934: The Mary Austin Letters,* ed. T. M. Pearce, letter 66. Westport, Conn.: Greenwood, 1979.

Luhan, Mabel Dodge. "Mary Austin: A Woman." In *Mary Austin: A Memorial.* Santa Fe: Laboratory of Anthropology, 1944.

Manning, Frank E. "Victor Turner's Career and Publications." In *Victor Turner and the Construction of Cultural Criticism: Between Literature and Anthropology,* ed. Kathleen M. Ashley. Bloomington: Indiana University Press, 1990.

Matsukawa, Yuko. "Cross-Dressing and Cross-Naming: Decoding Onoto Watanna." In *Tricksterism in Turn-of-the-Century American Literature,* ed. Elizabeth Ammons and Annette White-Parks. Hanover: University Press of New England, 1994.

McClellan, Robert. *The Heathen Chinee: A Study of American Attitudes Toward China, 1890–1905.* Columbus: Ohio State University Press, 1971.

McConnell, Grant. "The Conservation Movement—Past and Present." In *Readings in Resource Management and Conservation,* ed. Ian Burton and Robert W. Kates. Chicago: University of Chicago Press, 1960.

McGee, W. J. "The Relation of Institutions to Environment." In *Annual Report of the Board of Regents of the Smithsonian Institution, 1895.* Washington, D.C.: 1896.

Melville, Herman. *The Confidence-Man.* 1857; New York: Penguin, 1990.

Miller, Jay. Introduction to *Coyote Stories,* by Mourning Dove. 1933; Lincoln: University of Nebraska Press, 1990.

———. Introduction to *Mourning Dove: A Salishan Autobiography,* by Mourning Dove. Lincoln: University of Nebraska Press, 1990.

———. "Mourning Dove: The Author as Cultural Mediator." In *Being and Becoming Indian: Biographical Studies of North American Frontiers,* ed. James A. Clifton. Chicago: Dorsey, 1989.

Mooney, James. *The Ghost Dance Religion and the Sioux Outbreak of 1890.* Part 2. 1892–93. Washington, D.C.: Government Printing Office [U.S. Bureau of American Ethnology], 1896.

———. *Myths of the Cherokee.* 1900. Michigan: Scholarly, 1970.

Mott, Mary T. "Poor Ah Toy." *Californian* 5 (April 1882): 371–81.

Mourning Dove. *Cogewea, the Half-Blood.* Lincoln: University of Nebraska Press, 1981.

———. *Coyote Stories.* 1933; Lincoln: University of Nebraska Press, 1990.

———. *Mourning Dove: A Salishan Autobiography.* Ed. Jay Miller. Lincoln: University of Nebraska Press, 1990.

Murray, David. *Forked Tongues: Speech, Writing and Representation in North American Indian Texts.* Bloomington: Indiana University Press, 1991.

Myres, Sandra L. *Westering Women and the Frontier Experience, 1800–1915.* Albuquerque: University of New Mexico Press, 1982.

Nash, Gerald D. *Creating the West: Historical Interpretations, 1890–1990.* Albuquerque: University of New Mexico Press, 1991.

————. "New Approaches to the American West." In *Old West–New West: Centennial Essays,* ed. Barbara Howard Meldrum. Moscow: University of Idaho Press, 1993.

"A New Note in Fiction." *New York Times,* 7 July 1912, 405.

Norris, Frank. "After Strange Gods." *Overland Monthly* 24 (October 1894): 375–79.

Norwood, Vera. "The Photographer and the Naturalist: Laura Gilpin and Mary Austin in the Southwest." *Journal of American Culture* 5 (summer 1982): 1–28.

Oakes, Karen. "Reading Trickster; or, Theoretical Reservations and a Seneca Tale." In *Tricksterism in Turn-of-the-Century American Literature,* ed. Elizabeth Ammons and Annette White-Parks. Hanover: University Press of New England, 1994.

Ogawa, Dennis M. *From Japs to Japanese: An Evolution of Japanese-American Stereotypes.* Berkeley, Calif.: McCutchan, 1971.

Onoto Watanna. *A Japanese Blossom.* New York: Harper & Brothers, 1906.

————. *Me: A Book of Remembrance.* New York: Century, 1915.

————. *Miss Numè of Japan: A Japanese-American Romance.* New York: Rand, McNally, 1899.

O'Sullivan, John. "Nationhood: An American Activity." *National Review,* 21 February 1994, 36–45.

Oswald, Delmont R. Introduction to *The Life and Adventures of James P. Beckwourth* as told to T. D. Bonner. Lincoln: University of Nebraska Press, 1972.

————. "James P. Beckwourth." In *The Mountain Men and the Fur Trade of the Far West,* ed. Leroy R. Hafen, vol. 6. Glendale, Calif.: Arthur H. Clark, 1968.

Owens, Louis. *Other Destinies: Understanding the American Indian Novel.* Norman: University of Oklahoma Press, 1992.

Paredes, Americo. *"With His Pistol in His Hand": A Border Ballad and Its Hero.* Austin: University of Texas Press, 1971.

Paredes, Americo, ed. and trans. *Folktales of Mexico.* Chicago: University of Chicago Press, 1970.

Parins, James W. *John Rollin Ridge: His Life and Works.* Lincoln: University of Nebraska Press, 1991.

Pearce, Roy Harvey. *Savagism and Civilization: A Study of the Indian and the American Mind.* Berkeley: University of California Press, 1988.

Pearce, T. M. *Mary Hunter Austin.* New York: Twayne, 1965.

————, ed. *Literary America 1903–1934: The Mary Austin Letters.* Westport, Conn.: Greenwood, 1979.

Plummer, Norman B. *Crow Indians.* New York: Garland, 1974.

Porterfield, Amanda. "American Indian Spirituality as a Countercultural Movement." In *Religion in Native North America,* ed. Christopher Vecsey. Moscow: University of Idaho Press, 1990.

Pratt, Mary Louise. *Imperial Eyes: Travel Writing and Transculturation.* New York: Routledge, 1992.

Radin, Paul. *The Trickster: A Study in American Indian Mythology.* New York: Philo-
     sophical Library, 1956.

Ramsey, Jarold. *Coyote Was Going There: Indian Literature of the Oregon Country.* Se-
     attle: University of Washington Press, 1977.

————. *Reading the Fire: Essays in the Traditional Indian Literatures of the Far West.*
     Lincoln: University of Nebraska Press, 1983.

Ray, Verne F. *Cultural Relations in the Plateau of Northwestern America.* Los Angeles:
     Southwest Museum, 1939.

Reuter, Edward Byron. *The Mulatto in the United States.* New York: Haskell House,
     1969.

————. *Race Mixture: Studies in Intermarriage and Miscegenation.* New York: McGraw-
     Hill, 1931.

Ricketts, Mac Linscott. "The North American Indian Trickster." *History of Religions*
     5, no. 4 (1966): 327–50.

Ridge, John Rollin. *The Life and Adventures of Joaquin Murieta.* 1854. Norman: Uni-
     versity of Oklahoma Press, 1955.

————. *Poems.* San Francisco: Payot, 1868.

Roberts, John W. *From Trickster to Badman: The Black Folk Hero in Slavery and Free-
     dom.* Philadelphia: University of Pennsylvania Press, 1989.

Robinson, Forrest G. "The New Historicism and the Old West." In *Old West–New
     West: Centennial Essays,* ed. Barbara Howard Meldrum. Moscow: University of
     Idaho Press, 1993.

Rohner, Ronald P., and Evelyn C. Rohner. "Franz Boas and the Development of
     North American Ethnology and Ethnography." Introduction to *The Ethnography
     of Franz Boas,* ed. Ronald P. Rohner. Chicago: University of Chicago Press, 1969.

Ross, John R. "Man over Nature: Origins of the Conservation Movement." *American
     Studies* 16 (spring 1975): 49–62.

Rowlandson, Mary. "A Narrative of the Captivity, Suffering, and Removes of Mrs.
     Mary Rowlandson." In *Puritans among the Indians: Accounts of Captivity and Re-
     demption, 1676–1774,* ed. A. T. Vaughan and E. W. Clark. Cambridge, Mass.: Belk-
     nap, 1981.

Ruby, Robert H., and John A. Brown. *Dreamer-Prophets of the Columbia Plateau: Smo-
     halla and Skolaskin.* Norman: University of Oklahoma Press, 1989.

Rudnick, Lois Palken. *Mabel Dodge Luhan: New Woman, New Worlds.* Albuquerque:
     University of New Mexico Press, 1984.

————. "Re-Naming the Land: Anglo Expatriate Women in the Southwest." In *The
     Desert Is No Lady: Southwestern Landscapes in Women's Writing and Art,* ed. Vera
     Norwood and Janice Monk. New Haven: Yale University Press, 1987.

Ruoff, A. LaVonne Brown. "American Indian Authors, 1774–1899." In *Critical Essays
     on Native American Literature,* ed. Andrew Wiget. Boston: G. K. Hall, 1985.

————. *American Indian Literatures.* New York: MLA, 1990.

————. "Three Nineteenth-Century American Indian Autobiographers." In *Redefining American Literary History,* ed. A. LaVonne Brown Ruoff and Jerry W. Ward Jr. New York: MLA, 1990.

Ruppert, James. "Discovering America: Mary Austin and Imagism." In *Studies in American Indian Literature: Critical Essays and Course Designs,* ed. Paula Gunn Allen. New York: MLA, 1983.

————. "Mary Austin's Landscape Line in Native American Literature." *Southwest Review* 68 (autumn 1983): 376–90.

————. *Mediation in Contemporary Native American Fiction.* Norman: University of Oklahoma Press, 1995.

Said, Edward W. *Orientalism.* New York: Pantheon, 1978.

Saldivar, Jose David. *The Dialectics of Our America: Genealogy, Cultural Critique, and Literary History.* Durham: Duke University Press, 1991.

Sands, Kathleen Mullen. "Indian Women's Personal Narrative: Voices Past and Present." In *American Women's Autobiography: Fea(s)ts of Memory,* ed. Margo Culley. Wisconsin: University of Wisconsin Press, 1992.

Sargent, Aaron A. "The Wyoming Anti-Chinese Riot." *Overland Monthly* 6 (November 1885): 507–12.

Scheick, William J. "Mary Austin's Disfigurement of the Southwest Landscape in *The Land of Little Rain.*" *Western American Literature* 27 (spring 1992): 37–46.

Schlissel, Lillian. *Women's Diaries of the Westward Journey.* New York: Schocken, 1982.

Schlissel, Lillian, Vicki L. Ruiz, and Janice Monk, eds. *Western Women: Their Land, Their Lives.* Albuquerque: University of New Mexico Press, 1988.

Schoen, Lawrence M., and James L. Armagost. "Coyote as Cheat in Comanche Folktales." *Western Folklore* 51 (1992): 202–7.

Shaw, Rosalind, and Charles Stewart. "Problematizing Syncretism." Introduction to *Syncretism/Anti-Syncretism: The Politics of Religious Synthesis,* ed. Charles Stewart and Rosalind Shaw. New York: Routledge, 1994.

Simonson, Harold P. *Beyond the Frontier: Writers, Western Regionalism and a Sense of Place.* Fort Worth: Texas Christian University Press, 1989.

Slotkin, Richard. *Regeneration through Violence: The Mythology of the American Frontier, 1600–1860.* Middletown, Conn.: Wesleyan University Press, 1973.

Smith, Barbara Herrnstein. "Contingencies of Value." *Critical Inquiry* 10 (September 1983): 1–35.

Smith, Henry Nash. "Symbol and Idea in *Virgin Land.*" In *Ideology and Classic American Literature,* ed. Sacvan Bercovtich and Myra Jehlen. London: Cambridge University Press, 1986.

————. *Virgin Land: The American West as Myth and Symbol.* Cambridge: Harvard University Press, 1950.

Smith, Marian. "Boas' 'Natural History' Approach to Field Method." In *The Anthro-*

pology of Franz Boas: Essays on the Centennial of His Birth, ed. Walter Goldschmidt, vol. 61. N.p.: American Anthropological Association, 1959.

Smitherman, Geneva. *Talkin and Testifyin: The Language of Black America.* Detroit: Wayne State University Press, 1977.

Solberg, S. E. "Sui Sin Far/Edith Eaton: First Chinese-American Fictionist." *MELUS* 8, no. 1 (1981): 27–39.

Sollors, Werner. *Beyond Ethnicity: Consent and Descent in American Culture.* New York: Oxford University Press, 1986.

St. Clair, H. H. "Shoshone and Comanche Tales." *Journal of American Folk-Lore* 22, no. 85 (1909): 265–82.

Stabler, Marguerite. "The Sale of Sooy Yet." *Overland Monthly,* 2nd. ser., 35 (May 1900): 414–16.

Steckmesser, Kent L. "Robin Hood and the American Outlaw." *Journal of American Folklore* 79 (1966): 348–55.

Stepto, Robert B. *From Behind the Veil: A Study of Afro-American Narrative.* Urbana: University of Illinois Press, 1979.

Stern, Bernard J. *Lewis Henry Morgan: Social Evolutionist.* Chicago: University of Chicago Press, 1931.

Stewart, Charles, and Rosalind Shaw, eds. *Syncretism/Anti-Syncretism: The Politics of Religious Synthesis.* New York: Routledge, 1994.

Stewart, Patricia. "Sarah Winnemucca." *Nevada Historical Society Quarterly* 14 (winter 1971): 23–38.

Stineman, Esther Lanigan. *Mary Austin: Song of a Maverick.* New Haven: Yale University Press, 1989.

"Story of James P. Beckwourth." *Harper's New Monthly Magazine,* Sept. 1856: 455–72.

Stout, Joseph A., Jr. "Post-War Filibustering, 1850–1865." In *The Mexican War: Changing Interpretations,* ed. Odie B. Faulk and Joseph A. Stout Jr. Chicago: Swallow, 1973.

Sui Sin Far. "Betrothals in Chinatown" [1903]. In *Mrs. Spring Fragrance and Other Writings,* ed. Amy Ling and Annette White-Parks. Urbana: University of Illinois Press, 1995.

———. "Leaves from the Mental Portfolio of an Euarasian" [1909]. *The Heath Anthology of American Literature,* ed. Paul Lauter et al., 3rd ed. vol. 2. Boston: Houghton Mifflin, 1998.

———. *Mrs. Spring Fragrance.* Chicago: A. C. McClurg, 1912.

Takaki, Ronald. *A Different Mirror: A History of Multicultural America.* Boston: Little, Brown, 1993.

———. *Strangers from a Different Shore: A History of Asian Americans.* Boston: Little, Brown, 1989.

Teit, James A., Marian K. Gould, Livingston Farrand, and Herbert J. Spinden. *Folk-Tales of the Salishan and Sahaptin Tribes.* Lancaster: American Folk-Lore Society, 1917.

Tharp, Louise Hall. *The Peabody Sisters of Salem.* Boston: Little, Brown, 1950.

Theisz, R. D. "The Critical Collaboration: Introductions as a Gateway to the Study of Native American Bi-Autobiography." *American Indian Culture and Research Journal* 5 (1981): 65–80.

Thompson, Leonard, and Howard Lamar. "Comparative Frontier History." In *The Frontier in History: North America and Southern Africa Compared,* ed. Howard Lamar and Leonard Thompson. New Haven: Yale University Press, 1981.

Thompson, Stith. *European Tales among the North American Indians.* Colorado Springs: Colorado College Publications in Language, 1919.

———. *Tales of the North American Indians.* Bloomington: Indiana University Press, 1968.

Tisdale, Shelby J. "Women on the Periphery of the Ivory Tower." In *Hidden Scholars: Women Anthropologists and the Native American Southwest,* ed. Nancy J. Parezo. Albuquerque: University of New Mexico Press, 1993.

Toelken, Barre. "Life and Death in the Navajo Coyote Tales." In *Recovering the Word: Essays on Native American Literature,* ed. Brian Swann and Arnold Krupat. Berkeley: University of California Press, 1987.

———. "The 'Pretty Languages' of Yellowman: Genre, Mode, and Texture in Navaho Coyote Narratives." In *Folklore Genres,* ed. Dan Ben-Amos. Austin: University of Texas Press, 1976.

Tompkins, Jane. *Sensational Designs: The Cultural Work of American Fiction, 1790–1860.* New York: Oxford University Press, 1985.

Toor, Frances. *A Treasury of Mexican Folkways.* New York: Crown, 1947.

Tracy, Henry Chester. *American Naturists.* New York: Dutton, 1930.

Turner, Edith. "The Literary Roots of Victor Turner's Anthropology." In *Victor Turner and the Construction of Cultural Criticism: Between Literature and Anthropology,* ed. Kathleen M. Ashley. Bloomington: Indiana University Press, 1990.

Turner, Frederick. "'Hyperion to a Satyr': Criticism and Anti-Structure in the Work of Victor Turner." In *Victor Turner and the Construction of Cultural Criticism: Between Literature and Anthropology,* ed. Kathleen M. Ashley. Bloomington: Indiana University Press, 1990.

Turner, Frederick Jackson. *The Frontier in American History.* New York: Henry Holt, 1920.

Turner, Victor W. *From Ritual to Theatre: The Human Seriousness of Play.* New York: PAJ, 1982.

———. "Myth and Symbol." In vol. 10 of *International Encyclopedia of the Social Sciences,* ed. David L. Sills. New York: Macmillan, 1968.

———. *The Ritual Process: Structure and Anti-Structure.* Ithaca: Cornell University Press, 1969.

van der Veer, Peter. "Syncretism, Multiculturalism, and the Discourse of Tolerance." In *Syncretism/Anti-Syncretism: The Politics of Religious Synthesis,* ed. Charles Stewart and Rosalind Shaw. New York: Routledge, 1994.

van Gennep, Arnold. *The Rites of Passage.* Trans. Monika B. Vizedom and Gabrielle L. Caffee. Chicago: University of Chicago Press, 1960.

Van Hise, Charles R. "History of the Conservation Movement." In *Readings in Resource Management and Conservation,* ed. Ian Burton and Robert W. Kates. Chicago: University of Chicago Press, 1960.

Velie, Alan. "The Trickster Novel." In *Narrative Chance: Postmodern Discourse on Native American Indian Literatures,* ed. Gerald Vizenor. Albuquerque: University of New Mexico Press, 1989.

Vizenor, Gerald. "Trickster Discourse: Comic Holotropes and Language Games." In *Narrative Chance: Postmodern Discourse on Native American Indian Literatures,* ed. Gerald Vizenor. Albuquerque: University of New Mexico Press, 1989.

Walker, Franklin. *San Francisco's Literary Frontier.* New York: Knopf, 1939.

Werbner, Richard. Afterword to *Syncretism/Anti-Syncretism: The Politics of Religious Synthesis.* Ed. Charles Stewart and Rosalind Shaw. New York: Routledge, 1994.

White-Parks, Annette. *Sui Sin Far/Edith Maude Eaton: A Literary Biography.* Urbana: University of Illinois Press, 1995.

———. "'We Wear the Mask': Sui Sin Far as One Example of Trickster Authorship." In *Tricksterism in Turn-of-the-Century American Literature,* ed. Elizabeth Ammons and Annette White-Parks. Hanover: University Press of New England, 1994.

Wiget, Andrew. "His Life in His Tale: The Native American Trickster and the Literature of Possibility." In *Redefining American Literary History,* ed. A. LaVonne Brown Ruoff and Jerry W. Ward Jr. New York: MLA, 1990.

Wild, Peter. *Pioneer Conservationists of Western America.* Missoula: Mountain, 1979.

Wilkins, Thurman. *Cherokee Tragedy: The Ridge Family and the Decimation of a People.* Norman: University of Oklahoma Press, 1986.

Wilson, Elinor. *Jim Beckwourth.* Norman: University of Oklahoma Press, 1972.

Wilson, Robert A., and Bill Hosokawa. *East to America: A History of the Japanese in the United States.* New York: Morrow, 1980.

Wong, Hertha D. "Pre-literate Native American Autobiography: Forms of Personal Narrative." *MELUS* 14, no. 1 (1987): 17–32.

Wu, Cheng-Tsu. *"Chink."* New York: World, 1972.

Wu, William F. *The Yellow Peril: Chinese Americans in American Fiction, 1850–1940.* Hamden, Conn.: Archon, 1982.

Wynn, Dudley. "Mary Austin, Woman Alone." *Virginia Quarterly Review* 13 (April 1937): 243–56.

Xiao-Huang Yin. "Between the East and West: Sui Sin Far—the First Chinese-American Woman Writer." *Arizona Quarterly* 47, no. 4 (winter 1991): 49–84.

Young, Vernon. "Mary Austin and the Earth Performance." *Southwest Review* 35 (summer 1950): 153–63.

Zwinger, Ann H. *Writing the Western Landscape.* Boston: Beacon, 1994.

Index